QUALITATIVE
CONTENT ANALYSIS

QUALITATIVE CONTENT ANALYSIS

Methods, Practice and Software

2nd Edition

UDO KUCKARTZ
STEFAN RÄDIKER

Los Angeles | London | New Delhi
Singapore | Washington DC | Melbourne

Los Angeles | London | New Delhi
Singapore | Washington DC | Melbourne

SAGE Publications Ltd
1 Oliver's Yard
55 City Road
London EC1Y 1SP

SAGE Publications Inc.
2455 Teller Road
Thousand Oaks, California 91320

SAGE Publications India Pvt Ltd
B 1/I 1 Mohan Cooperative Industrial Area
Mathura Road
New Delhi 110 044

SAGE Publications Asia-Pacific Pte Ltd
3 Church Street
#10-04 Samsung Hub
Singapore 049483

Editor: Jai Seaman
Assistant editor: Hannah Cavender-Deere
Production editor: Ian Antcliff
Copyeditor: Richard Leigh
Proofreader: Richard Walshe
Marketing manager: Ruslana Khatagova
Cover design: Shaun Mercier
Typeset by: C&M Digitals (P) Ltd, Chennai, India

Library of Congress Control Number: 2022942312

British Library Cataloguing in Publication data

A catalogue record for this book is available from the British Library

ISBN 978-1-5296-0914-1
ISBN 978-1-5296-0913-4 (pbk)

CONTENTS

LIST OF FIGURES

LIST OF TABLES

PREFACE

Purpose of the Book

'Most people are not skilled in how to take text data and make sense of them. ... What they often do not realize is that text data are dense data, and it takes a long time to go through them and make sense of them' (Creswell and Creswell Báez, 2021, p. 159). The experience expressed in this quotation is also one we have noticed in many seminars and workshops. We have observed how unsure graduate students and doctoral candidates feel when analysing qualitative data. At a loss, they search for an appropriate analysis strategy and, specifically, for methods described as clearly as possible as well as techniques they can apply to the practical implementation of their analysis. This need has been the motivation for us to write a textbook, a hands-on guide to the systematic analysis of qualitative data that presents the central steps of the process of analysis in a straightforward way.

Qualitative content analysis (QCA) as a method for analysing qualitative data has been very well known in central Europe for a long time and is used in many research projects. In the last decade, QCA has also met with steadily growing interest worldwide, as is apparent in many publications. Particularly noteworthy are the two special issues of the online journal *Forum Qualitative Social Research* (www.qualitative-research.net), published in 2019 and 2020 and called 'Qualitative Content Analysis' (Janssen et al., 2019; Stamann et al., 2020). This book is the translation of the 5th edition of a German textbook on QCA (Kuckartz & Rädiker, 2022), the first four editions of which were authored by Udo Kuckartz (1st edition 2012). Translations of this book have been published in Japanese and Chinese; the English translation was published in 2014 by SAGE under the title *Qualitative Text Analysis* (Kuckartz, 2014a).

Eight years after the publication of the English book, we now present an expanded and updated edition. The aim of this book is to provide a detailed description of the QCA approach, using the analysis of qualitative interviews as an example. In principle, the methods presented are also suitable for other types of data such as documents, social media data, field notes, observation protocols, visual data, and images. The methods presented in this book are not intended to form a rigid, constricting structure, but they can be modified, expanded, and differentiated according to the approach adopted for actual analysis in a research project.

Audience for the Book

The target audience for this book are all those who are faced with the challenge of analysing qualitative data and want to do so in a rigorous, transparent, and documentable way. These are primarily empirical researchers and students who have already acquired a basic knowledge of qualitative and quantitative methods and are now faced with the practical problem of data analysis, for example in the context of a bachelor's or master's thesis or a dissertation. The task of analysing qualitative data is not peculiar to just one scientific discipline, it arises in many scientific disciplines and fields of practice, for example in education, sociology, political science, psychology, marketing, media and communication studies, the humanities, health and nursing sciences, and many others.

Outside the world of universities and academic research institutions, there is a great deal of interest in methods for analysing qualitative data, because qualitative research has become increasingly attractive for good reasons. It makes it possible to dig deeper into the data than is generally possible in quantitative research. Much can be learned about motives, subjective perceptions and preferences, interactions, and biographical decision-making processes. In a world in which facts or supposed facts no longer play an assured role, it is precisely these phenomena, formerly referred to as 'soft factors', that are increasingly moving to the centre of attention when aiming to 'understand' real life.

Outline of the Book

The aim of the book is to describe the procedures of QCA as comprehensibly as possible, using the analysis of qualitative interviews as an example.

The text is set out in nine chapters. In Chapter 1 we discuss the general issues regarding the method of QCA and its foundations. We outline our methodological position, argue for the central role of research questions in the whole process of analysis, and trace the historical path from classical quantitative-oriented content analysis to today's QCA.

Chapter 2 is dedicated to describing the most important instruments of QCA: the categories and coding. The categories are devices for structuring, indexing, and better understanding the material. In this chapter, we deal with the more general questions such as types of categories, category definition, and the characteristics of a good category system.

In Chapter 3 we turn to practice and deal with an activity that is eminently important for QCA, namely the practical process of developing categories and category systems. Both the formation of categories directly from the empirical data (inductive category formation) and ways of deductive category formation based on the current state of research, a theory, or a pre-structuring of the object of research (already existing before data collection) are dealt with. These methods are illustrated using examples from our own research projects as well as from our seminars and workshops.

In Chapters 4–7, we describe three different methods of QCA: structuring, evaluative and type-building QCA. Chapter 4 is an introductory chapter in which we first discuss the commonalities and differences of these three methods. It also deals with the first phase of the analysis, encompassing the initial work with the text, the writing of memos and of initial case summaries. These are activities that are common to all three methods. In the following chapters we describe the three methods in detail. Chapter 5 is dedicated to structuring QCA. We describe individual phases of the method and pay special attention to the analysis after coding. In the same way, we describe evaluative QCA in Chapter 6 and type-building QCA in Chapter 7.

Chapter 8 focuses on the possible assistance that special computer software for qualitative data analysis (QDA software) can provide throughout the entire analysis process. State-of-the-art QDA software like MAXQDA or NVivo offers powerful tools for analysis, ranging from different methods of coding, re-finding, linking, and writing notes to complex modelling and visualization of qualitative data. Closer connections with the data, better accountability, transparency, and comprehensive documentation are all likely to increase the quality and credibility of the analysis.

Chapter 9 focuses on the issues of quality standards, writing the research report, and documenting the analysis process.

This book has a linear structure, that is, it is designed in such a way that the individual chapters build on each other and ideally should therefore be read one after the other. However, we are aware of changes in reading habits. Often only selected chapters are read, and publishers take this into account in so far as they provide good online searchability for the individual chapters. We have also taken this into consideration in so far as we have made sure that the individual chapters are understandable on their own. Sometimes this results in minor redundancies, but these are hard to avoid given this objective.

Acknowledgements

We would like to thank all those who have contributed to this book since the publication of the first German edition and who have given us many further ideas and valuable feedback, especially the many students and young academics who have asked challenging questions or criticized our approach in seminars, workshops, and summer schools. We are especially grateful to Graham Hughes for his invaluable support in the English translation of this book. It is always a great joy when a book is finally done after many months of work. However, writing a book is usually a never-ending story. When browsing through a freshly printed copy for the first time, ideas for improvement arise and sometimes a few little mistakes are discovered right away that have crept in despite all the effort. We would like to encourage all readers of this book to give us feedback: simply send us your comments and suggestions by e-mail to kuckartz@uni-marburg.de or raediker@methoden-expertise.de.

Online Resources

We have set up a website at www.qca-method.net that includes many useful resources for students and instructors, for instance PowerPoint slides, lecture notes, discussion questions, suggested exercises, and selected illustrations from this book for download.

Udo Kuckartz and Stefan Rädiker

Summer 2022

ABOUT THE AUTHORS

Udo Kuckartz, Dr. phil. MA, is a professor emeritus of education and research methods at the Philipps University Marburg (Germany). He received his master's degree from RWTH Aachen (Germany), his doctoral degree from Technical University Berlin (Germany), and his habilitation degree from Freie Universität Berlin (Germany). He has authored 23 books (not including new editions) and numerous articles on qualitative and quantitative methods, on computer-assisted qualitative data analysis, and on environmental issues. His books have been translated in several languages (English, Chinese, Japanese, and Spanish). He was one of the pioneers of computer-assisted analysis of qualitative data, earning his doctorate as early as the 1980s with a thesis on 'Computer and Verbal Data. Opportunities for Innovation of Social Science Research Techniques'. With this, he created the foundation for the qualitative data analysis software which he developed in the following years (MAX, winMAX, MAXQDA). He has been principal investigator for projects and grants funded by the German Ministry of Environment and the German Environment Agency. His research focused on the topics of environmental attitudes and behaviour, sustainability, and perceptions of climate change. As part of this research, he conducted the nationwide survey 'Environmental Awareness in Germany' several times on behalf of the German Federal Environment Agency.

Stefan Rädiker, Dr. phil., is a consultant and trainer for research methods and evaluation located in Germany. He received his diploma in educational sciences, psychology, and computer sciences as well as his doctoral degree in educational sciences from the Philipps University of Marburg (Germany). His research focuses on the computer-assisted analysis of qualitative and mixed methods data. Stefan is a passionate lecturer and has given more than 200 workshops and webinars on analysing qualitative data, conducting mixed methods studies, and doing evaluation. His aim is to teach the application of research methods in a structured and easy-to-understand manner. In addition to several book chapters, he has co-authored and co-edited several books on qualitative and quantitative research methods, among others *Qualitative Evaluation, The Practise of Qualitative Data Analysis: Research Examples using MAXQDA, Analyzing Qualitative Data with MAXQDA: Text, Audio, and Video* and *Focused Analysis of Qualitative Interviews with MAXQDA: Step by Step.*

1

CONCEPTUAL FOUNDATIONS OF QUALITATIVE CONTENT ANALYSIS

―――――― Chapter objectives ――――――

In this chapter you will learn about:

- The distinction between qualitative and quantitative data
- The characteristics of qualitative, quantitative, and mixed methods research
- The basic problems of understanding texts; hermeneutic approaches
- The importance of the research questions for the analysis
- The need for methodological rigour in qualitative research
- The history of qualitative content analysis
- Important characteristics and a definition of qualitative content analysis
- Typical data types
- Relevant methodological issues.

1.1 Qualitative and Quantitative Data – A Few Clarifications

This book is about methods for the analysis of qualitative data, but what do the terms 'qualitative data' and its complement, 'quantitative data', mean? While the term 'quantitative data' is directly associated – even by laypersons – with numbers, statistics and, in the economic field, possibly with costs, the term 'qualitative data' is not equally self-explanatory, because it has very different meanings in different scientific disciplines as well as in everyday life. In human resources, for example, it includes such areas as employee satisfaction, motivation, and the work environment – in contrast to quantitative (hard) data such as personnel costs and headcount. For geographers, the population figures of different municipalities represent typical quantitative data, while classifying a municipality into use zones involves qualitative data. Somewhat confusingly, in the methodological literature on the analysis of quantitative data, the phrase 'qualitative data' often refers to data on nominal or categorical scales, that is, this data type is a subset within the field of standardized (quantitative) research. There you will even find textbooks that introduce the term 'qualitative data' in the title, but which actually involve quantitative analysis methods for categorical data.

In the context of this book, we will use the following pragmatic definition of 'quantitative' and 'qualitative':

> Quantitative data are numerical data (i.e., numbers). Qualitative data are more diverse: they can be texts, but also videos, images, photographs, audio recordings, cultural artefacts, and more.

Despite the multimedia revolution that has been taking place in recent decades, and despite the noted epochal shift towards the visual in our culture, texts are still the dominant type of qualitative data in social sciences, such as psychology and education. The methods of qualitative content analysis (QCA) described in the following are designed for the 'text' data type, and texts will be used in the examples shown. In principle, the methods can be transferred to other types of qualitative data such as videos, images, or photos.

Unlike the attitude often found in textbooks on social research methods, we do not view qualitative data as inferior to quantitative types of data. There is no hierarchy of analytical forms similar to that of scales – which includes nominal at the bottom, then ordinal, then interval and ratio at the highest level. Real science does not begin or end with quantification and the statistical analysis of quantitative data. One glance at other scientific disciplines proves this point. In many branches of science, not least in climate research, geophysics, and medicine, scientists work with non-numerical data, such as in the field of advanced medical imaging techniques (MRI, NMRI, etc.). Qualitative data are by no means a *weak* form of data; rather they are a *different* form that requires other, no less complex, and methodologically controlled analytical procedures.

An interesting aspect in this context has been introduced by Bernard and Ryan (2010, pp. 4–7). They have pointed out the ambiguity of the term 'qualitative data analysis' which is immediately apparent when the three words 'qualitative', 'data', and 'analysis' are bracketed together in different ways. While '(qualitative data) analysis' refers to the analysis of qualitative data in the above sense of texts, images, films, etc., 'qualitative (data analysis)' means the qualitative analysis of all kinds of data, that is, both qualitative and quantitative data. Differentiating between data and analysis results in a four-cell table[1] as presented in Table 1.1.

Table 1.1 Qualitative and quantitative data and analysis (according to Bernard & Ryan, 2010, p. 4)

	Qualitative data	Quantitative data
Qualitative analysis	A Interpretive text studies, hermeneutics, grounded theory, etc.	B Search for and presentation of meaning in results of quantitative processing
Quantitative analysis	C Turning words into numbers, quantitative content analysis, word frequencies, word lists, etc.	D Statistical and mathematical analyses of numerical data

The upper left cell A and the lower right cell D appear well known to us. Cell A contains the *qualitative analysis of qualitative data*, for instance in the form of hermeneutic analyses, grounded theory, or other qualitative analysis methods. Cell D, the *quantitative analysis of quantitative data*, is also familiar to us. This involves using statistical methods, that is, the typical process of analysing numerical data. However, the table also includes two unexpected combinations, namely the *qualitative analysis of quantitative data* (cell B) and the *quantitative analysis of qualitative data* (cell C). The latter may include, for example, the analysis of word frequencies and word combinations. The qualitative analysis of quantitative data (cell B), which involves interpreting quantitative data, begins when the statistical procedures have been done and the results are available in the form of tables, coefficients, parameters, and estimates. At this point it is time to identify and interpret the *meaning* of the results and to work out their substance. Without this qualitative analysis work, the mere numbers remain sterile and literally *meaningless*. As Marshall and Rossman emphasized, the interpretive act is inevitable:

> The interpretive act remains mysterious in both qualitative and quantitative data analysis. It is a process of bringing meaning to raw, inexpressive data that is necessary whether the researcher's language is standard deviations and means or rich descriptions of ordinary events. Raw data have no inherent meaning; the interpretive act brings meaning to those data and displays that meaning to the reader through the written report. (Marshall & Rossman, 2011, p. 210)

---

[1]The table is based on the earlier differentiation by Alan Bryman (1988) of qualitative and quantitative *research* rather than qualitative and quantitative *data*. Bryman classified cells B and C of the table as 'incongruent'.

Bernard and Ryan's differentiation makes it clear that the type of data does not necessarily determine the type of analysis. If one moves away from such a strict connection between data type and analysis type, it is clear that both a quantitative analysis of qualitative data and a qualitative analysis of quantitative data are possible. Thus, there is no reason to assume a deep divide between the qualitative and quantitative perspectives. In everyday life, as in science, we humans have a natural tendency to combine methods. We humans always try to keep both perspectives – the qualitative and the quantitative aspects of social phenomena – in mind.

1.2 Qualitative, Quantitative, and Mixed Methods Research

In a book on methods of analysing qualitative data, one might expect not only a definition of the terms 'qualitative data' and 'quantitative data', but also a definition of the term 'qualitative research' which goes beyond the phrase 'collection and analysis of non-numerical data'. There are many relevant definitions and many attempts to contrast quantitative and qualitative research (e.g., in Johnson & Christensen, 2020, pp. 33–34).

Flick's textbook *An Introduction to Qualitative Research*, now in its 6th edition (Flick, 2018a), begins with a note on the dynamics of qualitative research:

> Qualitative research continues to be in an ongoing process of proliferation with new approaches and methods appearing and … being taken up as a core part of the curriculum in more and more disciplines. (Flick, 2018, p. xxix)

In the latest edition of their handbook on qualitative research, Denzin and Lincoln emphasize the diversity of qualitative research, which shows how impossible it is to provide a 'one-size-fits-all' definition:

> The open-ended nature of the qualitative research project leads to a perpetual resistance against attempts to impose a single, umbrella-like paradigm over the entire project. There are multiple interpretive projects, including the decolonizing methodological project of indigenous scholars and theories of critical pedagogy; new materialisms and performance (auto)ethnographies; standpoint epistemologies, critical race theory; critical, public, poetic, queer, indigenous, psychoanalytic, materialist, feminist, and reflexive, ethnographies; grounded theorists of several varieties; multiple strands of ethnomethodology … (Denzin & Lincoln, 2018, p. xv)

Today, qualitative research presents itself as an almost unmanageable field of individual, sometimes exotic, methods and techniques.[2] In the early 1990s, Tesch tried to order

---

[2]At least, this is the impression one gets when reading Denzin and Lincoln (2018) or the abstracts of the Qualitative Inquiry conferences (www.icqi.org).

the diversity of approaches to qualitative research. The result was a tableau of almost 50 different qualitative approaches, trends, and forms of analysis, ranging from 'action research' to 'transformative research' (Tesch, 1990, pp. 58–59). Tesch arranged the various approaches in a *cognitive map* and differentiated them according to whether the research interests were focusing on the characteristics of language, the discovery of regularities, understanding the meaning of the text or the act, or reflection.

It seems as if almost every author of a textbook on qualitative methods feels committed to creating a new systematization of qualitative approaches. The results of such systematizations differ greatly. For example, Creswell and Poth (2018) distinguish five (main) approaches of qualitative research: 'narrative research', 'phenomenology', 'grounded theory research', 'ethnography', and 'case study'. In contrast to Tesch's differentiation based on research interests, Creswell and Poth focus on epistemological and pragmatic aspects.

This is not the place for a synopsis of this multitude of systematizations; we merely point out the existence of a great variety of qualitative approaches that do not share a uniform theoretical and methodological understanding (Flick, 2007, pp. 29–30). Accordingly, the definitions of 'qualitative research' vary greatly. Some elements, including case orientation, authenticity, openness, and integrity, can be found in almost every definition. It will suffice here to refer to the 12 characteristics of qualitative research practice listed by Flick et al. (2017, p. 24):

1   Spectrum of methods rather than a single method
2   Appropriateness of methods
3   Orientation to everyday events and/or everyday knowledge
4   Contextuality as a guiding principle
5   Perspectives of participants
6   Reflective capability of the investigator
7   Understanding as a discovery principle
8   Principle of openness
9   Case analysis as a starting point
10 Construction of reality as a basis
11 Qualitative research as a textual discipline
12 Discovery and theory formation as a goal.

In textbooks on research methods, however, the position of a strict opposition between quantitative and qualitative research is not the only one advocated. Oswald (2010), for example, argues that qualitative and quantitative methods are located on a continuum, that is, there are similarities and overlaps and a variety of useful combinations between them. According to Oswald, there are qualitative characteristics (usually called categorical data) in quantitative research and the results of statistical analyses are also *interpreted*. Conversely, qualitative research often includes quasi-quantifications, which is reflected in the use of terms such as 'frequently', 'rarely', 'usually', and 'typically'. The result of Oswald's reflections is the following instructive description of the difference between qualitative and quantitative research:

> Qualitative research uses non-standardized methods of data collection and interpretive methods of data analysis, where the interpretations are not only related to generalizations and conclusions, as in most quantitative methods, but also to the individual cases. (Oswald, 2010, p. 75)

What shines through in Oswald's position, namely that qualitative and quantitative methods are not mutually exclusive, is the focus of the discourse on *mixed methods*. Mixed methods approaches are – as the leading actors argue – a new contemporary understanding of methods that tries to overcome the old duality of approaches in a new, third paradigm. Scholars such as Bazeley (2018), Creswell and Plano Clark (2018), Mertens (2018), Morgan (2014), and Tashakkori et al. (2021) have elaborated mixed methods approaches in detail and developed a variety of precise design proposals for mixed methods research. In terms of *research practice,* the proposals of these authors are extremely interesting and relevant for research projects in many scientific disciplines. *Methodologically,* Udo Kelle's work to integrate methods should be taken into account in this context (Kelle, 2008). While the mixed methods movement is committed to pragmatism (Creswell & Plano Clark, 2011, pp. 22–36), Kelle's (2008) approach is episte-mological, beginning with the controversy regarding the role of explanation and under-standing that shaped the humanities and natural sciences for more than 100 years. His concept of the integration of methods is methodological and he attempts to substan-tiate the combination of methods at a much deeper level. Kelle goes back to the dawn of empirical social research and the qualitative–quantitative controversy, and asks how it is possible to develop empirically-based theories in the social sciences and arrive at a concept of 'causal explanation', which, in principle, was already present in Max Weber's research (Kuckartz, 2009).

1.3 The Challenge of Analysing Qualitative Data in Research Practice

The methodological orientation of empirical research in the social sciences, education, health sciences, political science and, to a lesser degree, psychology has shifted in recent decades: qualitative research has established itself and is very popular today, especially among young researchers. Meetings and conferences such as the Berlin Methods Meeting (www.berliner-methodentreffen.de) or the International Congress of Qualitative Inquiry (www.icqi.org) are evidence of the great resonance that qualitative research produces worldwide today.

Along with this shift of research methods towards qualitative methods, the amount of appropriate methods literature that is available has increased, especially literature in English. This literature is mainly concerned with data collection and design in qualita-tive research, while questions of analysing qualitative data are often dealt with in quite general terms and it is not clear how exactly to proceed.

In an online German doctoral forum, for example, a graduate student posted the following plea for help:

> Hello,
>
> I really wanted to create an online survey for my MA thesis (it's about differentiation/separation in the relationship of adult children to their parents). Since my constructs are difficult to understand, my supervisor recently said: Have you ever thought about tackling the whole research project qualitatively and conducting interviews?
>
> Hmm. Now I am rummaging through a lot of literature, mostly from the social sciences. But I simply cannot find anything tangible for analysing qualitative data. This is all very vague. And I would really like to report some results at the end. Feeling a little hopeless at the moment. Can anyone here give me any tips?
>
> Regards,
>
> Dana

Dana is right: a tangible and concrete method for analysing qualitative data is not easy to find. And that is where this book comes in: our aim is to show systematically and methodically ways in which qualitative data can be analysed. *Collecting* qualitative data is not only interesting and exciting but also usually feasible without major *methodological* problems. The difficulties with which researchers are faced in the early stages of a project are more related to field access or one's own behaviour in the field, rather than the methods employed to collect in the narrower sense. But what comes after you have collected the information, when the interviews or videos have been recorded and the field notes are written?

Students are not the only ones who feel unsure at this point in the research process, and many avoid the risks associated with qualitative research, because the analysis process and its individual steps are not described precisely and in enough detail in the literature and are therefore difficult to carry out. Even in the reports of large-scale funded research projects, there are often only very imprecise descriptions of the approach to data analysis. Researchers often use empty phrases or merely describe that they 'based their analysis on the grounded theory', 'interpreted according to Silverman', 'on the basis of qualitative content analysis', or by 'combining and abbreviating different methods'. A precise, well-understandable representation of the procedure is often omitted.

On the other hand, the mentality of 'anything goes'[3] can often be found in the discourse on qualitative data analysis methods. Researchers who read qualitative methods

---

[3]The slogan 'anything goes' of the American philosopher of science Paul Feyerabend was not meant as a licence for researchers to do anything they wanted methodically speaking, but as an invitation to use creative methods in their research.

texts and come to such a conclusion believe that they can more or less do what they want, make glorious interpretations, and let their own imaginations and associations have free rein, without the danger of strict methodologists rejecting them and/or putting them in their place. They can even call on the constructivist and postmodern positions encountered in the discussion of the quality standards for qualitative research, which emphasize that the social world itself is constructed cognitively and that multiple worlds and world-views exist side by side; thus, the question of universal and objective quality standards can be regarded as obsolete. Such positions are not shared in this book. For us, Seale's position of a 'subtle realism' (Seale, 1999a) is convincing: in the discourse on the quality of qualitative research, Seale pleaded pragmatically (building on Hammersley, 1992) for a compromise between the two extremes, namely between the adherence to the rigid rules of classical research concepts (objectivity, reliability, validity) on the one hand and the rejection of general criteria and standards on the other. Promoting the formulation of appropriate quality standards and precise descriptions and documentation of analytical procedures (see Chapter 9) would undoubtedly increase credibility and reputation when addressing a 'sceptical audience' (Seale, 1999a, p. 467) as well as research-funding institutions.

1.4 Understanding Meaning, the Role of Prior Knowledge, and Hermeneutics

How can you analyse a text in the context of social research? Without *understanding* a given text, you can only analyse its characters and words or its syntactic properties. This makes it possible to find out more about the length of the text, the total number of words and the number of different words, the average sentence length, the number of subordinate clauses, and so on. However, if you want to analyse the semantics of the text, you will have to address the question of how to understand and interpret it. In everyday interactions, we naively take it for granted that we can *understand* each other, as if we could open the newspaper, for example, and *understand* an article about the euro debt crisis in 2010 and how European countries are dealing with it. However, at second glance, it becomes clear that real understanding requires a wealth of prerequisites and extensive prior knowledge. First and foremost, we have to understand the language in which people are communicating. If the same newspaper article were written in *Kinyarwanda*, few of us would understand it. Most readers probably do not even know what Kinyarwanda is at this point.[4] Even if you understand the language, you must also have a good deal of previous knowledge in order to understand, to continue the above

---

[4] It is a language spoken in the East African country of Rwanda and the eastern Congo.

example, what the euro, the different countries in the EU, and the different financial policies are in order to understand the article. Finally, in order to really understand it, you have to know the history of the euro and be familiar with the aims of having a single currency in the EU.

The more we know, the better we are able to recognize that a text has different levels of meaning. For example, only with previous knowledge on the subject could you recognize that the politician quoted in a newspaper article who used to be a strict opponent of financial support for Greece has now given surprisingly balanced and convincing arguments in favour of such support. Moreover, if you know that that same politician is an active member of the state government, you can assume that that governmental body may be changing its stance on the issue as well.

It is impossible to gain an inductive understanding of a text by itself. Middle Age biblical illustrations serve as a good example of this: the more you know about the iconography of the time and the better your knowledge of Christian symbolism, the better you will understand a given illustration. This sort of understanding cannot be deduced from the illustration alone, as Christian symbolism goes beyond the illustration – and the Bible cannot be construed inductively based on illustrations of different biblical scenes.

Important points of orientation for the analysis of qualitative data are general considerations about understanding, specifically understanding and interpreting texts. In the German-speaking world, this is often associated with *hermeneutics*. But what exactly is meant by hermeneutics? What does this term mean, which hardly plays any role in the Anglo-Saxon social science methodological literature?

The term 'hermeneutics' is derived from the Greek word ἑρμηνεύειν, which means to explain, interpret, or translate. Hermeneutics, then, is the art of interpretation, the techniques involved in understanding written texts. As a theory of understanding, hermeneutics has a long history that extends as far back as the medieval interpretations of the Bible or even to Plato. Within the context of scientific thought, hermeneutics appeared in the late nineteenth century as leading philosophers, including Schleiermacher and Dilthey, proposed it as the scientific approach of the humanities in contrast to the explanatory methods of the natural sciences. Cultural products such as texts, illustrations, pieces of music, or even historical events were to be developed and understood within context. Dilthey wrote that we explain nature, but in the human sciences we have to establish a different methodological foundation based on understanding and interpretation (*Verstehen*). Dilthey's famous sentence 'We explain nature, we understand psychic life' is programmatic (Dilthey, 1894/1977, p. 27).

The contrast between explaining and understanding has been discussed a great deal in the literature on the philosophy of science and we will not address it any further here. If you are looking for an instructive text on the topic, see Kelle (2008, pp. 159–164), who tries to overcome the opposition of explaining versus understanding with a new approach. Kelle relies on the concept of multiple causality developed by the Australian philosopher John Mackie.

Over time, hermeneutics has evolved – from Schleiermacher and Dilthey to the modern-day approaches of Gadamer, Klafki, Mollenhauer, and others,[5] there is no single, uniform hermeneutical approach today. Some time ago, Anglo-American philosophers also became aware of hermeneutics through the work of Richard Rorty (1979). For the purposes of this book, we are interested less in the historical, theoretical, and philo-sophical aspects of hermeneutics and more in the guidelines hermeneutics offers for the analysis and interpretation of data collected in qualitative research projects. How do we take a hermeneutical approach to analysing the content of texts? Klafki presented a comprehensive example based on an interpretation of a Humboldt text about how to construct the Lithuanian city school system (Klafki, 1971/2001). In his text, Klafki formulated 11 methodological insights for his hermeneutical approach, which still apply today. Four of the main points are important within the context of QCA.[6]

First, pay attention to the conditions under which the text was created. Bear in mind the conditions under which the text to be analysed (e.g., an open interview) was cre-ated. Who is communicating with whom, under what circumstances? How much and what kind of interaction did the researcher have with the field prior to the interview? How would you characterize the interaction between interviewers and interviewees? What information have the research participants received about the project in advance? What are the mutual expectations? What role does social desirability in the interaction possibly play?

Second, the hermeneutic circle. The central principle in the hermeneutic approach is that a text can only be understood as the sum of its parts and the individual parts can only be understood if you understand the whole text. One approaches the text with a pre-understanding, with assumptions about the meaning of the text, reads it in its entirety, works through the text, which leads to a further develop-ment of the original pre-knowledge – always provided, of course, that one shows openness in working through the text and is prepared to change previously existing judgements.

Any attempt to understand a text presupposes some prior understanding on the part of the interpreters. Klafki noted that reading through the text and/or parts of the text multiple times results in a circular process (Klafki, 1971/2001, p. 145); how-ever, it would seem that a spiral serves as a more suitable illustration since you do not circle back to your starting point. Instead, you develop a progressive under-standing of the text. The hermeneutic circle or spiral is often visualized as shown in Figure 1.1.

---

[5]Gadamer elaborated a concept of philosophical hermeneutics; in his book *Truth and Method* (2013) he dealt with the nature of human understanding.
[6]In this section, we draw on central statements on hermeneutics in Vogt (2016).

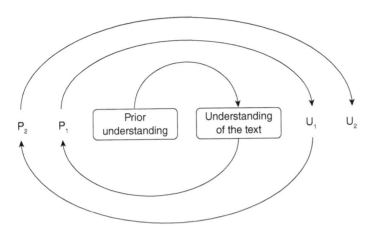

Figure 1.1 The hermeneutic approach

Third, the hermeneutic difference. The notion of the hermeneutic difference points to the central problem of all verbal communication, namely that we can only understand texts and communication in general – or think we understand them – through an interpretive process. The hermeneutic difference can vary greatly in degree. It is very high when, for example, we visit a foreign country and cannot understand the language that is spoken, even higher when – as in Chinese – the character system is foreign to us, and we cannot even look up the unknown words in a dictionary.[7] In everyday communication, the hermeneutic difference seems small or even obsolete to us. According to Schleiermacher, no hermeneutics is necessary to talk about the weather or when we order 'Five rolls, please' at the bakery. As Gadamer noted, hermeneutics takes place in the grey area between foreign and familiar: 'Hermeneutics is situated in this place in between' (Gadamer, 1960, p. 279).

Four: Accuracy and suitability. Hermeneutic procedures attempt to understand cultural products such as texts, images, and art. As Mollenhauer and Uhlendorff (1992) emphasize, they attempt to understand accurately. However, no methodology can guarantee accuracy. In hermeneutics, it all depends on the person trying to understand or interpret something, and each person always has some sort of preconception about the object or subject at hand. Gadamer stressed that these are preconceptions or assumptions. Thus, a hermeneutic interpretation that fulfils the criteria for intersubjective agreement cannot be postulated per se. There is no right or wrong interpretation, only a more or less suitable interpretation.

---

[7]Generally, we can distinguish between three forms of hermeneutic difference: linguistic, historical, and rhetorical. In the example above, it is a linguistic difference. Historical difference can manifest itself as a factual or linguistic difference, such as in the form of outdated terms or sayings, or unknown persons, facts, and situations.

In summary, hermeneutics provides five rules for understanding qualitative data in the context of social science data analysis:

1   Reflect on your own preconceptions and any assumptions you may have regarding the research question.
2   Work through the text as a whole, setting any unclear passages of the text aside until you gain a better understanding of the entire text which may shed light on the unclear passages.
3   Make yourself aware of the hermeneutic difference by asking yourself, 'Does the text contain a different language or culture with which I am unfamiliar?' Try to reduce these differences, such as by learning the new language or finding an interpreter.[8]
4   During your first reading of the text, pay attention to the topics or themes appearing in the text which are important to your research.
5   Differentiate between a logic of application (i.e., the identification of existing themes and categories in the text, as when the text is indexed) and a logic of discovery (i.e., the identification of important new, perhaps even unexpected things, in the text).

It is sometimes claimed that hermeneutics is a method that only partially corresponds to the scientific claims of intersubjectivity and validity. However, this is a very narrow view, since hermeneutic methods are indeed a part of empirical research, particularly in proposing hypotheses and interpretating results. Moreover, even strictly quantitative research cannot be conducted without hermeneutic considerations, that is, without thinking about the meaning of results. Klafki addressed the idea that research questions and research designs always have hermeneutic prerequisites. In the field of education, he noted:

> I suspect that every hypothesis in empirical research is based on considerations that aim to determine the meaning or significance of something and can thus be considered hermeneutical considerations. This does not, however, mean that all empirical researchers would recognize the thought processes leading up to their hypothesis as hermeneutical steps or practise the necessary precision in formulating hypotheses as in hermeneutics. The fact that researchers arrive at hypotheses hermeneutically in empirical research is often overlooked because many professionals in the field already have common preconceptions. For example, they may find particular questions meaningful for a given time period or for their research as a whole because they already have a previous common understanding of the subject. (Klafki, 1971/2001, p. 129)

---

[8]This is true in cross-cultural research, but it can also be useful for research conducted in a familiar environment. Sprenger (1989) tells of a social science project about the use of technology in critical care and how medical experts were invited to help the research team interpret the phenomena they observed, which made a scientific analysis possible.

1.5 The Importance of the Research Questions

The pivotal point of any research project are the *research questions*. What exactly is to be investigated in the research project? What is the specific problem about which the research should yield more insights? Why, with what practical purpose, and what benefit? What type of investigation should be conducted to obtain information about the research questions? What methods are most suitable for the research questions?

Miller and Salkind (2002) distinguish between three basic types of research, which are reflected in the corresponding research designs: *basic, applied,* and *evaluation research.* Although basic research is ideal for experimental methods and hypothesis testing, in general all three types of research may work with both qualitative and quantitative methods. According to Miller and Salkind, the various directions of research questions constitute the differences between the methods:

> They are not another way to answer the same question. Instead, they constitute a relatively new way to answer a different type of question, one characterised by a unique approach with a different set of underlying assumptions reflecting a different worldview of how individuals and group behaviour can best be studied. (Miller & Salkind, 2002, p. 143)

Diekmann makes a somewhat more differentiated distinction between the forms of empirical studies. He distinguishes four types of studies (2007, pp. 33–40): *explorative, descriptive,* and *hypothesis-testing* studies and, as a fourth type, *evaluation* studies. Both qualitative and quantitative methods can be used in all four types of study, and it is also possible to combine both methods within one type of study. According to Diekmann, the proportion of qualitative methods is different for the different types of studies. While mostly qualitative methods can be found in exploratory studies, descriptive studies, which will give the most generalized overview possible, rely on more quantitatively oriented survey research.

The starting points for all of the above forms of research are the *research questions.* Without such questions, research is difficult to imagine. Because no matter whether you are planning a bachelor's, master's, or doctoral thesis or you are writing a research proposal to receive third-party funding, the first step is always to face the challenge of drawing up an exposé, a research plan, or research proposal, in which the presentation and discussion of the research question plays a central role.

When *formulating research questions,* you should always reflect on the theoretical background and your own prior knowledge, that is, ask yourself: How much have I thought about this field of research. What research already exists? Which theories seem to have explanatory power regarding my research questions? What prejudices do I have myself and what prejudices are common among the scientific community of which I am a part?[9]

---

[9]Those looking for further suggestions on how to formulate research questions will find them, among others, in Creswell and Creswell Báez (2021, pp. 95–104), Creswell and Poth (2018, pp. 127–146), Flick (2018a, pp. 83–95), and O'Leary (2018).

To ask such questions is not in conflict with the idea of openness that is characteristic of qualitative research. The common assumption that researchers can be a 'tabula rasa' or a 'blank slate', able to devote themselves to a research subject entirely without prior knowledge is an illusion (Kelle, 2007). Prior knowledge is always a factor, as the researcher's brain is never 'empty'. Even if after well founded consideration, you choose not to refer to existing research results because you would like to approach your research question and approach the field 'without prejudice', you should reflect on your reasons for doing so and record them on paper. A mere reference to scholars who recommend such a theory-free and unprejudiced approach is not sufficient to justify it; instead it requires reflection regarding exactly why such a theory-abstinent approach to answering your research question is appropriate and why this promises better results. It is not uncommon to come across statements referring to grounded theory, according to which reading books on the topic of the research is said to be counter-productive in terms of research methodology. This is grotesque nonsense that is at best suitable for discrediting qualitative approaches in the scientific community and the wider public. In grounded theory itself, this misunderstanding found in the reception of the early grounded theory texts (Glaser & Strauss, 1998) has long been corrected (Corbin interviewed by Cisneros-Puebla, 2004; Kelle, 2007; Strauss interviewed by Legewie & Schervier-Legewie, 2004).

Of course, there are situations in social research in which it is advantageous to gain experience in the field first. For instance, anyone who wants to observe and experience how homeless people live should not simply plan to sit in the library reading the sociological and psychological literature on homeless people. However, it would make sense to consider the state of research either following the observation and in the course of the data analysis, or at the latest when discussing the results. On the other hand, it is hard to imagine that anyone who wants to analytically explore the causes of right-wing thinking in adolescents would consistently ignore all of the research literature that already addresses that very problem. In this book, the position is taken that it is wise and necessary to start with the existing research when exploring social phenomena. We agree with Hopf and Schmidt who encouraged researchers to delve into the current state of research on the chosen topic:

> Therefore, there is no reason to prematurely view the independence of your own judgement pessimistically, thus destroying many opportunities for gaining insight that are associated with theory-driven, empirical studies based on existing research. (Hopf & Schmidt, 1993, p. 17)

1.6 The Need for Methodological Rigour

What is the justification for analysing qualitative data in a systematic manner and according to strict rules? Does such an approach hinder the creativity and openness of qualitative methods? In qualitative research since the mid-1990s, issues of quality and validity have been discussed intensively. Three principal positions are taken regarding the acceptance and transferability of existing quality standards for quantitative research:

- *Universality.* The same standards are valid for qualitative research as for quantitative research.
- *Specificity.* Specific standards that are appropriate must be formulated for qualitative research.
- *Rejection.* Quality standards are generally rejected for qualitative research.

Flick (2018a, pp. 559–560) adds a fourth position, namely, that researchers should be able to answer the question of quality beyond the formulation of standards, such as in the form of total quality management, which takes the entire research process into account. For the general discourse on the quality standards for qualitative research, it will suffice here to refer to relevant contributions (Flick, 2020; Seale, 1999a; Steinke, 1999). In this book, the topic will be considered through a focus on the method of qualitative content analysis, and the second of the above positions will be used as the basis, namely that specific, appropriate standards for qualitative research must be formulated and not simply carried over from quantitative research. Inspired by psychological test theory, standards for objectivity, reliability, and validity have been established in quantitative research, which can be found in almost every textbook of social research methods. These quality standards are based on the scientific logic of measurement and are more oriented towards measurable variables (e.g., reliability coefficient). Standards for the quality of qualitative research, however, cannot be based on calculations and measures, as the data for such a calculation is missing. Thus, following Flick (2018a), the standards themselves must be more process-oriented.

In recent years, increased efforts have been made to canonize qualitative research procedures and to discuss aspects of quality (Flick, 2018a, pp. 539–568). In particular, the work of Clive Seale has been given a lot of attention. Seale and Silverman (1997, p. 16) pleaded, as shown above, in favour of ensuring rigour in qualitative social research and the construction of quality criteria. Does this mean that we have to take over the logic behind the quality standards of quantitative research and apply fixed technical evaluation instruments? Seale's position of 'subtle realism' is a middle way, beyond loose acceptance or rejection of the classical quality standards. The standards within quantitative research cannot be carried over directly to qualitative research.

Qualitative research is carried out in natural settings and differs from the hypothetico-deductive research model. There, the focus is on testing hypotheses and the goal is to find correlations and create causal models that can be generalized. Qualitative research can generalize, too, but this is not its main purpose. In particular, the broad generalization that is inherent in the research logic of the hypothetico-deductive model is a foreign concept in qualitative analysis (Seale, 1999a, p. 107). Ultimately, the goal of the hypothetico-deductive model is to discover patterns and even laws with universal and long-term validity, while in qualitative research, in particular in the theory-building grounded theory approach, the goal is to establish middle-range theories.

What, specifically, are the reasons for proceeding with methodological rigour when analysing qualitative data? Five aspects are important arguments for systematic kinds of analysis and qualitative text analysis in particular:

- *Against anecdotalism.* Systematic analysis avoids the trap of 'anecdotalism', since all of the data are included in the analysis and not just selected quotes are presented.
- *Transparency.* A detailed and transparent description of the analysis process increases the general understanding for the scientific community and other interested readers.
- *Trustworthiness.* Trust in the researchers and the results of their research is increased when specific standards are followed.
- *Reputation.* Methodological standards allow qualitative researchers to improve their reputations beyond their scientific communities.
- *Increased interest* and acceptance among funding institutions.

The application of methodological rigour also deals with the problem of quantification in qualitative research:

> Yet, as I showed in the last chapter, numbers have a place within qualitative research, assisting, for example, in sensitive attempts to learn lessons in one place that have relevance for actions and understanding in another place. There is a variety of other uses of numbers which can enhance the quality of qualitative research ... (Seale, 1999a, p. 120)

As a result of his very instructive overview of the benefits and use of numbers in qualitative research (Seale, 1999a, pp. 119–139), Seale formulated the principle of 'counting the countable'. Numbers can assume different functions: they can represent not only simple frequencies or percentages, but also be used for more complex statistical calculations, such as crosstabs with the chi-square test or cluster analysis. They can clarify arguments and support theories and generalizations. Seale's emphasis on 'avoiding anecdotalism' expresses the importance of using numbers quite concisely (Seale, 1999a, p. 138).

1.7 The History of Qualitative Content Analysis

Qualitative content analysis has evolved from classical, quantitative content analysis; therefore, it is useful to briefly describe this history. In many respects, Max Weber's suggestion at the first German Sociological Association Conference in 1910 that an 'inquiry be conducted of the content of newspapers' marks the birth of content analysis as a method of social science research.

To be clear, we will have to start simply by using scissors and a compass to measure how newspaper content has shifted quantitatively over the past generation, not only in the advertisement section and in the feuilleton, between the feuilleton and the main article, between main article and news – everything that is presented as news and what is not presented anymore .... Such studies are only in their beginnings – and from these beginnings, we will move on to qualitative analyses. (Weber, 1911/1988, p. 440)

Weber's suggestion included four aspects that were quite characteristic of the subsequent development of content analysis:

- First, content analysis references some form of media – Weber analysed newspapers, while radio, television, and other forms of mass media communications were included in later analyses over the history of content analysis, particularly in the golden age of content analysis in 1930s (Krippendorff, 2018, pp. 10–23; Schreier, 2012, pp. 9–13).
- Second, thematic analysis was and still is prototypical of classical content analysis, particularly in the form of frequency analyses of mass media themes. Textbooks (such as Früh, 2017) and text collections on content analysis often use these kinds of analyses as practical examples.
- Third, quantitative argumentation is central to traditional content analysis – Weber even wanted to cut out newspaper articles and measure their size, while we look at the size of files in bytes today as an indicator of the relevance that a given topic has.
- Fourth, quantitative analysis can be thought of as the beginning, the first step of analysis. More important are qualitative analyses that follow after one has obtained a quantitative overview. Quantitative analysis should therefore not be considered superior to or as a replacement for qualitative analysis.

What makes classical content analysis so interesting for the development of methods for systematic qualitative text analysis is that it is based on nearly 100 years of experience in systematically analysing texts, even a large quantity of texts. This means that it has already encountered (and often solved) a variety of problems that arise when analysing written texts or verbal data, which in fact are qualitative data.

Scholars like Krippendorff and Merten note that the history of content analysis began a long time ago. Merten sees precursors of content analysis in the exegesis of the Bible or in Sigmund Freud's interpretation of dreams. Within this context, Merten mentions an 'intuitive phase', which extends to approximately 1900 (Merten, 1995, pp. 35–36). The actual beginning of scientific content analysis is dated around the beginning of the twentieth century and marked by Max Weber's speech at the first German Sociological Association Conference, and his proposal for an 'inquiry of the newspapers', as noted above. Numerous studies and analyses were completed in the field of communications in this 'descriptive phase'. The golden age of content analysis came with the invention of the radio and particularly with the analysis of the impact of reporting on the war during the 1940s. Famous projects, such as the 'World Attention Survey' in 1941 and Lasswell's study of war reports and propaganda (for the Experimental Division for the Study of Wartime Communication, sponsored by the US government and the Hoover Institute), make it evident that content analysis in the field of communications was also politically important at the time. Under the leadership of Lazarsfeld and in occasional cooperation with Adorno, the Rockefeller Foundation's outstanding 'Radio Project' researched the effects of mass communication ('propaganda analysis').

The term 'content analysis' was first used in 1940 and many other terms that are central to content analysis, such as 'sampling unit', 'category', and 'intercoder reliability', stem from that time and were coined by leading content analysts like Lasswell, Berelson, and Lazarsfeld. Methodically, content analysis made considerable progress: Berelson wrote the first dissertation using methods of content analysis in 1941 and later co-authored the textbook *The Analysis of Communication Content* with Lazarsfeld (Berelson & Lazarsfeld, 1948). In addition, numerous publications and conferences made it possible for researchers to exchange their ideas and methodologies (Früh, 2017, pp. 11–15).

Since the end of the 1940s, content analysis has taken on more of a quantifying and statistical character. This must be viewed within the context of a general shift in the social sciences towards behaviourism after the Second World War and into the 1950s and the early 1960s. Empirical research focused on testing hypotheses and theories. Qualitative research was considered unscientific and more and more qualitative elements disappeared from content analysis, which was then limited to the quantitative analysis of the manifest content of communication. Thus, Berelson defined content analysis as follows:

> Content analysis is a research technique for the objective, systematic and quantitative description of the manifest content of communication. (Berelson, 1952, p. 18)

Critique of such a methodically narrow form of content analysis soon followed. Kracauer, for example, criticized Berelson's content analysis of being too superficial and not grasping the more subtle meanings. It was Kracauer who first advocated a 'qualitative content analysis' (Kracauer, 1952). Such a qualitative type of content analysis should also address latent meaning, not in the sense of objective meaning, of probable and improbable readings, but as latent meaning that can be intersubjectively agreed upon. This raises the general question of understanding the meaning of texts, for which a consideration of hermeneutics as the classical theory of interpretation is recommended (cf. Section 1.4).

A 'qualitative content analysis', such as Siegfried Kracauer's counter-position to the mainstream content analysis of that time, was a type of content analysis that wanted to put an end to the restriction to manifest content imposed by the prevailing behaviourist paradigm. Kracauer argued for a content analysis that also takes into account latent aspects of the meaning of texts, or of communication content in general (Kracauer, 1952). The QCA that we conceptualize in this book refers on the one hand to historical social science pioneers as Kracauer, who did not want to limit the method to the manifest content and its quantification, and on the other hand to hermeneutic traditions, from which one can learn a lot about the basic principles of understanding text and meaning.

What are the stages that mark the way to the method of QCA presented in this book? Kracauer had already conceived the method of QCA not as an antithesis to classical content analysis, but as a necessary extension of content analysis, which had become increasingly narrow in the course of time. Leading content analysts of that time had argued that different kinds of texts are situated on a continuum. Statements that do not require additional interpretation, such as facts or alleged facts, are situated at one end of the continuum while texts that require interpretation are situated at the other end. For example, the news of a train accident would be at the factual end of the continuum while an example of modern poetry would be at the other end.

Kracauer argued, however, that in social science analyses events such as train accidents that do not require additional interpretation are very rare. In such cases, counting and statistical analysis are indeed appropriate and useful. But even beyond the interpretation of modern poetry text analysis is not possible without subjective understanding and interpretation of text. The crucial point is that quantitative approaches are not as accurate as interpretive approaches when it comes to understanding communication. This can be seen, for example, if the attempt is made to rate a complex communication on a scale with only three points from 'very favourable' to 'very unfavourable' (Kracauer, 1952, p. 631).

Kracauer praised QCA as a necessary extension of and supplement to mainstream content analysis, which was becoming more and more quantitative this time. He concluded that a new kind, a *qualitative content analysis* had to be established. In the following decades, QCA played only a marginal role in the methods literature. If it was dealt with at all, it was done in a rather dismissive manner, as Devi Prasad (2019) describes. However, many qualitative researchers have used content analysis techniques in their research practice and have thus put Kracauer's advocacy of QCA into practice. For decades, methodological development took place in research practice rather than in the methods literature. The marginalized role of QCA then changed with the emerging discussion of qualitative research in the 1970s and 1980s. Texts dealing with QCA now appeared, especially in German-speaking countries (e.g., Ritsert, 1972). Of particular importance in this context is a book on QCA by Philipp Mayring (1983). This book was widely read, so that the term 'qualitative content analysis' was often associated with

Mayring's book in the German-speaking world. Nevertheless, there were numerous forms of qualitative data analysis in research practice that called their approach 'content analysis' without following Mayring's approach.

Since the turn of the millennium, QCA has gained steadily increasing popularity. On the one hand, books have been published that deal specifically with QCA (Gläser & Laudel, 2004; Mayring & Gläser-Zikuda, 2005; Schreier, 2012; Steigleder, 2008). On the other hand, QCA is now the method of choice in many research projects. However, this applies primarily to Germany and other parts of continental Europe, where there is a relatively strong hermeneutic tradition. In the English-speaking world, there are a number of textbooks on qualitative data analysis that contain basic ideas and techniques of QCA, but do not themselves use the term 'qualitative content analysis', such as Miles and Huberman (1984, 1994), Boyatzis (1998), and Guest et al. (2012). The reason for the avoidance of the term is presumably the association of 'content analysis' with quantitative methods that has occurred over decades, as well as the continuing disregard that leading representatives of content analysis have shown for forms of qualitative analysis in general. In his textbook *Content Analysis: An Introduction to its Methodology*, Krippendorff (2018) devotes only a few pages to qualitative approaches.

For the past decade or so, however, QCA has also become more widespread in the English-speaking world: articles in international journals address the method (e.g., Elo et al., 2014; Hsieh & Shannon, 2005) and textbooks by Schreier (2012), Kuckartz (2014a), and Mayring (2014, 2021) have been published in English. Two special issues of the online journal *FQS – Forum: Qualitative Social Research* (Janssen et al., 2019; Stamann et al., 2020) have played an important role in dissemination. There you will find more than 50 German- and English-language articles on both the foundation of the method and applications in the various academic disciplines. These two issues of *FQS* impressively demonstrate that Kracauer's call for a type of content analysis expanded to include elements of interpretation has fallen on fertile ground in recent decades and has been taken up very productively in many research projects.

1.8 Definition of Qualitative Content Analysis and Typical Data Types

Definition of Qualitative Content Analysis

In the previous section on the history of QCA, Berelson's well-known definition of quantitatively oriented content analysis has already been cited, in which he named the *objective, systematic and quantitative description of the manifest content* as central characteristics. The claim of a systematic approach is also adhered to in QCA today, but it should be clear that in a definition of QCA, the terms 'quantitative' and 'objective' will not be found as central features any more. It is precisely the claim to include latent content in the analysis that Kracauer used to justify his plea for QCA. In short, a different definition is needed, one that clearly differs from the definitions of quantitative content analysis that can be found in the literature (Früh, 2017; Krippendorff, 2018; Rössler, 2017).

Stamann et al. (2016) have compiled numerous definitions and attempted definitions of QCA. They identify the core of QCA as 'the systematic analysis of the meaning of material in need of interpretation by assigning it to the categories of a category system' (2016, para. 5) and formulate the following definition:

> In our understanding, all qualitative content analysis methods have in common the systematization of communication content with the aim of a highly rule-guided interpretation. Therefore, qualitative content analysis is a research method for systematizing manifest and latent communication content. The method is characterized by a variety of procedures specific to the research context. Category systems serve as a basic instrument for the desired systematization of content. The object of analysis are texts of all kinds in the sense of an expanded concept of text. (Stamann et al., 2016, para. 9)

For us it seems reasonable to go beyond the definition of Stamann et al. at essential points. As a basis for the concept of QCA presented in this book, we have formulated a detailed definition (see box).

Three differences from Stamann et al. are important to us: firstly, the specification with regard to the possible types of category development; secondly, that the analysis is primarily qualitative; and thirdly, that QCA not only is category-oriented but also can have a case orientation. A fourth difference

> Qualitative content analysis is the systematic and methodologically controlled scientific analysis of texts, pictures, films, and other contents of communication. Not only manifest but also latent contents are analysed. At the centre of qualitative analyses are categories with which all the material relevant to the research question(s) is coded. Category development can be deductive, inductive, or deductive-inductive. The analysis is primarily qualitative but can also integrate quantitative-statistical evaluations; it can be both category-oriented and case-oriented.

seems less relevant to us, but should be mentioned: we do not work with an extended concept of text that also includes videos, films and images, but differentiate between these types of data.

This definition also differs significantly in some points from the definition formulated by Margrit Schreier:

> QCA is a method for systematically describing the meaning of qualitative material. It is done by classifying material as instances of the categories of a coding frame. (Schreier, 2012, p. 1)

Two aspects of Schreier's definition seem problematic to us:

- Firstly, the definition of QCA as the systematic *description of* qualitative material. In our opinion, QCA can do much more than description. Qualitative content analysis can also *discover* relationships and even *test* hypotheses or theories; it is therefore a method of analysis and not merely of description.
- Secondly, the view of coding as a process of finding *instances of categories*. This is likely to create a misunderstanding, namely that pre-defined categories are always *applied to the* material, a procedure that critics of QCA call 'subsumption-logical'. Here we seem to be missing the discovery process in the definition, namely that it is through coding the material, inductive coding, that categories are first discovered and further developed in the course of the analysis.

We see another significant difference in the fact that – as in the definition by Stamann et al. – Schreier's definition does not include a case-oriented perspective, which, unlike in quantitative research, plays a very important role in qualitative social research.

In Mayring (2015), who now prefers the term 'qualitatively oriented category-guided text analysis' instead of QCA (Mayring, 2020, p. 500), there is no definition in the actual sense, but a list of 15 principles for the development of QCA (2015, p. 49):

1 The need for a systematic approach

2 Need for a communication model

3 Categories at the centre of the analysis

4 Verification against quality criteria

5 Conditions of origin of the material

6 Explication of the pre-understanding

7 Attention to latent meaning

8 Orientation towards everyday processes of understanding and interpreting

9 Adopting the perspective of the other

10 Possibility of re-interpretation

11 Basic semiotic terms

12 Pragmatic theory of meaning

13 Using linguistic context theories for explications

14 Psychology of text processing

15 Use of categorization theories to form a coding guide.

Such a list of 'principles' far exceeds the usual framework of definitions, whose function would be the concise determination of the essence of something, here QCA. Mayring's collection of 15 principles, on the other hand, comes from a *tour d'horizon* through different traditions and research approaches, which of course immediately raises the question of their compatibility (Stamann et al., 2016, para. 6). This will be discussed in more detail below in Section 1.9.

However, the relevance of a definition should not be set too high. Here it is worth recalling Karl Popper's rejection of the traditional view that one must first define terms, that is, reach agreement on the vocabulary to be used, before beginning a discussion. 'It is not by definition that the use of a term is established, but the use of the term establishes what is called its "definition" or its "meaning". In other words, there are only definitions of use' (Popper, 1979/2010, p. 447).

In this respect, it is more informative for the assessment of the variant of QCA proposed by Mayring to trace his practical use of the method instead of the definition. This can be understood both from the description of a practical example that the author included in the 12th edition of his German book (Mayring, 2015, pp. 88–89), and from the defined flow logic of the various analysis steps in the QCAmap software designed by Fenzl and Mayring (2017).

Typical Data in Qualitative Content Analysis

What types of data can be processed with QCA? In principle, almost all data types commonly used in qualitative research can be analysed, for example:

- Interviews of all kinds (narrative interviews, problem-centred interviews, online interviews, telephone interviews, etc.)
- Focus groups and group discussions
- Documents (e.g., files of the youth welfare office, annual reports, sustainability reports of companies)
- Observation protocols
- Field notes
- Film recordings (e.g., classroom interaction, educational behaviour)
- Videos (e.g., from the internet)
- Pictures, drawings, and photos
- Answers to open questions in surveys
- Data from social media (e.g., from Twitter and Facebook, YouTube comments, posts in online forums, comments on newspaper reports).
- (Learning) diaries.

In addition to the analysis of these data, which are prototypical of qualitative research, QCA can also be successfully used for the analysis of other data, such as:

- Articles in newspapers, magazines, and other media
- Speeches and debates (e.g., in parliament)

- Podcasts
- Internet data (e.g., blog posts, company websites)
- Scientific publications
- Textbooks.

Interviews and focus groups are usually analysed in written form and not as audio recordings, that is to say, in this case it is first necessary to transcribe the audio recording. With regard to the types of data, no order of appropriateness can be stated, for example, in the sense that QCA would be better suited for the analysis of interviews than for the analysis of documents or social media data. In social research, QCA is very often used for the analysis of interviews and focus groups, but this does not mean that it is less suitable for documents or social media data. Whenever qualitative material needs to be analysed systematically and with the help of categories, QCA is an excellent method.

If you look at the latest volumes of scientific journals, you will see that social media data are playing an increasingly important role in research. This has consequences for QCA, because in the analysis of these types of data, considerably more data are to be expected than is the case in a study with open interviews or focus groups. Given the volume of such data, for example more than 10,000 tweets in the analysis of Twitter data, it is no longer possible to skim or even read all the material. The initiating work with texts and the exploration of the data must be limited to a specific selection. It is quite natural that with these types of data there is a desire to integrate automated or semi-automated steps into the analysis process.

In summary, QCA is suitable for all forms of analyses, for which systematic procedures and methodological control are considered to be very important. As has been made clear in the definitions above, categories play a central role in QCA. There are no restrictions with regard to the data to be analysed, but the objective of systematics and the comparison of data requires that the data must have a certain comparability. Qualitative content analysis is therefore less suitable if only a small amount of data has been collected scattered over a long period of time and is intended to record developments and changes. This is prototypically the case in ethnological field research, where participant observation may take place again and again over a very long period of time in order to find out about certain customs, rites, and rules. Here, however, QCA can be used to evaluate certain sub-questions and sub-surveys, such as interviews conducted specifically with a certain group in the context of field research.

Differences between Qualitative and Quantitative Content Analysis

What differences exist between QCA and classical content analysis (which, as shown in Section 1.7, has increasingly developed towards quantification over the decades)? Three characteristics of qualitative and quantitative content analysis appear very similar at first glance:

1   The category-based approach and the key position of the categories for the analysis
2   The systematic approach with clearly defined rules for each step of the analysis
3   The classification and categorization of the whole data set and not just a small part of it.

However, a closer look reveals relevant differences even in these three points. For example, with regard to the systematic approach, which in QCA includes several steps and often also has a circular character, whereas it proceeds linearly in classical content analysis. The decisive point, however, is that QCA is a type of analysis in which understanding the meaning of a text and text interpretation play a much more important role than in classical content analysis, which is focused on the manifest content. Authors of textbooks of classical content analysis such as Krippendorff (2018) and Früh (2017) argue that the differences between classical content analysis and QCA are not so substantial as to justify a dichotomy. In principle, we agree with this, but this does not include the empirical examples presented by these two authors, such as the topic frequency analysis presented in detail by Früh. The differences from this type of quantitative content analysis are significant.

The difference between qualitative and classical content analysis is particularly significant for computerized automated content analysis, which aims exclusively at statistical analysis, as it has developed since the mid-1960s, primarily in the USA. In this type of analysis, words are coded automatically by means of a dictionary, whereby the ambiguity of words and the question of meaning are largely ignored. In contrast, QCA is an interpretive form of analysis, where coding is done on the basis of interpretation, classification, and evaluation; the text evaluation and coding are thus linked to a human performance of understanding and interpretation.

In conclusion, QCA differs in essential points from classical quantitative content analysis:

- First, the formulation of hypotheses at the beginning of the planning phase is not obligatory and is rather rare in the field of QCA. Here, an open approach without pre-formulated hypotheses is normal.
- Second, the phases of analysis in qualitative content analyses are not as strictly separated from each other as in the quantitative content analysis model, but rather data collection and data analysis can certainly take place in parallel, and feedback loops are often run through.
- Third, the process of coding the data is more interpretive and inspired by hermeneutic thinking. It includes reflection on the data and the interactive manner of their emergence.
- Fourth, the original data, also the audio recording, remains of great interest even after coding, that is, it has not been 'disposed of' by the coding and has not become superfluous.

- Fifth, the categories in QCA have above all a function of structuring and systematizing and not of transforming data from the empirical into the world of numbers.
- Sixth, QCA does not necessarily mean statistical data analysis. Statistical analyses can take place within the framework of QCA, but unlike in classical content analysis, statistics may play only a secondary role or QCA might do without statistical analyses altogether.

1.9 Methodological Issues

Method or Methodology?

In workshops on QCA as well as in the context of the relevant literature, questions are frequently raised that do not directly concern the methodology and practical application of QCA but are methodological and epistemological in nature. Thus Stamann et al. (2016) raise the question of the 'methodological positioning' of QCA and criticize the lack of a location in a 'background theory'. According to Stamann et al., following Uhlendorff and Prengel (2013), there is a dilemma: either QCA is a qualitative method without a theoretical foundation or it is not a qualitative method at all because it follows the tradition of quantitative content analysis and thus adopts the basic assumptions of critical rationalism:

> Either one conceives of a genuinely qualitative content analysis – which, however, lacks a theoretical foundation. Or one argues in favour of a qualitative content analysis that has developed out of the quantitative tradition and continues to lean heavily on it, and for which the assumptions of critical rationalism that are fundamental to quantitative research and the accompanying demands on the conduct and meaningfulness of empirical research also apply accordingly. (Stamann et al., 2016, para. 6)

This reasoning seems to us to contain two assumptions that do not hold.

First, the statement that quantitative research is based on the fundamental assumptions of critical rationalism is simply not true. It can be refuted in terms of the history of science, because Karl Popper, the founder of critical rationalism, was not even born when the sociologist Max Weber conducted empirical research for the Verein für Sozialpolitik (Association for Social Policy) at the end of the nineteenth century, using typical methods of quantitative survey research. More than a decade earlier, Karl Marx had also suggested research that would today be described as quantitative. It is difficult to suggest that his 'A Workers' Inquiry' of 1880 breathed the spirit of critical rationalism (or even positivism).

Second, the reasoning of Stamann et al. implicitly contains the postulate that methods must have a background theory, a theoretical foundation. In our view, QCA is a *method*, it is not a methodology, and it does not presuppose a particular way of approaching this world and its social problems. The term *method* comes from the Greek word μέθοδος, meaning a pursuit of knowledge, an investigation, or a mode of prosecuting such inquiry. A method is a tool for gaining insights, a planned procedure based on rules, just as the principle of the diesel engine, for example, is a procedure for generating energy through combustion so that a BMW can be powered. Methods can be applied in very different contexts: internal combustion engines are also used in lawnmowers, hedge trimmers, ships or aeroplanes. As a method, QCA can be used, for example, in the context of grounded theory research or in the context of discourse-analytical research; followers of the rational choice approach can also make use of it. Unlike variants of discourse analysis, which have developed as methods out of Foucault's discourse theory (Keller, 2011), QCA has no background theory. This is by no means a shortcoming. Quantitative methods such as variance analysis, multiple regression, and approaches of causal modelling, such as the LISREL approach, do not have a background theory either, but can be used in very different theoretical contexts. Sometimes there are close relationships between methods and theoretical approaches, such as between Bourdieu's theory of habitus and correspondence analysis (Blasius, 2001) but then the method of correspondence analysis can also be used in the context of other theoretical approaches.

Another suggestion by Stamann et al. (2016, para. 11) is to make a conceptual separation of method and procedure. This does not seem reasonable to us. A quick look in any encyclopaedia or dictionary shows that the two terms are rather to be understood as synonyms. For example, Wikipedia states that 'In recent centuries it [method] more often means a prescribed process for completing a task' (accessed 27 May 2022).

Possibility of Combining QCA with Other Methods

We are often asked about the possibilities of combining QCA with other approaches and methods, for example, 'Is QCA at all suitable for my project in which I am following the approach of critical discourse analysis?' or 'Can I combine QCA with grounded theory?'.

The question of whether QCA is 'compatible' with certain research styles or theoretical approaches cannot be answered from the viewpoint of QCA, but only from that of the respective research tradition. It is thus the responsibility of the grounded theory *sensu* Charmaz, for example, to formulate statements of compatibility or incompatibility.

On the part of QCA as a method, there is nothing to prevent its use within the framework of approaches that are bound to a certain theory and certain terminology. Qualitative content analysis can certainly be combined with discourse-analytical approaches or interactionist or phenomenological approaches. Whether this is productive or 'allowed' from the perspective of the approach depends, of course, on the approach in question.

Qualitative content analysis is very often used in mixed methods research for the analysis of qualitative data. We attribute this, among other things, to the fact that these projects often involve semi-structured open interviews using an interview guide. Systematic and effective analysis techniques are needed for these data. Qualitative content analysis not only makes it possible to process large numbers of cases systematically and effectively, but its results can also be integrated excellently into so-called 'joint displays' (Guetterman, Creswell, & Kuckartz, 2015; Guetterman & Fetters, 2022). In Kuckartz and Rädiker (2021), we describe numerous integration strategies for presenting qualitative and quantitative data and/or results of a mixed methods study in such joint displays. In practice, there are numerous joint displays in which typical results of qualitative content analyses (identified themes, case-by-case thematic summaries, etc.) are presented (Guetterman, Fetters, & Creswell, 2015). The frequent use of QCA in mixed methods projects is also due to the fact that the results of qualitative analysis can be transformed into quantitative data ('quantitizing') and analysed in combination with the quantitative data.

Openness and Understanding of Meaning

'How qualitative is QCA in relation to the central requirements of openness and under-standing of meaning in the qualitative research process?' This question seems to implicitly assume that there is a *continuum of qualitative methods*, that is, that different methods of analysis can be more or less qualitative. In fact, some groups of qualitative researchers have cultivated such views and see themselves as the representatives of 'true' qualitative research. Other approaches to qualitative research are then described as less qualitative or only half-heartedly qualitative, or even denied the attribute of being qualitative altogether. Their users are criticized for not spending enough time doing truly qualitative research, possibly due to the constraints of externally funded projects and/or clients to which the projects are subject. In this context, it is worth recalling Ryan and Bernard's four-field table of qualitative and quantitative data and qualitative and quantitative analysis presented in Table 1.1. There, as well as in the works of other scholars, qualitative and quantitative data and qualitative and quantitative analysis are just as clearly and unambiguously defined. Just as it does not seem reasonable in the quantitative field to speak of a bit of a number, a bit of a mean or variance calculation, so it does not seem reasonable to us to assume a valence in the qualitative field. There is a general consensus that openness and under-standing of meaning are central characteristics of qualitative research. In this respect, questions about the openness of QCA as a method, and the role played by the under-standing of meaning in this framework, are clearly justified.

Openness of Qualitative Content Analysis

As far as 'openness' is concerned, it is necessary to make explicit what exactly is meant by 'openness'. Openness can be localized on different levels within the framework of a research project. For the research project as a whole, openness means being open to discovering the new. For the research participants, openness means being able to respond to a question or a posed topic completely freely and openly. This means that, unlike in a standardized survey, no pre-formulated answers are presented, between which research participants have to choose and which thus provide the framework for thinking. At the level of the researcher, the question of openness presents itself differently, namely as openness in terms of communication during data collection and (theoretical) prior knowledge. Does the postulate of openness here mean that the researchers are not allowed to ask any specific questions? Does it mean, for example, that in an open-ended interview, the researchers have to wait for narratives from the research participants after an initiating stimulus and are not allowed to ask any further questions? Or does the postulate of openness in relation to the researchers mean that they should approach the research field and the research participants without prior knowledge? As a consequence, this would mean that researchers should go into the field as a tabula rasa, and not read any literature beforehand, but should engage in the research situation without bias and not blinded by existing theories.

These questions can only be answered from the perspective of the chosen research approach and the design of the research project. Qualitative content analysis, it should be emphasized again, is not a research style, methodology, and certainly not a paradigm according to which research is shaped and research designs are conceived. It is a method of analysis and as such can be used in many research contexts and disciplines. It can be used to analyse the material by means of categories; these can be defined in advance or developed directly based on the material, whereby mixed forms are possible. In this respect, the openness of QCA may vary, depending on the research approach chosen. A characteristic of QCA is a high degree of flexibility; it can work with a category system derived from theory as well as with categories developed entirely from the material. Qualitative content analysis can be used to analyse very open interviews, such as narrative interviews, as well as problem-centred interviews and strongly structured answers to open questions in surveys.

Understanding Meaning in the Context of Qualitative Content Analysis

The question of understanding meaning in the context of QCA is of central importance, so it is necessary to argue more fundamentally here. The category of meaning is primarily a philosophical and theological category. Many readers will immediately think of fundamental questions when they hear the term 'meaning', such as the question of the meaning of a professional career or even the meaning of life. Is there a way to understand the meaning of life, and to understand it correctly? The leading minds in philosophy have been racking their brains over this question for millennia: some have found a short answer, such as Douglas Adams in his book *The Hitchhiker's Guide to the Galaxy*, where the answer '42' was found to be the answer to the ultimate question of life – after 7½ million years of calculation. Of course, the question 'What is the meaning of life?', like many other questions about meaning, implicitly contains the premise that there is such a thing at all. But obviously not every statement or action is connected with a subjective meaning. In everyday life, for example, there are routines of behaviour that happen over and over again without being connected to a subjective meaning. For example, what meaningful considerations might be behind the fact that, according to citizens in Germany, underwear is usually changed daily, but pyjamas are only changed every few days? Modern personal assistance software such as Apple's Siri, Cortana (Microsoft) or Alexa (Amazon) also formulate answers in natural language without themselves associating any subjective meaning with them, unless this software has already taken on a life of its own behind the developers' backs and is now producing meaning. As you can see, we quickly get into a philosophical discussion that would transcend the question of understanding meaning in the context of the method of QCA.

The term 'sense' has many meanings; for example, it can mean the senses of our perception or the inner relationship of a person to something ('I have no sense of classical music'). But secondly, according to Wikipedia, it can also mean the meanings and ideas associated with a linguistic expression and thirdly, the state, the orientation of a person's thoughts. The above question about understanding meaning in the context of QCA presumably aims to understand the *meaning of a linguistic expression*. But perhaps it also means understanding the *state and thoughts of a person*. However, these are two fundamentally different orientations of understanding meaning. To put it clearly, QCA is not really well suited to the latter, it does not want to and cannot understand the inner states of a person; this is the professional field of psychology, and understanding meaning in this way is probably not easily practised by people without psychological training. Moreover, everyday life shows that it is very difficult to understand other people's state of mind in a valid or real way. Qualitative content analysis is not a method of individual psychological understanding of meaning, in terms of empathizing with inner worlds. Projects that work with QCA are mostly concerned with understanding the meaning of social action and understanding the meaning of statements and arguments. How the interpretive understanding and explanation of social action is to take place needs to be decided before QCA starts. Researchers can, for example, use Max Weber's widely known types of action (Prosch & Abraham, 2006) or Esser's (2001) framing model as a guide. As we have described in Section 1.4, we believe that hermeneutic techniques can provide important guidance. With the method of QCA, no model of understanding is mandated here, but it is required that the researchers develop a category system with consistency of meaning on the application of the categories when coding the material.

Qualitative Content Analysis and Development of Theory

Regardless of the questions to be investigated in an empirical study, researchers always have prior knowledge. This may be large or small, but in any case researchers should ask themselves self-critically what prior knowledge and (pre-)judgements they have. Depending on the scientific disciplines in which they have been trained, researchers also have a theoretical sensitivity, that is, they know the basic theories of their discipline, their categorical tools, and the fundamental interrelationships of empirical phenomena. In most cases, researchers also have profound knowledge of the current state of research in relation to the research questions they are investigating, because research-funding processes usually require such reference to the state of research in the respective application guidelines. In principle, prior theoretical knowledge for QCA does not have a special role that would differ from that for other methods. Regardless of which method is chosen, the question is how to deal with one's own prior knowledge, how to maintain sufficient openness to new perspectives and hitherto unknown factors. One of the strengths of QCA is the possibility of directly translating prior knowledge into categories of analysis. Frequently, such prior knowledge has already been incorporated into the strategy of data collection, for example, in the development of an interview guide for problem-centred interviews, which can be closely linked to the category development. Although such procedures are frequently encountered, QCA can also be applied to completely different situations and can also be used for the analysis of data that were collected with little or no prior knowledge.

Description or theory, what are the results of QCA? First of all, it has to be stated: there is no either/or here. Many research projects aim at description, typical research questions being: 'What contribution can families make to the care of Alzheimer's patients?', 'What is the everyday life of school children like in times of pandemic lockdown?', and 'How can households be convinced to modernize their home in terms of energy efficiency?'. The precise and differentiated answering of such research questions can be done in a descriptive manner with the help of QCA. In these research questions, the focus is not on theory building, but on obtaining practically usable knowledge through appropriate research. The situation is quite similar in the field of evaluation, where the aim is to optimize programmes and processes and where questions of theory building do not play an important role. However, QCA is not a method limited to description. It can also be used to discover relationships and contexts, formulate hypotheses and theories, and, under certain conditions, test theories. Similarly to grounded theory, this usually involves medium-range theories and not 'grand theory' (Breuer et al., 2019). In this context, questions about generalization in the context of qualitative research emerge, that is, questions that are not specifically about theory building in the context of QCA. In Section 9.5 we address such questions in more detail.

1.10 Summary and Concluding Remarks

In this introductory chapter we have discussed the foundations of qualitative content analysis and basic questions of methodology. What is the methodological position of QCA? We conceptualize QCA as a systematic method for the detailed analysis of qualitative (i.e., non-numerical) data. In accordance with the diversity of qualitative data, which ranges from individual interviews, focus groups, documents, and scientific publications to images, photos, videos, and social media data, the QCA method must be adapted to the type of data in each specific situation. In most research projects, QCA is used to analyse textual data, very often transcribed interviews (narrative, episodic, problem-centred interviews, etc.) or focus groups as well as documents of all kinds and social media posts.

We think it is important for researchers to know that QCA has long history as a method of social research. As a classic, predominantly quantitative content analysis, QCA emerged as early as the first half of the twentieth century. For more than 60 years, researchers have now used the term QCA to describe a decisively qualitative method. We see an important connection between QCA and principles of text understanding, such as those developed in hermeneutics: to understand the meaning of a text as a whole, one must understand the meaning of its parts – and vice versa. We conceptualize QCA as a qualitative method with a systematic approach and a claim to produce inter-subjectively valid results. In this regard, it differs from strongly constructivist approaches.

As a method of analysis, QCA is not in competition with methodologies and research styles such as grounded theory methodology or critical-rational approaches. Therefore, QCA can also be used within the framework of various overarching approaches such as the documentary method, discourse analysis, or even grounded theory.

2

ON CATEGORIES

━━━━━━━ Chapter objectives ━━━━━━━

In this chapter you will learn about:

- The meaning of the term 'category'
- Different types of categories
- The relationships of the terms 'category', 'code', 'theme', and 'concept'
- Category systems and their structure
- The structure and usefulness of category definitions
- The process of coding qualitative data.

As Berelson, one of the founding fathers of classical content analysis, noted:

> Content analysis stands or falls by its categories ... since the categories contain
> the substance of the investigation, a content analysis can be no better than its
> system of categories. (Berelson, 1952, p. 147)

In principle, this statement also applies to QCA. Here, too, (almost) everything revolves around categories and so it is obvious to pay special attention to the term 'category'.

2.1 The Term 'Category'

The term 'category' stems from the Greek word κατηγορία, which originally meant class, charge, or even accusation and can be found in many different scientific disciplines, from philosophy and the social sciences to biology, linguistics, and mathematics. Within the context of the social sciences, the term 'category' is mostly used in the sense of 'class': a category is the result of the classification of units. The classified entities can be, for example, persons, ideas, institutions, processes, statements, discourses, objects, arguments, and much more. We are familiar with the term 'category' within the context of knowledge systems, such as those presented in encyclopaedias, indexes, or even taxonomy charts. Numerous synonyms are in use for the term 'category'; thesaurus.com gives the following terms as synonyms, among others: class, division, grade, group, kind, league, level, section. Other synonyms that can be found frequently are family, genus, order, rank, and classification. Closely related to the term 'category' is the human ability to categorize, for which the following concise definition can be found in the English-language Wikipedia:

> Categorization is the ability and activity of recognizing shared features or
> similarities between the elements of the experience of the world (such as
> objects, events, or ideas), organizing and classifying experience by associating
> them to a more abstract group (that is, a category, class, or type), on the basis
> of their traits, features, similarities or other criteria. Categorization is
> considered one of the most fundamental cognitive abilities, and as such it is
> studied particularly by psychology and cognitive linguistics.[1]

Developing categories is therefore an elementary process for every mental activity. As a fundamental cognitive process, category development is the subject of both developmental psychology and epistemological thought. We need such processes of category development to perceive the world around us and organize what we perceive, for example, to form concepts, make comparisons, and decide which class we should assign a given observation or event to. Such fundamental cognitive processes are necessary

---

[1]https://en.wikipedia.org/w/index.php?title=Categorization&oldid=1023744955 (accessed 2 August 2022).

for everyday life and decisions as well as for practising science because objects in the world around us do not themselves dictate to which category or class they should be assigned. Thus, we have to assign objects and ideas to categories, and our perceptions and thought processes influence every categorization we make.

The question of what exactly a category represents in empirical research is hardly addressed in the literature on research methods, even in textbooks that focus on methods of qualitative data analysis. It is apparently assumed that people already know what a category is based on common sense. Instead of a definition, you often find a collection of category attributes, particularly in the context of the method of classical, quantitatively oriented content analysis. For example, Pürer (2003, p. 551) states that text features should be recorded 'with the help of a systematically developed category system with clearly defined categories. The categories must be clearly distinguishable from each other'.

2.2 Different Types of Categories

The following collection of examples in Table 2.1, all of which can be found in the social science literature, illustrates the diversity of the spectrum of what is referred to as a category in the social sciences. Obviously, the spectrum of what is considered a category is quite broad. We propose to distinguish at least the following types:

Table 2.1 Examples of categories

Category	Source
42 Energy consumption/energy demand	Category with number 42 from a quantitative content analysis (Früh, 2017, p. 169)
13100 Afghanistan conflict	Category with number 13100 from a quantitative content analysis (Rössler, 2017, p. 131)
Societal impact	Category from a qualitative content analysis on climate awareness
Baker	Category for occupational classification
Protective governing	Category developed in a grounded theory study (Strauss & Corbin, 1990, p. 121)
Personal affectedness by climate change with the following values: – high level of affectedness – low to medium level of affectedness – not affected – not ascertainable	Evaluative category developed in a study of social science environmental research
Scope (length/duration)	Category in a media analysis (Rössler, 2017, p. 116)
Critique of multiform racism with marking of resistance options between discourse orientation and use of violence	Category developed in a grounded theory study in the research field of digital youth cultures (Dietrich & Mey, 2019)

Factual categories. These are categories that refer to certain objective or seemingly objective occurrences, such as to classify different occupations (someone is a 'politician'; someone says, 'I am a baker'), a place ('I live in Surrey', 'I live in a redevelopment area') or an event ('train accident at Rome Central Station').

Thematic categories. Here, a category refers to a specific content, such as a topic, a specific argument, a specific figure of thought, etc., such as 'political commitment', 'consumer behaviour', or 'environmental knowledge'. Within an interview, the text passages are marked that contain information on these thematic categories. The categories have the function of pointers here, they point to a certain position, a certain segment in the text. The quality criterion in this case is that the right positions are marked. An exact determination of the boundaries of the segment is not a priority.

Evaluative, scaling categories. With the help of these categories, assessments of specific data are made on the basis of the researchers' evaluation standards. Evaluative categories have a defined number of values that are used to assess the data. Evaluative categories often have an ordinal scale level; for example, the category 'helper syndrome' may have three values, namely 'strong', 'little', 'none'. Dichotomous rating scales (a characteristic is 'present' or 'not present') can also be used. Coders process relevant passages of the material and make a rule-based classification.

Analytical categories. This type of category is the result of the researchers' intensive examination of the data, that is, the categories move away from the description that is provided by thematic categories. For example, an analysis of the thematic category 'environmental behaviour' and its dimensions 'mobility behaviour', 'energy behaviour', etc. leads the researchers to the realization that the research participants often talk about the financial costs and benefits of certain behaviours; they then define the analytical category 'cost–benefit calculation'.

Theoretical categories. This category type represents a special form of analytical categories. The categories refer to existing theories or are derived from them; for example 'cognitive dissonance reduction' according to Festinger's (1957) theory.

Natural categories. These are the terminology and concepts used by the actors in the field themselves. In the English literature on research methods, especially in grounded theory, the term 'in vivo code' is used for this purpose (Strauss & Corbin, 1990, p. 69). An example of this is the term 'tradition bearer of the unit' mentioned by Strauss, by which a head nurse refers to another ward nurse (Strauss & Corbin, 1990, p. 69). The transition to analytical categories is fluid because actors use these terms to explain to themselves and others the phenomena of their everyday world. Often natural categories are very vivid and pictorial, for example, when young people, during interviews, refer to a particular teacher as 'the eco-woman'.

Formal categories. This category type refers to dates and information about the unit being analysed. For an open interview, for example, this could be the length of the interview in minutes, the date of the interview, and the number of words.

In qualitative content analysis, another form of categories often plays a role, the so-called *ordering categories*. These are not used to code the material, but to structure the categories themselves. In this way, the ordering categories have a similar function to the headings in a book or in an article. This considerably improves the clarity.

We see the importance of such a distinction of category types primarily in the fact that it promotes analytical sensitivity in a qualitative content analysis. Furthermore, it initiates a probing and comparative reflection on the appropriateness of category types for the respective research questions. Although in principle it is always a matter of assigning a category to a certain segment of the material, for example a certain passage of text, the processes of coding differ depending on the type of category. This soon becomes clear when you compare the use of natural categories and factual categories: in the one case, one searches for particularly apt ways of speaking by research participants in an exploratory and interpretive way; in the other case, it is about identifying facts, features, and attributes that are directly related to the research questions. Category types and the forms of coding are thus intimately connected. While we approach the relationship of categories and coding from the side of the categories and distinguish category types, Saldaña (2013) takes the perspective from the side of the coder. He distinguishes numerous types of coding, including 'attribute coding' and 'in vivo coding' corresponding to the 'factual categories' and 'natural categories' examples above. Saldaña's almost encyclopaedic presentation of coding forms in research practice stimulates the analytical imagination and is especially helpful if one wants to know in which studies certain types of coding, for example, 'narrative coding', 'emotion coding', or 'dramaturgical coding', were practised. Saldaña distinguishes 32 types of coding and invites readers to fill in other coding forms they encounter in the literature or discover for themselves in the blank forms included in his book (Saldaña, 2013, p. 183). Whether it is really useful to distinguish between so many different types of coding for QCA work seems questionable, especially because, on closer inspection, many types of coding overlap and because they are located at completely different levels of abstraction.

2.3 The Relationship of 'Category', 'Code', and 'Theme'

As shown in the previous section, we are dealing with very different types of categories. Beyond the differences described, categories also differ in terms of their breadth of content, their degree of complexity, their degree of abstraction, and their significance and relevance for the core topic of the research project. Finally, they also differ in terms of the time of their emergence in the research process – and this leads to a problem that is also perceived by many as a confusion of terms: many different terms such as 'main category', 'parent category', 'sub-category', 'core category', and 'key category' circulate without generally accepted definitions and delimitations. Apparently, the terms reflect the above-mentioned distinguishing features. But what actually is a main category, what distinguishes it from a core category, when can a category be called a 'key category', and how many of them should or may an analysis have?

The confusion increases even more because in qualitative social research the term 'code' and corresponding specifications (sub-code, higher-level code, parent code, top-level code, etc.) are also frequently used (e.g., in Bazeley, 2021, pp. 155–260; Miles et al., 2020, pp. 61–102). This applies first and foremost to grounded theory, where the term 'code' appears in several forms, namely as 'open' and 'axial code' in the early stages of analysis and as 'substantive code', 'key code', 'selective code', or 'theoretical code' in the later phases of analysis (Strauss & Corbin, 1990, pp. 57–142). Corresponding to the different analysis activities in the different phases of the analysis process, the term 'code' sometimes denotes an abstract concept encompassing many dimensions, but sometimes only a first ad-hoc developed concept, which possibly develops into a category within the further analysis. This now introduces another term, namely 'concept', whose relation to the terms 'code' and 'category' is also not quite clear. Although Strauss and Corbin (1990) have endeavoured to provide some clarity regarding the different uses of the terms, it is difficult to deny that although some grounded theory writings differentiate between the terms 'code' and 'category', often their use is not uniform and consistent. This applies, for example, to the various editions of the textbook by Strauss and Corbin. In addition, scholars advocating grounded theory usually work with an expanded concept of coding, which includes analysing, naming, and categorizing as well as the theoretical classification of the data as a whole.

Obviously, there are different traditions and conceptual cultures in qualitative research, and also within grounded theory itself. For example, the constructivist variant, as represented by Charmaz (2014), uses some of the same terms as Glaser (2005) and Corbin and Strauss (2015) but also others, such as 'focused code'. Overall, in the field of qualitative data analysis, one encounters numerous inconsistencies and confusing phenomena in relation to the use of the terms 'code' and 'category'. Thus, with regard to the activity, one speaks almost always of coding, but far less often of categorizing. Moreover, in translations from English into other languages, 'code' is often translated in the same way as 'category'.

A look beyond qualitative research shows that in communication studies and the prevailing form of content analysis there, people usually talk about categories and not codes. However, the application of categories to research data, such as media products, is referred to as coding and not categorizing, and the people who do this are called coders (Früh, 2017; Krippendorff, 2018). Those who are at home in quantitatively oriented social science research will be particularly surprised, because code, category, and coding mean something quite different there than they do in the context of qualitative data analysis: there, 'code' refers to the assignment of a number, or to put it more generally, a sign, to a certain attribute (also called a 'category'). For example, in a data matrix, respondents from rural areas can be coded '1' and respondents from urban areas '2'. For them, coding is therefore a transformation process from the empirical world to the numerical world.

Of particular importance is that in qualitative data analysis software (see Chapter 8), the term 'code' is used almost exclusively, whether it is a code, a category, a main or key category, a concept, or a theme.

All this makes efforts to delineate the terms appear very difficult and unpromising. Even if it were possible in this book, readers would be confused as soon as they picked up other relevant books. The question may therefore be asked whether all the terms mentioned do not ultimately mean the same thing and only a blurred use of terms needs to be stated. This can certainly be said in the affirmative for some methodological texts and research approaches. As described, particularly in the literature on grounded theory, there is often no systematic, continuous distinction between concept, code, and category. There is therefore a case for using the terms 'code' and 'category' synony-mously, including the fact that some composites are more common than others in English (e.g., 'coding frame' instead of 'category frame' or 'categorizing frame', and 'code memo' rather than 'category memo'), while in other languages, such as German, the opposite might apply. One argument against such synonymous use is that there are plausible efforts to ascribe differentiated meanings to the terms and to establish a chronological order oriented to the research process. For example, Creswell and Creswell Báez (2021, pp. 158–171) describe the path from the raw data (texts) to the themes in the following sequence: first, read texts and assign codes to text segments; second, order codes and summarize codes into themes; third, create a 'map of the themes' and describe their interrelations in the 'qualitative report'. In this inductive approach, the initial, still poorly developed, codes become themes in the course of the analysis, or categories in the language of qualitative content analysis. Such a development from simple to more abstract and complex analytical tools is typical of many analytical approaches that work with codes or categories, and that is why we also want to recom-mend it for qualitative content analysis. Thus, in inductive approaches (what exactly these are is described in Chapter 3), as far as the beginnings of the analysis are con-cerned, we speak of codes. But when it comes to the main phases of qualitative content analysis, we should always speak of categories and not of codes. The title of Chapter 3 of this book is therefore 'Developing Categories' and not 'Developing Codes and Concepts'. We will try to maintain a consistent use of terms in relation to QCA. However, in so far as we refer to grounded theory or positions close to it in the rest of the text (such as the technique of open coding), we will not attempt to impose a consist-ent use of terms on grounded theory ex post and will not attempt to introduce a kind of standard language. The same applies to Chapter 8, in which we describe the imple-mentation of qualitative content analysis with QDA software. In the current QDA programs, only the term 'code' and its composites (e.g., 'sub-code', 'code name', etc.) exist – we cannot change this and so we naturally also use these terms, which some-times seems a little strange, for example, when we describe how new categories are inserted with the option 'new code'.

As far as the relationship of the terms 'theme' and 'category' is concerned, we under-stand these terms to be synonyms if they are thematic categories. For example, when summarizing the coded text segments of the category 'personal environmental behav-iour', we would speak of a thematic analysis rather than a categorical analysis.

We understand the term 'concept' as transversal to the terms code, category, and theme. A concept can be both a designation for individual events, phenomena, and occurrences in the first phase of the analysis (Strauss & Corbin, 1990, pp. 61–69) as well as an elaborated idea, a complex plan, for example, the 'sustainability concept of the Green Party' (resulting from the analysis of documents) or 'Heidi Klum's concept of beauty' (resulting from the analysis of various episodes of *Germany's Next Topmodel*). In this sense, a concept can be a code, a theme, or a key category that emerged through analysis only at a late stage of the research.

2.4 The Category System

The set of all categories is usually referred to as a 'category system', 'code system', or as a 'coding frame'. A category system can be organized as a linear list, a hierarchy, or a network.

A *linear list* is a string of categories that are all at the same level (e.g., 'environmental knowledge', 'environmental attitudes', 'environmental behaviour').

A *hierarchical category system* consists of various superordinate and subordinate levels (e.g., the category 'environmental behaviour' with the sub-categories 'energy behaviour', 'mobility behaviour', 'consumption behaviour', 'recycling behaviour', etc.). Such category systems are probably familiar to us from everyday life and science. We encounter them in the structuring of offers at Amazon or eBay as well as in the form of organizational structures in academic libraries and public libraries and as organizational charts of administrations and institutes. Hierarchical structures can be depicted as tree structures; the number of levels and ramifications is not limited. As far as terminology is concerned, in the case of hierarchical category systems one speaks of main categories or parent categories and sub-categories or child categories. As soon as a category is being subdivided, it can be referred to as a *parent category* and the categories of the subordinate level as *child categories*. When using QDA software for the analysis, the terms are correspondingly parent code and sub-code, since most QDA software packages use the term 'code' instead of 'category'. In a hierarchical category system, there can of course be more than two levels, thus sub-categories of sub-categories can also exist. In this respect the term 'parent category' or 'parent code' is no longer unambiguous with regard to the designation of the level in the category system. Often the term 'main category' is used instead of the formal term 'parent category'. This could lead to the wrong conclusion that these are particularly important categories for the research project, a kind of *key categories*. However, this is by no means always the case; the prefix 'main' often only denotes the difference with respect to the subordinate sub-categories. However, we advocate using the term 'main category' only when it is actually a category that is particularly important for the research project in question. It is also not mandatory for a main category to be further subdivided and to have sub-categories. In research practice, however, this will almost always be the case, because in the case of a particularly important category, the analysis process will almost always be to identify dimensions and specify characteristics and to define sub-categories on this basis.

The third type of category system organization, the *network structure,* is characterized by the fact that the elements (nodes) of the network can be connected to each other in many ways (and not only hierarchically). Networks are usually represented as graphs with nodes and edges. Networks allow different connection paths, a fact that is used, for example, in the organization of websites.

The category systems of qualitative content analysis are almost always structured hierarchically. This also applies to the examples presented in this book. Compared to linear lists, hierarchical category systems have the advantage that they can be structured, and the groupings can convey meaning. This suits a multi-level approach that wants to go into detail and discover dimensions and specifics through the analysis. Compared to network-like category systems, hierarchical category systems are clearer, and they allow one to search for connections at different levels. The advantage of hierarchical structuring may be illustrated by the following example of geographical structuring. With appropriate structuring, we can compare countries with each other (e.g., Germany and Canada), regions of these countries (Bavaria and Quebec), cities of these regions (Munich and Montreal), certain neighbourhoods in these cities, and so on. It is easy to aggregate and disaggregate, an advantage that is particularly useful when using QDA software.

Are there certain demands to be made on category systems? The question can be answered with a clear 'yes'. Category systems should have an inner coherence and their structure should be plausible and comprehensible. The main categories should share a similar degree of abstraction and generality.

Furthermore, how can you recognize a good and useful category system and how does it differ from a less good one? The following standards should be met (according to Rädiker & Kuckartz, 2020, pp. 46–49):

The categories are closely related to the research questions. This is the most important condition; after all, the categories should contribute to answering your research questions. It is therefore important to ask of each category to what extent it helps to achieve the goal of a study. The usefulness of a category can, of course, also consist in capturing important contextual knowledge, that is to say, a category does not have to be removed just because the connection to the research question is not immediately obvious. The examining gaze should also grasp the overall construct: Does the category system offer sufficient analytical depth? It can be helpful to anticipate the finished results report and its structure: does the category system cover all important aspects to be investigated or are categories relevant to the research questions possibly missing?

The categories are exhaustive. This means that for every aspect in the data that is important for answering the research questions, and hence should be covered, there is a category. Whether this criterion is met can only be said with certainty when the categories are applied to the empirical data, (i.e., it is primarily an empirical question). Often, at the beginning of the analysis, it is a good idea to create a category 'other', duplicated if necessary at several levels of the category system. This category can then be used to capture aspects beyond the categories already developed. In the course of the analysis, it can then be decided whether these are individual aspects that do not require a category of their own, or whether a further category is added inductively from the data.

The categories are selective (distinct) but, depending on the application, they can also be mutually exclusive. 'Selective' means that it must always be clear which category is assigned to a particular section of text – and which is not. If you constantly fluctuate between two similar categories when assigning categories, this is an indication of low selectivity. Absolute unambiguity cannot always be achieved; nevertheless, special attention should be paid to precise category definitions. Precise definition of categories, however, does not mean that only one category may always be assigned to a text passage. Very often in the application of QCA, several main categories or sub-categories are assigned to the same text section, sometimes even overlapping, because several aspects are addressed. In some cases, however, the multiple assignment of categories is not desired, and it is necessary that categories are mutually exclusive. In these cases, categories are not allowed to overlap. Typical examples are evaluative sub-categories, such as 'low', 'medium', and 'high' pro-environmental attitudes.

The categories are well formulated. It is important to pay attention to how category names are formulated. Are equivalent sub-categories also formulated linguistically in an equivalent way? It also makes a difference whether you choose 'climate' or 'climate crisis', 'motivation' or 'attitude' as a category. It is helpful to look at a dictionary or thesaurus to include distinctions from other terms in the category definition and to select terms that are as appropriate as possible.

Taken together, the categories form a 'gestalt'. We have already addressed this aspect in the introductory sentences above. The point is that a category system has an inner coherence and that the categories do not merely stand next to each other loosely and without connection. To check this criterion, it is helpful to pay attention to the level of abstraction of the categories; in particular, equivalent sub-categories should have a comparable degree of generality. The main categories should also generally have a similar level of abstraction and generality.

The sub-categories are dimensions, values, or sub-aspects of their parent category. The degree of abstraction sensibly decreases with each lower hierarchy level, since the sub-categories should always be aspects, values, or dimensions of the parent categories. While this seems logical, it can entail a longer development process in category development on the material. Is, for example, 'nature' mentioned in the interview as a sub-aspect of 'environment' or is it on the same level so that it would be better called 'nature and environment'? Should 'climate change' be a separate main category or a sub-category of 'environmental issues'?

The categories are understandable. The category names should not be too complicated. Names should be used that are easy to understand for the coders as well as for the later recipients of the study. This does not mean that no technical terms should be used and category names should be formulated in simple language. However, when formulating and constructing the category system, it is useful to keep in mind who will be working with the categories and to whom they will later be presented in publications, lectures, and posters.

2.5 Category Definition, Code Book, and Coding Guide

Working with categories and developing a category system is of great importance for the QCA method. The construction of the category system requires careful work, takes a lot of time, and is the basis for further analyses. For QCA as a systematic method, it is very important to formulate category definitions at the same time as constructing the category system. A category definition explains what exactly is meant by a category in a research project, for example, what 'environmental attitude', 'global politics', or 'resilience' are taken to mean in the context of the current research. It does not matter how the categories were developed, whether inductively based on the data or concept- or theory-oriented without regard to the empirical data: categories should be defined, and the definitions should be as precise as possible so that all coders have the same understanding of the categories and can thus code the material in the same way. Of course, this does not apply to categories such as proper names, place names, and the like. Some categories may not seem to need definition at first glance, such as 'ball sports', but a particular research question may result in problems of classification. For example, should Harry Potter's favourite sport of Quidditch be categorized as a sub-category of ball sports? Then a category like 'ball sport', which actually seems self-explanatory, still needs a definition.

Name of the category:	Concise label as meaningful and precise as possible
Content description:	Description of the category, if applicable with theoretical background
Category application:	'This category is coded if the following aspects are mentioned ...'
Examples of applications:	Quotations with reference (document; paragraph or page)
Other applications (optional):	'The category is also coded when ...' Quotations with reference (document; paragraph or page)
Differentiation from other categories (optional):	'The category is not coded if ...: ... but in this case category z is used' Quotations with reference (document; paragraph or page)

Figure 2.1 General scheme for category definitions

A category definition should have the structure shown in Figure 2.1. Quotations from the texts should help to illustrate the concrete application of a category, that is, examples must be selected that are as typical as possible for a category. It is not always possible to find a truly typical example that covers all use cases of a category. In this case, several quotations can be integrated into the category definition, or a typical example can be constructed as an alternative or supplementary example, which must of course be marked as such.

Category definitions have a twofold function. First, they document basic elements of QCA for the recipients of the study and for the scientific community as a whole. Without knowledge of these basic elements, the results of the analysis may be difficult for outsiders to interpret. Second, the category definitions – supplemented by concrete instructions for action – represent the coding guidelines for the coders. This means that the more accurate the definitions are, and the more illustrative the examples of the applications of each category are, the easier it is to code and the more likely it is for a high level of agreement among coders to be achieved.

The *category manual* is to be distinguished from the *coding guide*; alternatively, the term *code book* is also used. The term 'code book' has nothing to do with secret services or with cryptology but refers to a document that contains all categories and their definitions.

The difference between the coding guide and the category manual can be expressed most simply by an equation: category manual + instructions for coders = coding guide. The coding guide is a document that is primarily intended for internal use and gives coders specific instructions for their work. The code book, on the other hand, is designed for the world outside of the research project. Categories are central to QCA, and in this respect the code book has a very important function, as it documents the accuracy and precision with which the work was done.

2.6 About Coding

The terms *category* and *coding* are closely linked in QCA. Although the category system as a structural and ordering system has its own relevance, the actual purpose of the categories is the coding of the data or parts of the data, which are then referred to as 'coded segments'. Thus, in the case of verbal data, a coded segment is understood to be a passage of text that is associated with a particular category, a particular content (e.g., a theme, a behaviour, or a motive). The direction of view can be twofold. On the one hand, one can look from the category to the text passage – this passage is then a coded segment that is tagged with a particular category. On the other hand, starting from the text passage (i.e., based on the data), one can develop concepts and categories (i.e., code the material in an extended sense).

The process of identifying and classifying relevant text passages and the associated coding can thus be both an act of *subsuming under* a category already existing, and an act of *generating* a category, possibly also the invention of a completely new term, for a phenomenon that one has discovered in the empirical data.

The result of both views is ultimately the same, namely a connection between the text passage and the category. Figure 2.2 illustrates this basic principle: on the left is the original text, on the right the coded segment. The section with a grey background was coded with the category 'learning via values education'.

I: So it also makes sense for an individual to start there?

R: It makes sense because if all individuals started sweeping their own front door, then we wouldn't have any problems.

I: Good, and do you think that it is possible to learn how to deal with the problems, and if so, how and where?

R: Yes it is. It starts at a very young age. It starts with the fact that you only put as much on your plate as you eat, that you don't throw away your lunch, but that you say, I have something here that will be eaten, that is food, that is valuable, that you don't waste, that is available, that you don't give away wastefully, that you make it clear even to small children that there are people who don't have such things

R: You can learn. It starts at a very young age. It starts with the fact that you only put as much on your plate as you eat, that you don't throw away your lunch, but that you say, I have something here that will be eaten, that is food, that is valuable, that you don't waste. These are the basic attitudes, the values we have, that we don't give it away wastefully, that we make it clear to young children that there are people who don't have such things.

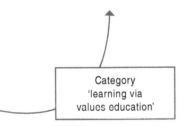

Category 'learning via values education'

Figure 2.2 The coding process: original text, category, and coded segment

The bidirectional perspective described above represents a decisive difference between classical and qualitative content analysis. In classical content analysis, a step towards a new, higher analytical level takes place through coding, and a reference back to the source material is no longer intended after this step; work continues with a data matrix consisting of numbers (units of analysis by categories). In QCA, on the other hand, the relationship between category and source material remains throughout the analysis: first, it may be of interest to be able to refer back to the underlying coded text at any time; and second, the qualitative forms of analysis are based on these original data as well as their summaries and abstractions.

Classical content analysis only looks at the text from the point of view of the categories and accordingly uses different terminology: it does not speak of a 'coded segment' but of a 'coding unit'. This refers to the individual element that triggers coding, that is, the assignment of a category. The assignment of the category 'American president' is triggered by the words 'Joe Biden', 'Donald Trump', 'Bill Clinton', 'Barack Obama', 'George W. Bush', 'George H. W. Bush', etc. According to the understanding of classical content analysis, a coding unit should address only one category, so that 'Bill Clinton' is only considered an indicator of 'American president' and not also an indicator of 'lawyer'. Margrit Schreier (2012) follows this logic of classical content analysis in her book *Qualitative Content Analysis*. For her, it is central to segment the data into coding units before coding:

> Before you can get started on trying out your coding frame, you first have to divide your material up into smaller units, which you will then code using your coding frame. This is called segmentation. (Schreier, 2012, p. 126)

In QCA, we believe that coding has a broader meaning than mere indexing or 'tagging' and that a predetermination of coding units is not necessary but rather alien to the process of the analysis. In the context of QCA, researchers usually code units of meaning instead of determining coding units in advance, which means that coded segments may well overlap or be nested within each other. The criterion for determining the segment boundaries is comprehensibility 'out of context', which means that the segments should be comprehensible in themselves when seen outside their context. Of course, it does not necessarily have to be units of meaning that are chosen as coded segments. In the case of factual categories or natural categories (in vivo codes), the situation is different; also, the occurrence of certain persons or places, certain metaphors or idioms can be coded, that is, in this case the coded segments are very short and do not represent units of meaning.

Often, especially when the amount of text to be processed is very large, assistants beyond the scientific research team are called in specifically for the coding of the material. For QCA, a certain degree of interpretive competence is necessary: the coders must be well informed about the research questions, the theoretical constructs and the meaning of the categories. Typically, team coding sessions and coding workshops are conducted to achieve as much coding agreement as possible. While in quantitatively oriented content analysis appropriate coefficients of agreement, such as Krippendorff's alpha, Cohen's kappa, or Scott's pi (Krippendorff, 2004b) are calculated to determine the so-called intercoder reliability or interrater reliability, in QCA there is a tendency to adopt a procedural approach that seeks to minimize non-matches through discussion and consensual decision-making within the research team. Chapter 9 describes this approach and the options for determining intercoder agreement in more detail.

2.7 Summary and Concluding Remarks

Categories are the most important instrument for all QCA strategies. As instruments, the categories are not an end in themselves, but have a specific function in the research process: they are used to code the data, which usually means coding parts of the data, prototypically text segments, parts of an image, or specific film clips. The categories are thus devices for structuring, indexing, and better understanding the material; all this not from a general perspective but from the specific perspective of the research questions.

It is important for researchers to be able to distinguish between different types of categories. Which types of categories researchers decide to use when processing their data depends on the research questions. Different types of categories can be combined in one study.

All the categories and sub-categories taken together form a category system, a framework that is central to the analysis of the data collected. Category systems can vary in terms of complexity: They can be simply structured and consist of a linear list of categories, for example. However, category systems can also be highly complex and differentiated with multiple levels and sub-categories. Category systems should have a plausible overall shape and cover as many relevant aspects of the research questions as possible.

For each category and sub-category, a definition should describe as precisely as possible what the category means and what phenomena it is intended to capture. A category manual contains all category definitions as well as examples from the original data. A coding guide also provides the researchers with precise instructions for the coding process, so that consistency can be achieved across multiple coders. The final category system developed in a project after intensive analysis work should be documented in detail.

Researchers should make sure that their category system remains manageable. Beginners in particular tend to form too many categories and use far too many hierarchical levels.

3

DEVELOPING CATEGORIES

Chapter objectives

In this chapter you will learn about:

- The topic of category development in the methods literature
- Developing a priori categories independent of the empirical material (deductive category development)
- Developing categories using the material (inductive category development) in different ways
- Mayring's approach of inductive category development via summarizing, paraphrasing content analysis
- The development of categories from the material in grounded theory
- Mixing forms of category development (deductive-inductive category development).

If you choose to conduct a qualitative data analysis, you will likely ask yourself, 'How do I determine which categories to use?', 'How many categories are necessary?', or 'What rules do I have to follow in constructing the categories?'

In the literature on research methods, little information is given about how exactly categories are constructed because it is assumed to follow common sense. You may come across rather unhelpful statements, such as that there are no patent remedies for developing categories (Kriz & Lisch, 1988, p. 134). However, the same textbooks point out that category construction is very relevant for the analysis and protagonists argue that content analysis stands or falls with its categories. So, you may be asking yourself, how in the world can you construct something as important as a category?

The most suitable way to develop the categories depends largely on the research questions at hand and any previous knowledge that researchers have about the given research subject or field. The more theory-oriented the project, the more extensive the previous knowledge, the more focused the research question, and the more specific the existing hypotheses, the easier it is to develop categories while reading through the collected data.

Looking at empirical studies, a spectrum of theoretical and empirical category development can be observed:

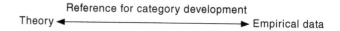

Reference for category development

Theory ◄————————————————————► Empirical data

The two poles represent an exclusively theory-oriented and an exclusively empirically oriented category development. However, we prefer to distinguish different types of category development according to the role the empirical data play in the development of the category system. The left-hand side of the continuum is then formed by *deductive category development*, which can also be called *a priori category development*. In this case, a priori categories are developed independently of the collected data but based on an already existing systematization. This can be a theory or a hypothesis, but also an interview guide, or an already existing system for structuring content. This means that a priori category development is not necessarily oriented towards a theory.

The right-hand side of the continuum is often referred to as *inductive category development*. Here, the categories are developed directly using the empirical data.

A priori category development and inductive category development using empirical data are not as contradictory as one might assume when it comes to applying the categories. In general, for qualitative content analysis, it is characteristic that the entire material is coded, that is, systematically processed using a category system. The same rules and standards always apply to the use of the category system, regardless of whether the categories were developed directly from the data or independently of it.

In the following, procedures of deductive and inductive category development are described. Subsequently, frequently encountered mixed forms of category development will be discussed.

3.1 Developing Categories Deductively (without Using Empirical Data)

Deductive category development is largely independent of the data collected. However, the term 'deductive category development' is not really an optimal description of the procedure researchers use in developing categories and the cognitive processes taking place in the background. 'Deductive' means that the particular is deduced from the general, that is, a logical derivation is made. Thus, the word 'deductive' seemingly gives the impression that everything follows a set path, similar to the derivation of a mathematical function. If everything is done according to the rules, so the assumption goes, everyone comes to the same result. This is (unfortunately) not the case at all, which is why an alternative term, such as 'a priori category development independent of the empirical data', would actually make more sense to us, because it only describes the procedure and does not suggest that, if the rules are followed, a clear and 'correct' result will emerge. The term 'deductive category development', however, has become a standard in the language used in the context of qualitative research, so that everyone immediately believes they understand what is meant by this term. That is why we have decided – grudgingly – to retain the term and use it here.

Sources for Deductive Categories

In qualitative content analysis, various sources are available that can be used to develop deductive categories.

Interview guide. If an interview is conducted with an interview guide, numerous preliminary considerations that reflect the research interest have usually already been incorporated into their development. In this respect, it makes sense to develop categories directly based on the interview guide. The resulting category system often consists of thematic categories, which follow the structure of the guideline in their sequence. If the guide is structured by thematic blocks, these can be adopted as ordering categories.

Theory. If a theory guides a study, the constructs and concepts contained in the theory can be translated into categories. For example, if an interview study examines media literacy in assessing (fake) news on climate change, the interview will certainly not directly ask about this media literacy. Nevertheless, the theoretical elaborations on media literacy should be consulted in the category development to ensure that important theory-based constructs are accessible in the analysis. The important constructs of the guiding theory are usually also found in the research questions, that is, there is a triad with the three interrelated elements of theory, research questions, and categories that need to be reconciled in the development of deductive categories.

State of research. It also makes sense to consider the current state of research during the development of categories. If connections between media literacy and the assessment of (fake) news have already been empirically verified, these can be incorporated into the category development. There may even be existing category systems of thematically similar studies that can at least be adopted as a starting point.

Process models. In classroom research, a school lesson can be subdivided according to certain aspects: an analysis process follows a typical sequence, as does a visit to a doctor's office. These chronological orders, which are inherent to an object under study and for which process models are often available in the literature, can be translated into categories.

Hypotheses and assumptions. If qualitative content analysis is to be used to verify hypotheses and assumptions about a certain field or object of interest, the categories must reflect these in some way. It does not matter whether the conjectures originate from earlier empirical studies and were used there as abductively obtained explanations for the research results or whether the researchers noted down their conjectures about the phenomenon under study for purposes of reflection in a first step of analysis.

Everyday knowledge. There is nothing wrong with using everyday knowledge to develop deductive categories as long as the result contributes to answering the research questions in a meaningful way. If the aim is to investigate why young adults drop out of university, or what motivates students to spend a semester abroad, categories can be developed a priori on the basis of everyday knowledge without reference to theory or collected data. The categories developed in this way can supplement theory-based categories or be compared with the result of a later inductive category development.

Personal experience and subjective theory. A special form of everyday knowledge is personal experience, which can also be coupled with a subjective theory. If I have spent several years in education for sustainable development giving courses to school classes and decide to write a dissertation on the learning processes that might occur, then I can draw on this experience and can take my hypotheses and subjective theories into account in the category development.

These sources of deductive categories are not mutually exclusive. On the contrary, different sources of deductive categories should always be considered in a research project to increase the chance of including valuable and innovative categories.

Example of Deductive Categories Based on Everyday Knowledge

A well-known daily newspaper distinguishes between the following seven categories:

1 Politics
2 Business

3   Finance

4   Sport

5   Local

6   Culture

7   Miscellaneous

These seven categories were developed by the newspaper editors independently of the data (i.e., the news items). The different categories seem plausible because they are based on everyday knowledge and the perceived social realities in our culture, in which these categorical differentiations can be found in scientific disciplines and governmental agencies. Another newspaper can of course work with completely different categories such as 'Technology & Motor' and 'Life'. Now, any new story that appears on the news ticker can be 'coded' accordingly and forwarded to the appropriate editor or division, as can be seen in Figure 3.1.

Time	Headline	Assigned department/ category
18:48	Buried victims freed by companions	Miscellaneous
18:24	EU debt limits remain suspended in 2022	Finance
17:58	Spectacular prison break in Athens	Miscellaneous
17:22	Will Israel's coalition be sworn in as early as Wednesday?	Politics
16:17	Another avalanche in the Alps	Miscellaneous
16:05	World's largest meat company ramps up production again	Business
15:52	The giant batteries from Wittenberg	Business
15:16	NASDAQ at lowest point since autumn 2004	Finance
15:10	David Diop wins British International Booker Prize for Literature	Culture
15:08	Why laziness is important for democracy	Miscellaneous

Figure 3.1   News headlines sorted into pre-defined categories

Clearly, some stories or topics are difficult to assign. For example, it is not clear if the story with the headline 'NASDAQ at lowest point since autumn 2004' should be assigned to the 'business' or 'finance' category. Thus, it is imperative to formulate criteria to be able to differentiate between the categories and encompass the intentions behind the classifications so that coders can reliably assign the headlines and code the data. In content analysis, such a written assignment rule is called a *category definition*. In our example, such a definition could be as shown in Figure 3.2.

Name of the category:	Finance
Content description:	All reports that deal with aspects of national or global finance.
Application of the category:	Reports on public finances, taxes, national and international financial markets, stock exchange, assets, etc.
Examples of applications:	NASDAQ at lowest point since autumn 2004
Delimitations:	The category is not coded if: – messages refer to local finances; these are assigned to the category 'Local'. – messages relate to economic policy and labour, transport and technology; these are assigned to the category 'Business'.

Figure 3.2 Category definition for the category 'finance'

A category definition must at least contain the name of the category and a description of its content. Furthermore, it is very useful if concrete examples and delimitations to neighbouring categories are included. When applying the categories, concrete examples from the data should be added.

The biggest difficulty in constructing categories deductively lies in formulating precise category definitions so that the categories do not overlap. Furthermore, there is the need for completeness of the categories. For example, the category scheme with seven categories presented above could hardly be used if we forgot to include a category like 'business'. Also, it is always important to include a category for topics that may not fit any of the other categories ('miscellaneous' here); this will allow you to assign all of the data. In the methodological literature, the requirement for categories in deductive category development is therefore often that categories *should be mutually exclusive and exhaustive* (e.g., Diekmann, 2007, p. 589; Krippendorff, 2018, pp. 138–139). In the above example this means that a news item from the news ticker should not be forwarded to two departments at the same time, otherwise one would risk the same story appearing in several places in the newspaper. In a newspaper, it does not make sense to run a news item twice. In QCA, on the other hand, a statement can also contain several aspects and therefore be assigned to several categories if necessary. Only by defining the categories as precisely as possible can sufficient quality be achieved in the application of the categories.

Example of Deductive Category Development from an Interview Guide

If structuring instruments are used for data collection, the inherent structure is often used as a starting point for the development of deductive categories. In the case of interviews conducted with an interview guide, the categories can be developed directly from the guide at the beginning of the QCA. The further development of the categories and the development of sub-categories are then carried out directly on the data. Such a mixed form of category development is described in Chapter 5.

Table 3.1 Categories developed deductively from an interview guide

Topics and questions of the interview guide	Category
CONCEPTIONS OF THE WORLD	
1. In your view, what are the world's biggest problems in the 21st century?	Biggest world problems
2. How can these problems be dealt with? Can they be dealt with at all? By whom?	Societal efficacy
3. When you think of climate change and the necessary reduction of carbon dioxide emissions: can a change in consumer habits in developed countries have a positive effect?	Consumption and climate
CONCEPTIONS OF OTHERS	
4. We often talk about the discrepancy between attitude and behaviour. People talk a certain way but act differently. What do you think are the reasons for this?	Causes for discrepancy
SELF-IMAGE	
5. How do you see yourself in relation to global development?	Relation
6a. Through which behaviours do you think you can influence this development?	Action
6b. And how do you actually behave?	
6c. Would you like to do more?	
7. Do you feel a responsibility to deal with the problems of the 21st century?	Responsibility
CLOSING	
8. Do you think it is possible to learn how to deal with these problems? If so: How? And where?	Learnability

Source: Rädiker and Kuckartz (2020, p. 44)

Table 3.1 shows how categories can be generated from an interview guide on climate awareness. The category names refer to the main focus of the interview questions and summarize it in one or more words, taking into account the research questions. The names can be very short and concise, as in the example, which is usually very practical for further presentation and use in QDA software. However, they can also be formulated in more detail, as we describe in Section 5.4. For example, instead of 'Learnability', 'Learnability of dealing with global problems' could also be used as a category name. In any case, it is necessary to record the meaning of the categories in category definitions as far as possible a priori.

Example of Deductive Category Development Based on the State of Research

In several workshops we gave the participants the task of developing a category system on the topic of 'quality of life' independently of empirical data. The following scenario was given: as part of an online study, citizens were asked 'What do you think constitutes quality of life in Germany?'.

The task for the small groups was to develop a category system of *thematic* categories for a QCA in advance (i.e., without looking at any of the answers). The categories were to build on the state of research on 'quality of life'. For this purpose, the workshop participants were asked to explore the state of research on the internet – for example, in the online encyclopaedia Wikipedia.

Group 1	Group 2	Group 3	Group 4	Group 5	Group 6	Group 7
Health	Health	Health	Health	Health	Health	Health
Self-determination	Social integration	Free choice of lifestyle	Freedom	Chance for self-realization	Opportunities for self-realization	Diversity
Educational offer	Education	Access to education	Social integration	Education	Opportunities for education	Social policy
Educational offerings	Work; career opportunities	Work and occupation	Labour market	Security	Leisure activities	Solidarity
Appreciation	Culture	Social relations	Security	Freedom	Infrastructure	Can work in parallel
Time prosperity	Environment	Political participation	Sustainability	Family & friends	Environment	
Cultural offerings		Material wealth		Income	Security	
Material security					Standard of living	

Figure 3.3 Category proposals of different working groups

Figure 3.3 shows the category systems of seven different working groups (with three or four members each) that emerged in the course of these exercises. Comparing the category systems developed by the seven working groups, the following observations can be made:

1 The number of categories proposed by the groups varies; it ranges between five and eight categories (for pragmatic reasons a limit of 10 had been set).

2 It is noticeable that no two proposals are identical; however, there is sometimes a great similarity between different proposals – for example, between the category proposals of groups 1 and 3.

3 Not all category systems are exhaustive; for example, proposal number 7 obviously lacks important aspects of quality of life.

4 Only one thematic category, 'Health', is proposed by all groups.

5 A number of categories appear in several proposed category systems (e.g., 'education', 'social relations', 'work and occupation') but with quite different accentuations (e.g., 'education', 'educational offerings', 'opportunities for education', etc.).

6 There are proposals where the categories have obvious overlaps and therefore raise the question of principle delimitations; for example, for group 6, it may be

unclear how the statement 'material security' would be coded if there are the categories 'standard of living' and 'security'.

7   The proposed categories have different degrees of abstraction or generality; for example, 'Social integration' is much more general than 'Family & friends'.

In another workshop we combined the seven proposals into a single category system for a QCA. How did we proceed? Firstly, we followed the principle that frequently occurring categories are taken over into the common category system. Then we discussed in detail the delimitations between the categories and added definitions to the individual categories to ensure selectivity. The result was the following category system consisting of 11 categories:

1   Work and occupation (including labour market and career opportunities)
2   Education (including educational offerings and opportunities)
3   Political freedom (in the sense of participation and political involvement)
4   Health
5   Individual freedom (in the sense of self-determination, self-realization, and free choice of lifestyle)
6   Culture (including cultural and leisure activities)
7   Standard of living and prosperity
8   Security (from war, civil war, crime, personal assault, and also from personal poverty)
9   Social integration
10   Environment, nature, sustainability
11   Work–life balance, time prosperity.

In the process of creating the category system, decisions often have to be made that have a far-reaching impact on the subsequent analysis and the results of the research project. In case of doubt, the research questions should always be consulted as a decision-making aid and should be the deciding factor. At this stage very specific categories, such as 'Leisure activities' or 'Theatre' should be avoided, and instead more general categories, such as 'Culture' should be preferred, which include the more concrete aspects. In order to cover everything that could be mentioned about quality of life, a residual category 'other' should normally be included. If it turns out later that a large number of statements are coded with this residual category, it will be possible to add another category if there is an accumulation of certain aspects.

It is important that the categories are exhaustive and do not overlook a theme that is important from the perspective of the research questions. The subsumption under more abstract and general categories can have implications that can trigger criticism and contradiction in the later reception of the study in the scientific community. For example, the grouping of 'Nature', 'Environment', and 'Sustainability' under one umbrella category is not unproblematic; protagonists of the sustainability model emphasize precisely that this is not just an environmental concept, but that the model also includes social and economic dimensions. Furthermore, one should think ahead to the later work of coding the data and the desired agreement of the coders; a broad interpretation of sustainability could lead to a very, very large number of statements being identified as belonging to this category and the categories losing the required selectivity.

With the later communication of the results of the QCA in mind, it can also be very important to integrate new thematic aspects and to develop inventive categories that may, for example, not be as obvious as 'Health'. In the category system above, the category 'work–life balance, time prosperity' is an example of such an inventive category. These types of categories signal a new approach to the topic, they are innovative, and can advance research. In addition, one should also keep an eye on the communication and presentation of the study in the scientific community: in order to attract adequate attention in today's polyphonic scientific communication, a certain degree of originality is absolutely necessary.

Can a judgement be made as to which of the seven proposed category systems is 'better' and which is 'worse'? Yes – using the criteria presented in Section 2.4. It is relatively easy to determine whether a category system is exhaustive or not. According to this criterion, the proposal of group 7 is certainly worse than the proposal of group 1. A second important criterion for assessing a category system is the quality of the category definitions (cf. Section 2.5). In this context, the quality criterion of coder agreement – both intracoder agreement and intercoder agreement – comes into play as a third criterion. This is a highly important criterion for assessing the quality of any form of content analysis. If the categories formed are not selective, only a low level of agreement can be achieved. Fourth, a criterion for a good category system that should not be underestimated but is difficult to operationalize is the coherence and plausibility of the overall structure of the category system. There is a need to develop a plausible whole and not just individual (potentially even selective) categories that stand next to each other rather unrelatedly.

Deductive Category Development and Qualitative Research

When comparing qualitative and quantitative methods for developing categories, deductive category development is often associated with quantitative research. This is accurate for research that uses standard instruments and is based on theories. However, quantitative research can also have a descriptive nature and create categories inductively. In explorative factor analysis, there is even a statistical approach that helps quantitative researchers to differentiate between different dimensions and develop and explore categories inductively. The reverse case also exists, namely that qualitative research works with pre-formed categories. For example, in a qualitative study Hopf et al. (1995) investigate the extent to which attachment theory has explanatory power for the development of right-wing extremist attitudes among young people. The analysis categories 'insecurely attached', 'securely attached', etc. and their definitions come from attachment research; the category development is clearly independent of the empirical data being used. However, the research process itself, working with multiple biographical interviews, fulfils all the criteria of qualitative research such as openness, communicativity, etc. (Hopf & Schmidt, 1993; Hopf et al., 1995; Hopf, 2016). This means that we are dealing with a combination of deductive category development and qualitative research.

When using deductively developed categories, it may turn out that categories are not selective or that very many passages are coded into the residual category 'other'. This leads to categories being modified or even to new categories being defined. Deductive category development therefore in no way excludes the possibility of changes being made to the category system and the category definitions during the analysis and thus deviating from strict adherence to the a priori definitions.

3.2 Developing Categories Inductively (Using Empirical Data)

In qualitative research, the formation of categories is very often practised directly using the data, an approach that is usually referred to as *inductive category development*. The term 'inductive' should not, however, lead to the assumption that with this type of category development the categories virtually bubble out of the material and, like the news in a news ticker, have only to be picked up by the researchers. This is (unfortunately) not the case; inductive category development also requires active involvement. Although it may seem as though inductive categories simply emerge from the data, you should avoid this kind of naive assumption and keep the hermeneutical perspective explained in Chapter 1 in mind, which notes that you cannot gain an understanding of the text without solid prior knowledge and understanding.

The development of categories represents a 'very sensitive process, "an art",' as Mayring (2014, p. 79) states with reference to Krippendorff (1980). This sounds striking, but attending art school to acquire the competence to develop categories is not necessary and presumably not conducive either, for this is indeed a scientific activity that succeeds all the better the more social science knowledge, research experience, and theoretical sensitivity are present. However, category development using empirical data – and this is probably what is meant by the term 'art' in this context – is and remains an active design process that does not guarantee success. But because category development is dependent on individual competence and individual activity, no intersubjective agreement, no reliability, can be postulated for the act of constructing a category system. The possible claim that inductive coding by several persons or members of a team would result in the same categories cannot be fulfilled.

> Category development using empirical data is an active design process that requires theoretical sensitivity and creativity. The standards of coders' agreement and the claims of intracoder and intercoder agreement do not apply here. The situation is different with the *application of categories* to the data: here, the need for coders' agreement is usually justified.

For this reason, it does not make sense to calculate coefficients of agreement or intercoder reliability in general for the development of categories. In many workshops we have practised getting the participants to form categories from the material individually and/or in groups. There are always areas where the proposed category systems overlap (i.e., the same or very similar categories are proposed). But just as regularly there are non-overlapping areas and it is not uncommon that category systems are formed that are structured completely differently, are partly also very original and definitely represent a reasonable implementation of the research question.

Where can we find good examples of how categories have been generated directly from empirical data? Where have scholars given more detailed methodological reflections on the inductive development of categories?

This section first presents two approaches that have dealt with the inductive development of categories: Mayring's (2014, 2021) approach, which is based on paraphrasing and summarizing, and the multi-stage procedure of grounded theory, which begins with open coding and organizes the open codes into categories (Strauss & Corbin, 1990; Charmaz, 2014). We then present guidelines for inductive category development, which can be used as a guide for your own projects.

Approaches to Inductive Category Development

Mayring's Approach to Inductive Category Development

Since the first edition of his German-language textbook on QCA (1983 12th ed. 2015) more than 30 years ago, Mayring has developed an approach to inductive category development that builds on the technique of paraphrasing. The approach is based on the so-called 'psychology of text processing', a method of bundling and summarizing that was developed in the early 1980s by Mandl (Mayring, 2014, pp. 34–36). The text is processed line by line and a paraphrase is written in the adjacent column next to each individual statement in a multi-column table created for this purpose. Here is a short excerpt from the example given by Mayring in his English publication (2014, pp. 70, 125). The example is taken from a study of experiences during teacher training courses:

Text passage of the interview	Paraphrase	Generalization
Well, it certainly wasn't a strain for me, at least from the, well, the physical side of things.	No psychological strain experienced through practice shock	No practice shock experienced as very enjoyable because
The contrary in fact. I was sort of pretty keen to get down to teaching at last.	On the contrary, was very keen on teaching practice	Tended to look forward to teaching practice

This example not only illustrates the general procedure, but also shows problems of paraphrasing. For example, whether the generalization 'No practice shock experienced ...' really reflects the original statement of the respondent seems rather questionable. Anyone who reads the relevant pages in Mayring's text (2014, pp. 70–76) will come across many paraphrases and generalizations that seem rather problematic. At this point, however, problems of paraphrasing will not be discussed further and we will only focus on the subsequent procedure up to the development of the categories. After paraphrasing the text, a step described by Mayring as 'reduction' is carried out, with the help of deletions and bundling of paraphrases, to create a system of statements that summarizes each individual interview. The next steps of category development are then cross-case: the categories of all interviews previously paraphrased are again bundled and summarized in a second round of generalization and reduction, whereby Mayring forms the following four categories in the example presented:

K'1 No practice shock occurs, if one

- has had prior teaching experience;
- has favorable training conditions in the postgraduate phase;
- is flexible and adaptable;
- communicates openly with colleagues;
- has no 'unrealistic' pedagogical expectations (illusion of simple persuasion techniques)

K'2 Practice shock can reduce and strain self-confidence considerably, if

- no practice was experienced beforehand;
- destructive criticism and obligation to adapt to seminary instructor are not 'taken in stride';
- one is not completely convinced of oneself

K'3 A good relationship with students can always be attained

K'4 Wanting to try out pedagogical behavior strategies and still remaining consistent in one's treatment of the class presents a dilemma (Mayring, 2014, pp. 76–77)

The categories developed in this way are declarative sentences that are supposed to contain the core content of the material in a condensed form. It remains relatively unclear how contradictory statements of respondents can be reduced and summarized. The categories developed by continuous generalization apparently claim to be free of contradictions. Here is an example. Two of the four trainee teachers interviewed in the sample study reported great difficulties in dealing with students. However, in the category 'K'3 A good relationship with students can always be attained', which was developed through the summary procedure, nothing of this can be seen any more.

Another problem concerns the relationships of the sub-statements (sub-categories) to the main statement (main category). In the case of category K'1, five factors are mentioned as conditions for ensuring that trainee teachers do not experience practice shock. In the simplest case, assuming dichotomies (e.g., teaching experience present versus teaching experience not present), results in $2^5 = 32$ possible combinations of these five factors. In which of these constellations does practice shock not occur? Is it only in the one case when all five positive factors are present?

Developing categories based on paraphrasing in the style of the 'psychology of text processing' method can be extraordinarily time-consuming. The procedure of paraphrasing, summarizing, reducing, and bundling also carries the danger that conflicting statements are easily overlooked and fall victim to the compulsion to generalize. Often, however, it is precisely the dissonances and divergences that are particularly interesting, and indeed are sometimes welcome, in qualitative research, as a means to inspire new thoughts on a topic (Bazeley, 2018, pp. 263–276). If, in the first step of category development, paraphrasing is done in a very detailed way, clarifying phrases are deleted and the text is transformed to a uniform level of language, more complex connections – such as the relation of the sub-statements to each other – are easily lost.

In his English-language publications, Mayring (2014, 2021) has dissolved the close connection he previously postulated between paraphrasing and inductive category formation:

> Summarizing qualitative content analysis is, as we have seen, a very rule-bound, intensive analysis of texts. But this means that it is time consuming. The claim of content analysis, that huge amounts of text materials can be worked through, has not yet been fulfilled. So, we looked for a more economical way to extract summarizing categories from texts. The technique of inductive category formation was the result. This basic model of summarizing qualitative content analysis can also be used for inductive category formation. (Mayring, 2021, p. 81)

In fact, the time required for paraphrasing is enormous, so it is only reasonable to exclude paraphrasing a necessary preliminary stage of inductive category formation. Indeed, it is also hardly possible to analyse huge amounts of text with QCA if the texts must be paraphrased beforehand.

In Section 6.2 of his book, entitled 'Inductive Category Formation', Mayring (2021, pp. 81–85) presents a process model for this abbreviated way of inductive category building consisting of eight steps:

1   Research question, theoretical background
2   Establishment of a selection criterion; category definition; level of abstraction
3   Working through the material line by line; category formulation; subsumption or new category formation
4   Revision of the categories and rules after 10–50% of the material
5   Final working through the material
6   Building of main categories if useful
7   Intra-/intercoder agreement check
8   Final results, maybe frequencies, interpretation.

Mayring has formulated more than 20 specific rules for these eight steps. An example of this procedure can be found in Mayring (2014, pp. 83–87). This example illustrates not so much the process of category formation itself, more the result and the form of the categories developed. In this example, based on the research question and guided by Lazarus's theory of stress, firstly a category definition is formulated: 'Stressful experiences in and around teaching, experiences of harm, loss or challenge which are not automatically coped with (Lazarus)' (2014, p. 84). Then the material is gone through line by line and each text passage that contains a statement about stress factors is identified and categories are formulated. In this example, 12 categories are formed. The categories are called, for example, 'B1: Disappointments about students', 'B2: Little time for education', 'B3: Difficult students', 'B4: Problems in very large classes', and 'B5: Being forced to authoritarian behaviour' (2014, pp. 84–85).

Together with Thomas Fenzl, Mayring has developed the QCAmap computer software. This software offers a strongly structured implementation of Mayring's technique of inductive category formation. This technique, just like the paraphrasing and summarizing technique described above, works in a highly fragmented way. The small-scale approach, modelled on the psychology of text processing, is clearly different from a hermeneutically oriented approach aimed at understanding, in which, in the sense of the hermeneutic circle, a whole can only be understood if its individual parts are understood, and the individual parts can only be understood if the whole is understood. Paraphrasing in small parts carries the risk of creating categories that seem to stand next to each other unrelatedly. However, where the text data is not too voluminous, an initial phase of paraphrasing some texts may be quite useful, particularly when inexperienced researchers are learning how to form categories.

The Grounded Theory Approach to Inductive Category Development

Over its fifty-year history, grounded theory has addressed how categories should be constructed more intensively than most other methods (Glaser & Strauss, 1967; Bryant & Charmaz, 2007; Charmaz, 2014; Mey & Mruck, 2011; Strauss & Corbin, 1990). The approach of category development in grounded theory is quite different from Mayring's approach described above, but there is agreement on some key points, for example the requirement that categories should be as precise as possible: 'they must be clear enough to be readily operationalised in quantitative studies when these are appropriate' (Glaser & Strauss, 1967, p. 3).

Strictly speaking, it should not be referred to as the approach to building categories within *the* grounded theory because the theory itself has developed in a variety of different directions.[1] For space reasons, we will not discuss the different directions and alternatives here.

Grounded theory is a research style that explicitly focuses on generating hypotheses and middle-range theories. It aims to develop categories (i.e., the basic elements of the theory)

---

[1]Barney Glaser and Anselm Strauss founded the tradition of grounded theory in 1967 (Glaser & Strauss, 1967), which is not simply a method or an evaluation technique. Strauss later said that grounded theory is a research style or a methodology and that at the time, he and his co-author wanted to design an epistemological and political science approach that deliberately and provocatively went against the leading behaviourist research paradigm (Strauss interviewed by Legewie & Schervier-Legewie, 2004). Kelle sees an 'inductive misunderstanding of one's self' in the beginnings of the history of grounded theory (Kelle, 2007, p. 32). Grounded theory developed in three main directions: Strauss and Corbin; Glaser; and Charmaz, who gave grounded theory a constructivist flair.

directly from the data through a multifaceted and circular process. It should be noted that the original textbooks of grounded theory speak almost exclusively of *code* and not of *category*, but in more recent textbooks, such as Charmaz's (2014), both terms are used.

Open coding represents the first step in working through the data. It is centred on identifying and/or naming concepts. In grounded theory, concepts are labels or tags for phenomena, and they serve as the foundation for the theory to be generated. Strauss and Corbin (1996, pp. 43–46) name the following examples of concepts: 'attention', 'transfer information', 'offer support', 'monitor', 'satisfaction of guests', and 'experience'. In grounded theory, coding refers to the intellectual processing of empirical data and the development and assignment of codes, where a code is a label that, to a certain extent, theoretically sums up a segment of the data:

> Coding means categorizing segments of data with a short name that simultaneously summarizes and accounts for each piece of data. Your codes show how you select, separate, and sort data and begin an analytic accounting of them. (Charmaz, 2014, p. 111)

Furthermore, in the grounded theory approach – in contrast to QCA – the entire process of data analysis is conceived as coding. Concepts have a similar role to that in standardized quantitative research. Specifying concepts requires you to step away from the data and work towards developing theories. Strauss and Corbin also refer to coding as diving into the data. You can proceed line by line, or consider sentences, paragraphs, or even complete texts, asking yourself what is the main idea of this sentence, paragraph, or text. Researchers then name phenomena, pose questions, and make comparisons regarding the similarities and differences that can be found within the data. How open coding works in the style of grounded theory can be well illustrated by an example from Charmaz. It is an interview excerpt with a very ill patient Bonnie (48 years, living alone), who talks about how her daughter Amy only found out about her current state of illness through her neighbour Linda:

> She found out from Linda that I was, had been in bed for days and she called me up, 'You never tell me, and I have to find out from Linda', and 'Why don't you tell me who you are and what's going on and ...' Well, I don't know how long after that, but that Saturday the pain started right here and it, throughout the day it got worse and worse and worse. And she – I kept thinking that, well, I can deal with this, so I took some kind of a pain pill and nothing helped. (Charmaz, 2014, p. 119)

Charmaz develops the following codes for this text:

- Receiving second-hand news
- Being left out; Accusing mother of repeated not telling; (questioning ethical stance?) Being confronted

- Facing self and identity questions; Demanding self-disclosure and information
- Experiencing escalating pain
- Expecting to manage pain
- Inability to control pain.

The codes show very clearly the general action orientation of grounded theory that is particularly evident in Charmaz' approach. Charmaz explicitly calls for codes to be formulated preferably in the grammatical form of the gerund: 'Experiencing escalating pain'. This linguistic form of the codes expresses the fact that the focus is on action and not on topics; however, the latter also occurs in Charmaz's work, as the code 'Inability to control pain', which is not in the gerund, shows.

The raw data come to life as researchers conceptualize about them. As Strauss and Corbin noted, raw data are useless, for you cannot do much with them other than merely count words or repeat what was said. Concepts are always named on the current state of the analysis; they can also stem from the literature and do not have to be developed by the researchers. This can be advantageous because some such concepts are associated with analytical meaning, such as 'caregiver burnout', 'experience during illness', and 'loss of status'. However, many of these concepts are already connected to certain theories, which could be disadvantageous to your current study.

During the first open coding of a text, we recommend that you pay attention to the words and metaphors that the respondents use. In grounded theory, such words and statements are referred to as 'in vivo codes'. For example, Strauss mentioned the term 'tradition bearer of the unit', which the head nurse used to refer to another nurse in her unit (Strauss & Corbin, 1998, p. 116; Kuckartz, 2010a, p. 75). In the remaining steps of the analysis process, the grounded theory moves from the initial concepts to categories, which are more abstract concepts or summarized concepts at a higher level of abstraction (Strauss & Corbin, 1998). For example, concepts such as 'holding on', 'hiding', and 'moving out of the way' may arise when watching children play. Those concepts could then develop into the more abstract category 'anti-sharing strategies'.

Concepts within grounded theory should be as precise and specific as possible. They are not paraphrases, but they move towards a more abstract, general level. The following examples of concepts stem from Strauss and Corbin (1996, pp. 106–107): 'work in the kitchen', 'attention', 'transfer of information', 'unobtrusiveness', 'timing of service', and 'satisfaction of guests'. Once researchers have collected a good number of concepts, they can group them together and summarize them.

Grounded theory can be seen as an invitation to and instructions for arriving at a theory that is based on the data. The same idea of empirically grounded analysis is true for QCA: every category and sub-category, every relationship presented, every evaluation conducted, every typology constructed is rooted in the data, documented and traceable for everyone who receives the research, whether they are experts or people who read the research report. From the beginning, grounded theory aims to develop *theoretical* categories (see Kelle, 2007); however, this is not necessarily the case in qualitative text analysis. Grounded theory does not require all of the data to be coded because it focuses on moving forward, working with the categories, and developing theories, leaving the data behind.

As a summary, the following points can be noted for inductive category development within the framework of grounded theory:

- The open approach, in which everything that 'comes to mind' for researchers, what is 'induced' by the text, is recorded in the form of codes
- The multi-stage process of category building, which seeks to achieve a higher level of abstraction and analysis through integration and aggregation of those earlier codes
- The focus on a few categories that seem particularly important in the course of the analysis process
- Attention to words, terms, and metaphors used by the research participants
- Reflecting on the categories throughout the entire process of analysis.

3.3 Guidelines for Inductive Category Development

The presentation of different approaches in this section makes it clear that there are very different ways of inductively forming categories from the material. As shown in Section 2.2, there are also very different types of categories (factual categories, thematic categories, etc.) to distinguish. Instead of mixing different approaches as on a mixing desk and presenting only one true strategy for the formation of categories from the material, it seems more reasonable to us to present guidelines that leaves freedom to choose from different ways. Regardless of which approach is taken, for example, whether thematic, evaluative, or analytical categories are formed, working on the category system and reflexive handling of the categories should play a central role when performing a QCA. Categories are not an end in themselves, but the analysis stands and falls with them, whether it is a descriptive or a theory-generating analysis, in which the categories are the elements, the building blocks, of the theory being aimed at.

The guidelines consist of six stations, some of which can be passed through in a circular fashion:

1 **Determine the goal of category building based on the research question.** When you start developing inductive categories, you should ask yourself: What exactly do I want to achieve with the category system? For which questions will the systematization and compression achieved through category development and categorization of text passages be helpful? How openly do I want to approach the categorization? What prior knowledge about the research field do I already have?

2 **Determine category type and level of abstraction.** Based on the types of categories presented in Section 2.2, you should consider which types of categories

are most suitable for your own study. Mixing different types of categories is also possible. Furthermore, it is important to ask: How close do I want to stay to the language of the research participants when creating categories? How far do I want to work with more abstract categories or with analytical or theoretical categories? For example, a respondent describes her activities in terms of waste separation. A 'waste separation' category can now be defined, but also more abstract categories are possible, such as 'individual behaviour in the area of recycling' or even more generally 'individual environmental behaviour'.

3   **Familiarize yourself with the data and determine the scope of the segments to be coded**. With reference to the remarks on hermeneutics in Section 1.4, it is always important initially to familiarize oneself with the data and not to start forming categories with the first line one reads. Those who have collected the data themselves already have this familiarity, of course. In the case of very extensive material, it may be sufficient to make a conscious selection, for example, to start with particularly diverse interviews and then add others until a good overview of the material emerges. Before starting to code and create categories, one should also think about segmentation, that is, the scope of the text passages to be coded. In the simplest case, only the term or the core of the statement leading to the coding is coded. Alternatively, a formal criterion – a sentence, a paragraph – can be defined as the segment to be coded. In most cases, especially when working with QDA software, it is recommended that you code complete statements ('units of meaning') that can still be understood out of context during later analysis.

4   **Read the text passages sequentially line by line and develop categories directly using the text**. Assign existing categories or create new ones. The development of categories can be done in a single-phase run through all the data or through just a subset of the data. The order in which the texts are coded is not really important, but the risk of bias should be taken into account and randomly ordering the texts may help avoid this. The texts are now processed line by line. For example, highlight and mark the text on paper and write comments in the margins or use QDA software to do so electronically by assigning codes to the given text passage. One should be aware that the development of categories is a constructive activity on the part of the researcher and therefore one should reflect on the nature of the categories that are 'induced' by the text. Do the categories tend to denote themes or are they more analytical? How do I deal with particularly significant words or terms that research participants use? Do I code these as natural categories (in vivo codes)? The categories themselves may be comprised of single or combined terms or, as in the case of argumentation and discourse analyses, of an argument, phrase, or even a short sentence. The beginning of category development should be rather open; no specific degree of concreteness or abstractness of the categories should be prescribed yet. In the further process of category formation, the now steadily

growing category system must be taken into account. If a text passage corresponds to an existing category, simply assign it to it. Otherwise, you may need to create a new category. If this new category is similar to one of the categories that you have already defined, you could create a new, more abstract integrative category 'on the fly'.

5 **Systematize and organize the category system.** When the number of categories gradually threatens to become unmanageable and only a few new categories are being formed, it is time to deal with the question of how the categories can be ordered. Similar categories should be listed together and, if necessary, grouped into a more abstract category. In general, hierarchical category systems have proved to be very useful as they offer the possibility of aggregating within higher-level abstractions in the analysis. It is now time to reflect on the main categories: either new main categories are defined or some existing categories become the main categories. Inevitably, the question arises as to how many categories are reasonably needed for the analysis. This question can only be answered by considering the time available for the analysis and the goal, namely the kind of research report to be written. Another question that arises is what level of sophistication or generality is needed for the planned analyses? A typical interview study will rarely use more than 20 main categories, each with up to 10 sub-categories. It is also important to think now about how the later presentation of results (tables, overviews, visualizations, etc.) should look and what degree of differentiation can be communicated within this framework.

6 **Finalize the category system and create category definitions.** At some point in the circular progression through phases 4 and 5, the time will be reached when (almost) no new categories are created. If necessary, the category system can be systematized and (re)ordered again in between. At some point, however, the time comes when not much more is happening; a first 'saturation' has been reached. Now it is time to check the system of categories again for compliance with the important criteria (among others: selective, plausible, exhaustive, easily presentable and communicable) and to optimize it if necessary. From this point on, the category system is fixed, but this does not mean that it is fixed and unchangeable once and for all. The determination of this point of 'saturation' is not critical, because before the completion of the content analysis, a run through the entire remaining material takes place, so that one does not run the risk of overlooking important aspects. It is certainly possible to expand the category system at a later time by adding parent categories or sub-categories or by combining categories. A continuous adaptation of the category system to the empirical data is therefore possible – if necessary. Now is also the right time to turn to the category definitions and to create or

complete the coding guide (cf. Section 2.5). The definitions should be illustrated with concrete text passages (quotations). Special attention should be given to the selection of these examples. They should be as typical as possible, clarify the distinction from other categories and thus create confidence in dealing with the category. How much data should you process in this way to arrive at an optimal coding scheme? There is no fixed answer to this question, as you will have to work through as many text passages as necessary until you have the impression that no new aspects are surfacing within the text. Depending on the size and complexity of the data to be analysed, this may be the case after you have processed just 10% of the text; however, you may have to process as much as 50% of the text. Normally, you will have to process the data in several cycles: some categories can be grouped together according to their similarity, while other categories that may have started out too broad may have to be subdivided.

To illustrate the guidelines, we now show a practical implementation in two variants. The first variant of inductive category development works with focused summaries, while the second variant, which is much more common in practice, takes the shorter route of code development directly using the material without prior summaries of the content.

Inductive Category Development via Focused Summaries

Inexperienced analysts especially feel more confident in forming categories if they work closely with the text. They often feel insecure in their analysis because they fear that their approach seems too arbitrary and not sufficiently well founded. In such cases, it can be very helpful to work with focused summaries of the content after reading all the compiled text passages and then going through the text again. For this purpose, it is best to create a table consisting of at least three columns, with the left column containing the original text.

During the writing of the content summaries, one may notice that some statements are repeated or one may feel the desire to summarize statements into more general statements that form categories; these are then written in the third column of the table. In the middle column, you can use a highlighter or simply cross out which summaries have already been considered in the development of categories.

Such a procedure is illustrated in Figure 3.4. Here, categories were written directly in the third column and possible sub-categories were also entered below the higher-level categories. In this abbreviation procedure, the third column represents a kind of workspace that changes constantly as one goes through the material. The task of creating summaries in the first step forces one initially to stay very close to the text.

Original text	Summary	Category
B: I simply believe that climate change, as it is predicted everywhere or painted in black, will not happen. I mean, there are also physicists or meteorologists, I don't know, climate researchers, who are not of the opinion that climate change will happen. But they are not listened to in the media because the catastrophe report simply seems much, much more important or is simply more attractive for the media. But that doesn't change the fact that everyone should live in an environmentally-conscious way. And yes, whether you have to eat cherries from somewhere else in winter (...) you don't have to (laughs). I don't know. But I don't believe that the world will get 2 degrees warmer because you eat cherries from (laughs) 'Timbuktu'. I don't believe that humans can have such a big influence. And yes.	Doom-mongering about climate change (CC) is everywhere. CC will not occur as predicted. There are scientific counter-opinions that are being ignored. The media do not publish critical positions. News about disaster is more attractive for the media. People should live in an environmentally conscious way. Eating cherries in winter is not necessary. Does not believe in the effect of own purchasing behaviour on CC. Humans do not have much influence.	*Scepticism about CC* • Exaggerated pessimism • Scientific counter-positions *Media criticism* • Selection of the media • Preference for disasters *Perception of norms* • Living environmentally consciously *Personal environmental behaviour* • Consumption area *Influence of individual behaviour on CC* • No effect *Fundamental position*

Figure 3.4 Technique of inductive category formation via focused summary

Inductive Category Building via Open Coding

The following example describes the process of inductively developing thematic categories directly based on data. It works with publicly available data from the 'Living Well in Germany' project, in which citizens were asked the question 'What is important to you personally in life?' in an online survey.[2]

As is usual in online surveys of this kind, the answers vary greatly in terms of their scope and detail: while some respondents only give keyword answers (e.g., 'health, family, work – these are the most important basics for me in my life'), other respondents explain in great detail what they consider important in their lives. We describe how a (preliminary) proposal for a category system can be developed based on a subset of the material. The presentation follows the six stages of the 'Guidelines for Inductive Category Development' presented above.

---

[2]The study was conducted by the federal government in 2015 in the context of its citizens' dialogue on the understanding of quality of life. More detailed information is documented and generally accessible on the internet at www.gut-leben-in-deutschland.de (as of 20 March 2022).

1 **Determine the goal of category formation based on the research question.** The goal of the study is initially explorative and descriptive: we want to find out something about what Germans currently consider to be personally important in their lives. In doing so, we want to find out which topics are in the focus of attention and which terms are mentioned by the respondents. The frequency with which topics are mentioned is also of interest. As a result of the research a report is to be written in which the question of what is personally important to Germans should take up about 20 pages. In the first step of category development, the main categories are to be formed. The decision whether sub-categories should also be developed and if so, whether for all or only for selected main categories, should only be made after a first coding cycle.

2 **Determine category type and level of abstraction.** In accordance with the descriptive research questions of the project, it is appropriate to develop thematic categories. The question 'What is important to you personally in life?' is deliberately intended to encourage people to name important topics. Differentiated judgements are not asked for, so that the development of evaluative categories does not make sense. The following example of category development is based on a subset of the total of approximately 2500 statements. The cleanest selection procedure, methodologically, would be a random sample for the development of categories, but there is no overall file from which this could be drawn. In order to avoid distortions due to the timing of the survey (the period extended over several months), it makes sense to form a quota sample in which the selections are made at different points in the survey period. Initially, open coding is used, that is, without specifications regarding the degree of generality and abstractness of the categories.

3 **Familiarize yourself with the data and determine the scope of the segments to be coded.** Now it is important to get an overview of the data: many statements must be read through until the impression of a good overview is achieved. Even in real life, it is difficult to give exact information about how long it takes to get an overview. This is of course strongly dependent on the 'terrain' over which one would like to get an overview. In the case of this example study, the answers of the respondents are quite short and so interesting that one keeps on reading spontaneously. A reasonable amount of reading time should be planned: at least 100–200 answers to the question of what is important to you personally should be read before you start to develop categories.

After a first overview of the data has been gained, two questions need to be clarified next: the question of the scope of a segment to be coded in each case and the design of the category system. The reading of the responses shows that not only the scope but also the type of responses varies greatly: on the one hand quite extensive prose texts, on the other hand only a series of keywords. Coding units of meaning, the 'gold standard' of QCA, is therefore not always possible. It makes sense to establish the following rule for this data. For responses formulated in sentence form, meaning units of at least one complete sentence are coded. In the case of keyword-type responses, only the words of the individual key points are coded and, if necessary, only individual words.

With regard to the thematic categories to be formed, there is still the question of how to deal with valences, that is, positive or negative valuations in the answers given by the respondents. Take a statement like this: 'A good life means living in an environment worth living in. Large wind turbines that come extremely close to our houses make a good life impossible.' Here the topic of renewable energy is indirectly addressed, but the topic has a negative connotation. Is the conclusion that a decision is required whether each valence expressed is positive or negative? The reading of the responses shows that negative evaluations only occur very rarely, which is understandable in view of the positively worded question 'What is important to you personally in life?' Therefore, in this case it is appropriate that no specific categories are created for the valence, but it is taken into account in the later analysis of the category.

There is one more point to clarify, which has to do with the nature of the questions asked in this online survey. Respondents had been asked to give their statement a heading. How do you deal with the headings when coding the data? Should the headings be treated like the other text of the response and coded in the same way? A specific check showed that the headings often not only sum up the text but also contain information of their own. In this respect, it is logical to treat the headings like normal text when creating categories. At the same time, it can be assumed that headlines, similar to those in daily newspapers, still have a special informative value. When working with QDA software, headlines should therefore be marked and coded as such (with the code 'Headline') and then subjected to a separate analysis.

4   **Read the text passages sequentially line by line and develop categories directly using the text**. Assign existing categories or create new ones. Starting with the first text, proceed line by line. Figure 3.5 shows the answer of one person in the left-hand column and the codes developed, some of which already represent potential thematic categories, in the right-hand column.

If the aspects that appear in the answers are openly coded, as has been done here, one should proceed quickly and not think too long about the best choice of words when formulating codes. In the next step of the analysis, all codes are ordered and systematized – there is still time enough to find the most appropriate and fitting words for the categories. This is – by the way – also a great advantage compared to the development of categories via paraphrasing and focused summarizing, where one tends to spend a lot of time on formulating paraphrases. Also, no premature generalizations or abstractions should be made and far-reaching interpretations should be avoided.

Response	Codes/categories
Time for family and friends, mental and physical FREEDOM, nature	Time for social life
	Mental and physical freedom
Friends: this requires like-minded people and time. Many people around me have little time to meet with each other. Instead: Everyday stress (lots of work, lots of driving the kids around), short messages via WhatsApp. For me and my children, I would wish for more people with time and less media communication and planned leisure time – in other words, children who play outside (also in the forest!) with lots of time, as they used to!	Family
	Friends and like-minded people
	Leisure without stress
Freedom: The woman in the burqa in the supermarket the other day threw me off. Many Muslim women wear headscarves and cover their bodies with long clothes. Muslim women did not shake hands with my husband at the barbecue recently. Why, I asked – 'Because it says so in the Koran'. For me, these women and especially girls are restricted in their physical and mental freedom (criticism of religion). I think: Religion must not take precedence over the ideas of the Enlightenment (Kant) and the emancipation of women.	Children's play in nature
	Cultural commonality
	Personal freedom
	Self-determination
	Ideas of the Enlightenment
	Emancipation of women

Figure 3.5   Direct category development using the material – example 1

Conspicuous things should always be recorded, preferably in a memo (further discussion of memos can be found in Section 4.5). In the text in Figure 3.5, for example, a longer description makes it clear that it is important for the respondent *not* to experience certain religiously motivated behaviours in her immediate living environment. Since it was decided to only create categories for positively important topics, it should be noted in a memo at this point that attention should be paid to the occurrence of such negatively valued topics in the further coding process and that categories may still be developed for certain negatively valued topics.

Should codes or categories that have already been coded in a response be coded again in the same response? In longer interviews, such as narrative interviews, the answer would normally be 'yes', because whether some phenomena occur several times or even very often in a text or are only singular can be important. In the present case of the 'Living Well in Germany' survey, however, the material consists of rather short statements and therefore the same code is only used again in the same text if the corresponding text passage contains a new aspect, another dimension of the topic.

As the analysis progresses, it is also possible to form sub-categories and categories at a higher level of abstraction as they arise. Figure 3.6 shows an example in which the sub-category 'children' and the relatively abstract category 'material security' have already been formed for the category 'family'.

Response	Codes/Categories
All five are Important	
I need	
a family, today often a patchwork family, including the children	Family
who live with my 'ex' (but which is severely restricted for me).	– Children
a job that feeds me and is fun as often as possible, including	material security
employee rights that (somewhat) protect me.	fun work
	Security through workers' rights
Friends who support me and that can also be people from other	
cultures and social classes.	Friends
	Diversity
Health, healthy food, good medical care that is not solely	Health
oriented towards the monetary interests of big business.	Supply of healthy food
	Medical care
Safety, I want to be able to move around without fear, even at	Safety in the city
night in the metro	

Figure 3.6 Direct category development using the material – example 2

5 **Systematize and organize the category system**. Near the end, when it becomes difficult to keep track of all the codes and categories that have been formed, the work process should be interrupted and attention focused on the entire system of categories. The full set of codes and categories, at whatever level of abstraction, that have been created so far are now ordered and systematized. How does this work? First, identical or very similar codes can be merged into one code. Second, codes can be bundled together into a new or already existing category. Third, the overall shape of the category system should be thought about. Do the category system and the individual categories support the answering of the research questions? Is the category system coherent in itself? Is the relation of the categories to each other plausible? Is the category system exhaustive?

It also makes sense to start writing category definitions, which can be illustrated immediately with quotations from the already coded data.

Organizing and systematizing the codes and categories is technically best done by writing them down on moderation cards and using a large working surface (pinboard, tabletop, etc.) or – much more convenient and effective – with the help of QDA software. Here, the codes and categories developed can easily be organized and grouped on a sufficiently large-screen work surface. This way of working also has the advantage that there is always a link between the categories and the original text.

Figure 3.7 shows a category system[3] consisting of eight main categories, an intermediate result of the process of category development. The main categories are arranged around the centre of an imaginary individual in this graphic.

---

[3]The illustration was created with the function 'Creative Coding' in MAXQDA.

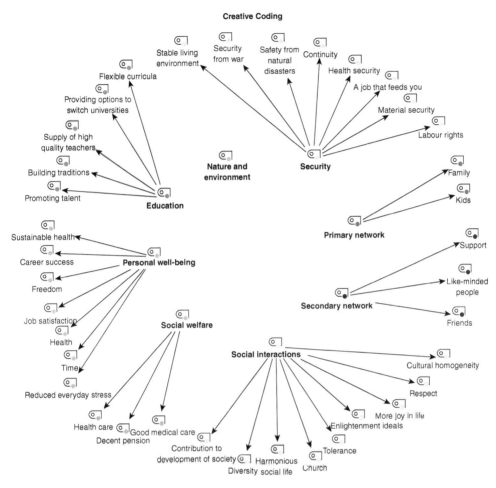

Figure 3.7 Systematizing and ordering codes into categories with QDA software (reprinted by permission from: Springer Nature. *Analyzing Qualitative Data with MAXQDA* by Udo Kuckartz and Stefan Rädiker © 2019)

The codes, so far developed in the process of open coding, are connected to the main categories by directional arrows. Behind the codes in the outer circle of the diagram are concrete text passages – at least one text segment. The codes are illustrative examples of what is hidden behind the main categories; in this case, they are not sub-categories, because the development of sub-categories was deliberately dispensed with at this point in the analysis.

As soon as a satisfactory order and systematization has been achieved, the coding process continues with the processing of further data. Of course, the results of the systematization step are taken into account when assigning further text passages to already existing categories, that is, the new main categories are used and, if necessary, supplemented by new codes and categories.

6 Finalize the category system and create category definitions. If nothing new or only singular aspects (i.e., only aspects specific to the life situation of a particular person) appear, the process of category development is terminated. Now follows the step that is significant for the coding of the further material, namely the final specification of the category system. As stated in the guidelines above, this does not mean that no more changes are permitted to the category system in the future. The final specification of the category system also includes formulating category definitions. Since the codes grouped into a category are assigned to existing text passages, it is easy to include concrete examples from the data in the definitions.

When working in a team, it makes sense to do the step of specifying the final category system together. It is important now to have the research question(s) in mind and to ask ourselves: Where do we want to go with the final category scheme and the subsequent coding and analysis using the categories? What do we want the product of our analysis to look like? In this example, the goal of the content analysis is to identify the topics that the research participants consider important for their lives and then, in the second step of the analysis, to get an overview of what is hidden in detail behind the major topics; in other words, to find out what exactly is declared to be important when, for example, someone talks about nature being very important to them personally.

There are now several strategies that can be adopted with regard to the final category system. One variant involves the development of a relatively large number of quite specific categories (20 or more). This strategy, which is often adopted in quantitative content analysis, is not adequate for qualitative research. It is more appropriate to keep the number of main categories smaller and above all to pay attention to the relation of the categories to each other – the shape (gestalt) of the category system.

The development of the category system is not just preparatory work for the analysis which will follow, but already a part of it and represents an analytical achievement, which should also be presented in the research report in appropriate detail. The report does not have to be limited to describing what is present but can also point out what is missing. In our example, in the selection of statements made for the development of categories, it is striking that an intact close environment (partner, children, family, friends) is very often considered important, as is the possibility of social influence in the sense of democratic participation, but that the middle ground of an intact neighbourhood or intact community is only mentioned relatively rarely.

3.4 Combining Deductive and Inductive Category Development

Qualitative content analysis is characterized by often combining different methods to develop categories. This can be seen in many of the examples of Mayring and Gläser-Zikuda

(2005), Gläser and Laudel's (2010) approach, as well as the methodically well-documented study on family and right-wing extremism by Hopf et al. (1995). In the latter, hypotheses and categories were formed first, derived from attachment theory. These categories were then assigned to the data, specified, modified, and differentiated as necessary. At the same time, unexpected elements in the data, such as those that could not be derived from the attachment theories, served as inspiration for new categories (Schmidt, 2010). The mixture of deductive a priori category and inductive category development based on the data occurs almost exclusively in one way: deductive categories are developed first and the development of categories or sub-categories using the material follows in the second step, which is why one can also speak of *deductive-inductive category development.*

Depending on the research question and schedule of a given project, there are different ways to develop categories in a deductive-inductive fashion. The general process is, however, always the same. You start with a category system that contains relatively few main categories (usually not more than 20) that have been derived from the research question, the interview guide and/or a reference theory. Unlike within pure deductive approaches, these categories are seen only as starting points here. They serve as search aids, meaning that you can search through the data for relevant content and roughly categorize it. In the second step, sub-categories are developed inductively, whereby only the material assigned to each main category is used.

A typical application of deductive-inductive category development is described in Chapter 5 on structuring QCA. In Rädiker and Kuckartz (2020) we present a method that works with such a deductive-inductive approach, in which the so-called basic categories are primarily developed from the interview guide and further differentiated by sub-categories developed using the empirical data.

3.5 Summary and Concluding Remarks

In this chapter, which is central to the use of QCA in research projects, the considerations on the topic of categories from Chapter 2 were continued. We discussed different strategies of category development. The central distinguishing criterion of the strategies is the role that the data play in this process. The more prior knowledge researchers have and the more precisely they have formulated the research questions, the more likely it is that categories will be developed in advance, before working with the data. In this chapter, we have shown that even such deductive category formation is a constructive act and that the categories by no means emerge automatically from the research state or the theoretical approach.

In qualitative research, when there is little prior knowledge and no preconceived theories, the categories are usually formed directly from the material, typically in a multi-stage process. We have developed guidelines for this strategy of category formation (inductive development) to guide and support researchers. It is rare to find either deductive or inductive category formation in its pure form, but in most projects mixed forms are practised, often in such a way that relatively broad categories are initially formed, which are then gradually elaborated on in a data-based manner in the further analysis process. This strategy of deductive-inductive development of categories offers the advantage that it can be linked initially to the current state of research, which also strengthens the feeling of being on safe ground and provides legitimacy for one's own research work.

When creating categories, it is important to keep the whole in mind – the entire system of categories. This analytical framework should be coherent and have a consistent and plausible overall shape so that it can be easily communicated in the scientific community. It must be clear at a glance, so to speak. In concrete terms, this means that the categories should be set at a similar level of abstraction and the category names should be formulated in a consistent way.

4

THREE TYPES OF QUALITATIVE CONTENT ANALYSIS

Chapter objectives

In this chapter you will learn about:

- The general process of QCA
- Three basic types of QCA
- Cases and categories as essential structuring dimensions
- The profile matrix as a starting point for further analyses
- Similarities and differences of the three basic types
- The possibilities and limits of quantification
- Starting the analysis by means of initial work with the texts and writing memos and case summaries.

Within social research there are a number of methods and techniques for qualitative content analysis. Mayring (2021), for instance, distinguishes between nine different forms of QCA: (1) summarizing, (2) inductive category formation, (3) narrow and (4) broad context analysis, (5) nominal deductive category assignment, (6) ordinal deductive category assignment, (7) content-structuring/theme analysis, (8) type analysis, and (9) parallel forms. However, some of these techniques, such as content structuring and type analysis, are only very briefly outlined there.

In the following chapters, three basic methods of qualitative content analysis are described in detail:

- *structuring QCA*, which can be regarded as the core method of QCA procedures and in which the material is typically coded in several coding cycles with deductively and/or inductively formed categories (Chapter 5)
- *evaluative QCA*, in which the material is assessed by the coders and assigned evaluative categories (Chapter 6)
- *type-building QCA*, which is usually based on structuring and/or evaluative analysis and whose primary objective is to develop a typology (Chapter 7).

These three methods use different strategies of analysis and are each used very frequently in research practice. This is especially true for the first type, structuring QCA. Interestingly, structuring analysis in form of thematic analysis (Früh, 2017) is also by far the most commonly used method in the field of quantitative content analysis. In this area, it is mostly done as frequency analysis of themes. What distinguishes *qualitative* content analysis from *quantitative* analysis can be seen particularly well in the way the themes are analysed. While the atomizing manner of quantitative analysis aims to convert the verbal data into precise categories (represented by numbers) and then to statistically evaluate the resulting data matrix, qualitative content analysis is interested in the text itself, notably based on the text in its entirety. Even after categories have been assigned, the text itself (i.e., the wording of the statements) is relevant and also plays an important role in the preparation and presentation of results. In quantitative content analysis, however, the results include merely statistical parameters, it is coefficients and models that are interpreted and presented. After the coding process, the verbal data in quantitative content analysis are no longer of interest, even as quotations, because the plausibility of the results of the statistical analysis cannot be demonstrated using selected text passages.

All three QCA methods described below include both topic-oriented and case-oriented methods. This means they can be viewed not only as category-based analysis but also at the case level as case analysis (e.g., in the form of case summaries). The comparison of cases or groups and clusters of cases plays an important role in the analysis process for each of the three methods. This also marks an important difference from Mayring's conception of QCA: there, the case-oriented perspective plays almost no role compared to the category-oriented perspective (Steigleder, 2008, p. 174).

4.1 General Processes of Qualitative Content Analysis

How do you proceed in qualitative content analysis? Which phases are passed through? The first question should correctly be formulated in the plural, because there are different types of QCA – three of these methods are the subject of this book – each of them proceeding differently. In the following, we will remain at the general level and describe the common core in a general model; the specific processes will then be focused on in Chapters 5–7.

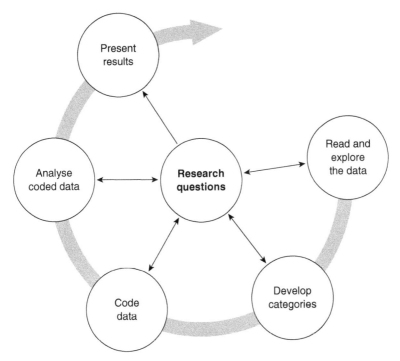

Figure 4.1 General process of qualitative content analysis

The sequence *research question* → *select or collect data* → *data analysis* is quite characteristic of all forms of empirical research, and QCA is no exception. In Figure 4.1, the five phases of QCA are illustrated, starting with the research questions placed in the centre, surrounded by the subsequent steps. On the one hand the figure shows the basic sequence, but on the other hand it also illustrates the possibilities for circular processes mediated by the research question. The core of every QCA is represented by the phases 'develop categories', 'code data', and 'analyse coded data', whereby the forming of categories and the coding of data can take place in several cycles. The figure is meant to illustrate that the flow of the analysis process is much less linear than in the classical model of the research process and that the different phases of analysis are not strictly separated from each other. It is even possible to acquire additional data after the category system has been established and the majority of the data has been coded. The figure also illustrates that the research questions play a different role in QCA than in other approaches. They are posed at the beginning of the research process, but they do not remain unchanged as in the classical hypothetical-deductive model only to be answered at the end of the analysis. Instead, the research question is central to each of the five method areas and can be changed dynamically during the analysis process (within certain constraints). For example, you may wish to make the research questions more precise, place new aspects at the forefront, or modify the research questions because of unexpected discoveries.

The phases centred on developing and modifying categories in which researchers progressively work with the data are very important phases of the analysis process. Even if a QCA is conducted in a theory-based manner with hypotheses in mind – which is not out of the question – you can fine-tune the categories during the analysis process and add new (sub-)categories if you deem it necessary while working through the data.

What role does theory play in QCA overall? Based on the identification of QCA as a method, the question needs to be asked differently: what role does theory play or should theory play in a research project in which QCA is used as a method of data analysis? That is, the role of theory in the specific research project must be questioned. There may be projects that want to describe a certain social phenomenon as precisely as possible (e.g., 'How do young fathers experience paternity leave?') and do not aim at theory building at all. Other projects are theory-oriented and take a specific theoretical approach such as the theory of planned behaviour (Kan & Fabrigar, 2017) as their starting point, for example, to investigate the connections between environmental attitudes and behaviour. Yet other projects explore a topic in a very open manner but aim to generate theory through their research. In all these projects, QCA can be used beneficially to some extent independently of the role of theory. In the process model outlined above, theory can serve both as a starting point in determining the formulation of the research questions and as the end point of a very open approach. Thus, the objective can be the generation of theory, the confirmation of theory, the refinement of theory, and finally, as mentioned, projects may also want to deliberately focus on description. Intentionally, we do not speak of 'limiting' here, because this sounds as if such research projects have a deficiency and, in a sense, stop halfway. However, the *usefulness* of a project (e.g., for addressing social problems or with regard to transformative questions) does not depend on whether theory building is the primary objective of the project. Rust (2019) suggests that theory generation should be an explicit phase in the process model of QCA. However, the different roles of theory in research projects argue against the integration of such a phase in the *general process* of QCA. On closer inspection, it becomes clear that Rust's proposal, based on experiences in teaching research projects, also refers only to the second type of project (open approach with the goal of theory building at the end). However, Rust points out a very significant problem, namely that in many projects the role of theory or of theory building is not sufficiently considered and that before writing down the results, a review of the state of research and the literature should be carried out.

4.2 Cases and Categories as Structuring Dimensions

The idea of structuring the material according to two dimensions, namely *cases* and *categories*, is essential for QCA. Cases are usually, as in an interview study, the research participants. But families, institutions, and organizations can also be defined as units of analysis, as cases.

The second structuring dimension is formed by the categories. Very often these are themes, but in principle all kinds of categories can be represented here. These two dimensions form the matrix for structuring the content, a *cases-by-categories* matrix. Usually, the cases are arranged in the rows and the categories in the columns. In the prototypical case, an interview study with thematic coding, the persons are placed in the rows and the themes are placed in the columns, so that one can also speak of a thematic matrix (Figure 4.2). If the columns do not only consist of thematic categories but also include socio-demographic data or other standardized information, the term *profile matrix* is more appropriate.

Organizing the data in a persons-by-categories form is comparable to creating a cross-tabulation when analysing quantitative data statistically. In quantitative analysis, the parameters and coefficients are of primary interest, and the relationships represented in a table are summarized in a single coefficient, for instance chi-squared, Pearson's *r*, or Cramér's *V*. Of course, qualitative analysis does not aim to identify and summarize numerical values and test for statistical significance; rather, it aims to create a clear and comprehensible interpretation of the information that is included in such a matrix. The individual cells of the matrix contain not numbers, but text, which you can access at any time during the analysis process. Thus, it is possible to select, separate, and abstract without losing sight of the context.

	Topic A	Topic B	Topic C	
Person 1	Person 1's text passages about Topic A	Person 1's text passages about Topic B	Person 1's text passages about Topic C	⇒ Case-oriented analysis for Person 1
Person 2	Person 2's text passages about Topic A	Person 2's text passages about Topic B	Person 2's text passages about Topic C	⇒ Case-oriented analysis for Person 2
Person 3	Person 3's text passages about Topic A	Person 3's text passages about Topic B	Person 3's text passages about Topic C	⇒ Case-oriented analysis for Person 3
	Category-oriented analysis for			
	⇓	⇓	⇓	
	Topic A	Topic B	Topic C	

Figure 4.2 Prototypical model of structuring in qualitative content analysis, here as a thematic matrix for an interview study

The *cases-by-categories* matrix can be analysed in two directions. Horizontally, you can follow a single row of the matrix (e.g., the second row, Person 2) to gain an overview of a particular person's statements. This gives you a case-oriented perspective structured by the thematic categories of the analysis. The results can take the form of a written case summary for several or all of the selected topics. Vertically, you can direct your attention to a specific column (e.g., Topic B), which gives you a *category-oriented* perspective, in this example topic-oriented. This enables you to view all of the respondents' statements regarding a given topic.

In the simplest case, summarizing one row or one column creates individual case summaries (which characterize one person) or thematic summaries (which describe the statements pertaining to a given topic in a systematic manner). However, the matrix can be used for much more complex analyses. You can compare multiple rows with each other, which would compare and contrast different individuals. You can also contrast the statements within different categories in order to evaluate how the statements correspond with each other.

Moreover, the rows and columns can be summarized in a vertical as well as horizontal fashion. This means that individuals can be assigned to groups according to specific characteristics, and topics can be grouped under broader or more abstract, overarching categories. The type-building QCA (described in Chapter 7) is specifically designed for the first variant – grouping cases according to similarity.

4.3 Similarities and Differences between the Three Types

All three of the methods described in Chapters 5–7 work with *categories*. Classical content analysis, which was developed as a systematic research method in the 1940s, is essentially based on the idea of creating categories and analysing the empirical material according to these categories. Over time, content analysis evolved more towards a form of quantitative content analysis, which often ignored the qualitative aspect of text analysis, text comprehension.

The methods of QCA described here in detail are also focused on categories, which are the most important tools of the analysis. The three methods build on each other in some respects, but this should not be interpreted as a hierarchical ranking. Thus, evaluative analysis should not be perceived as superior to thematic analysis and type-building analysis is by no means superior to evaluative analysis. In contrast, it is better to ask which method is more suited to answering a given research question. For example, it is not always beneficial to build types during the analysis. Type building is often described as a goal of qualitative research in methods textbooks, and it is often viewed as equivalent to the representative generalizations applied in quantitative research. However, if your goal is to describe the object of your research in detail or to test a hypothesis about how different concepts are related, building types is probably not particularly useful.

Intensely explorative or descriptive research will perhaps focus on the analysis of issues and arguments, examining the relationship between categories or, in the style of grounded theory, work to create core categories for the phenomena identified in the research field (Corbin & Strauss, 2015, pp. 187–190). In these cases, neither evaluative nor type-building analysis would be appropriate. Evaluative analysis would force judgement too early in the process, and both methods follow approaches other than the comparative method of grounded theory, which operates mainly in terms of minimum or maximum contrasts.

In the literature on QCA, there is agreement that structuring content analysis is *the* core content analysis procedure (Mayring, 2015; Schreier, 2012, 2014; Steigleder, 2008). For this reason, it takes up most of the space in this book. In a contribution comparing the different variants, Schreier (2014) notes that evaluative and type-building QCA are also structuring content-analytical procedures at their core. This is certainly true, but the processes of evaluative and type-building analyses are so different that separate descriptions seem appropriate – and of course the methods can also be combined.

What do the three methods of QCA presented in Chapters 5–7 have in common? We can identify six key points:

1 They are *methods of analysis*, that is, they do not prescribe a specific type of data collection. Different methods, such as structuring and type-building QCA, can easily be applied to the same data, for instance, during the secondary analysis of existing qualitative data.[1]

2 They are methods that *compress and summarize* the data rather than expand in the style of sequential analysis in order to interpret the data exegetically.

3 They are *category-based methods*. Thus, the analytical categories are the focus of the analysis process, although the way in which the categories are constructed may vary. Categories or topics can be developed from the theory or the research questions and applied to the data, or developed directly grounded on the data. It is quite common to combine various methods to build categories.

4 They are *systematic* scientific methods and not open to artistic interpretation, meaning the implementation of these methods can be described precisely and mastered by researchers and students. These methods do not involve the art of interpretation that is characteristic in fields such as literary or art history.

5 The three methods are *language-related* and are initially conceived as methods for systematic qualitative analysis of verbal or textual data. Nevertheless, they may also be applied to images, movies, and other products of culture and communications.

6 Because they are systematic, *rule-governed* processes, *quality standards* can be formulated for all three methods. Thus, we can distinguish between qualitative content analyses of better or lesser quality.

---

[1]For more information on secondary analysis of qualitative data, see Medjedović and Witzel (2010) and Medjedović (2014). Qualitative data for secondary analyses are provided by Qualiservice, a research data centre at the University of Bremen (www.qualiservice.org), and by the UK Data Service (https://discover.ukdataservice.ac.uk/qualibank).

For all three methods, analysis can begin even before all of the data are collected. All three methods are compatible with different sampling methods and can be combined with more conventional methods, such as a quota-based sampling, or theoretical sampling as is preferred in grounded theory. However, as systematic processes, the three methods require a complete coding of the entire data material, meaning that later changes to the category system require additional processing of the data and are therefore associated with substantial additional effort. The postulate that the entire data of a study can be analysed in a systematic, category-based manner prevents researchers from drawing premature conclusions based on individual cases. Regardless of which analysis method you use, it is recommended that you document the individual steps of the analysis process as accurately as possible in a research journal.

Differences from Other Approaches of Qualitative Content Analysis

How do the methods of QCA that we explain in this book differ from those proposed by other authors? What is different about a QCA according to Mayring (2014, 2015, 2021) or according to Schreier (2012)? First of all, let us look at the similarities and the commonalities. In our view, the above-mentioned six characteristics of the methods presented in this book also apply to the methods of QCA proposed by other authors. That is, QCA is not a method of data collection but of analysis that takes a compressive approach using categories. It is a systematic and descriptive method that is applied primarily to verbal data and must meet strong quality criteria. Instead of comparing individual approaches and taking the risk of presenting them in a different way from what the authors intended, it seems to us more purposeful to emphasize the special features of our approach and its presentation in this book:

- Our form of QCA always begins with an *introductory phase* that is primarily case-oriented. The deliberate entry into the analysis is intended, among other things, to help researchers not to equate QCA with only coding and categorizing text segments and not to lose sight of the overall picture by hastily starting to code.
- Regarding the interpretation of texts, we are guided by *hermeneutic principles* as the classical approach to understanding texts.
- Especially in the introductory phase, but also later, *word-based analysis methods* such as keyword-in-context or word frequencies can be integrated.
- The procedure for all three types is divided into phases and *described in as much detail and as concretely as possible.*
- The procedure considers the *support of the analysis by QDA software* from the outset. Accordingly, the book contains a detailed chapter on the implementation of the procedures using computer software.
- One focus of the descriptions is on the phase *after coding* – the analysis of the coded data – for which numerous procedures and possibilities beyond mere

category frequencies are presented. In this context, we also show possibilities for *summarizing coded segments* and integrating this into further analysis.

- A frequency analysis of the categories in some situations makes sense (if the number of cases is large enough), but the actual *analysis is qualitative*.
- Despite the focus on the research questions and the postulate of methodological rigour, there is a place for *serendipity* (Merton & Barber, 2004), the accidental discovery of important findings that were not the primary focus of the research, but which prove to be significant for the object of investigation.
- *Continuous writing of memos* to record working hypotheses, analysis ideas, and findings is a recommended part of the whole analysis process.
- *No pre-definition of segments to be coded* is required as the first step of the analysis. We recommend this only for the calculation of chance-corrected coefficients of intercoder agreement.
- *Consensual and discursive verification of intercoder agreement* is prioritized over the mere use of coefficients.
- *Theory orientation is not per se the starting point* for the analysis, analytical decisions, or the selection criterion for inductive category development, although the inclusion of theories can be valuable at many points in the analysis process. Theory orientation is also not regarded as the primary quality criterion by which a QCA should be evaluated.
- *No predetermination of the level of abstraction of categories is postulated*. But, of course, we consider a similar level of abstraction across the main categories as an important criterion for the assessment of the quality of category systems.
- During the entire analysis process, the focus can be directed both to the case level and the category level. Depending on the research questions, the case can remain relevant in its entirety, including its multi perspectivity, its multidimensional nature, and its possible inherent contradictions. The case does not necessarily lose its importance because of cross-case coding. *Case orientation and category orientation* can also be combined in a study. This 'double perspective' of cases and categories marks an important difference from Mayring's conception of QCA: there, the case-oriented perspective plays virtually no role compared to the category-oriented perspective, as the following quote illustrates:

> Text analysis is thus selectively limited to the category system. Contents that are not addressed in categories, as well as a holistic impression of the text, are not taken into account or would have to be addressed with other text interpretation procedures. (Mayring, 2019, para. 3)

The list could be continued in detail, but this would not be very useful. We have already mentioned further aspects in Section 1.9 when we pointed out the central characteristics and focal points of our definition of QCA in contrast to other definitions. Further explanations of the similarities and differences between various approaches to QCA can be found in Schreier (2014).

Differences from Grounded Theory Methodology

In workshops we are often asked about the differences from grounded theory methodology. Students want to assess which method is suitable for dealing with their research project and their research questions. The following main differences between QCA and grounded theory approaches seem relevant to us in this context:

- In a grounded theory study, the goal is always to develop a new theory (of medium scope) grounded in the data. This can also be a goal when using QCA, but it does not have to be.
- To achieve the purpose of theory building, it is not necessary to code all the material in a grounded theory project, because the end point of the analysis is the saturation of the theory generated, not the coding and category-based analysis of the complete material. It is also not necessary in grounded theory approaches to process and code all the material in the same systematic manner as is done in QCA.
- In a grounded theory study, changes to the category system are possible on an ongoing basis; in fact, continuous work on the codes and categories is a characteristic feature.
- The grounded theory approach not only describes an analysis method, but also includes data collection (its keyword is 'theoretical sampling'). Optimally, data are continuously collected and analysed; overall, the approach is very process-oriented and flexible. In contrast, projects that use QCA as a method of analysis usually work with predetermined samples. Such systematic selection plans make it possible, among other things, to conduct comparisons of sufficiently large groups.
- Due to its objective, grounded theory approaches are less suitable for descriptive analyses, and the same applies to their use in evaluation.

At this point we would like to point out a misunderstanding that we have often encountered in practice. Many times we have been presented with projects labelled as grounded theory studies which, on closer inspection, turned out to be qualitative content analyses with inductive category development. The mere fact that categories are developed using the data in the style of open coding does not justify a designation as a grounded theory study if there is no intention to work conceptually and analytically towards a theory (a keyword here is 'theoretical sensitivity').

4.4 Quantification in Qualitative Content Analysis

Even though in all variants of QCA the actual analysis is primarily qualitative in nature, quantifying analysis steps are also possible, because numbers can certainly play a role in qualitative research:

> Yet, as I showed in the last chapter, numbers have a place within qualitative research, assisting, for example, in sensitive attempts to learn lessons in one

place that have relevance for actions and understanding in another place. There is a variety of other uses of numbers which can enhance the quality of qualitative research. (Seale, 1999a, p. 120)

As a result of his very instructive overview of the benefits and use of numbers in qualitative research, Seale (1999a, p. 121) formulated the principle of 'counting the countable'. Numbers can assume different functions; they can not only be simple frequencies or percentages but also be used for more complex statistical calculations, such as crosstabs with the chi-squared test or cluster analysis. They can clarify arguments and support theories and generalizations. Seale's (1999a, p. 138) emphasis on 'avoiding anecdotalism' expresses the importance of using numbers quite concisely.

However, there should be careful reflection on the significance that quantification can have for every QCA. The main question here is: does frequent also mean important? Counting what can be counted always means that one acquires additional information but does not relieve one of the task of reflecting on the significance of quantification and statistics for the particular research project. For example, if in an online interview with relatively short answers a question asks about what is personally important in one's life, it is justified to describe in the analysis a topic mentioned by more people as 'important to more people' than a topic mentioned less frequently. So, if the category 'primary network' was coded for more people than 'secondary network', it is legitimate to write in the research report that the primary network is considered important by more research participants than the secondary network. The situation is different at the individual level: if someone has mentioned 'primary network' more often in relatively short answer texts, it is difficult to justify the conclusion about relevance.

One should also be careful not to draw conclusions from the category-based frequency analysis of the data about questions that were not asked at all. Assuming that, in the analysis of the question about what is important in one's life, the category 'security' was developed with corresponding sub-categories 'internal security in public space', 'external security, peace', etc., it cannot be concluded from a higher frequency of 'internal security in public space' compared to 'external security, peace' that internal security is more important to the research participants than external security. This was not the question that was asked. In general, it can be said that the further one moves away from the questions asked, for example in a guided interview, the less meaning numbers have. They remain important as additional information, but the meaning must be critically considered in the specific case. The more openly the interview was conducted, the less useful frequencies become.

A conscious approach to quantification in QCA requires reflection on what should actually be counted or what can be counted at all given the present data and the coding used. In this respect, it is helpful to take a look at quantitative content analysis, which uses the term *unit of analysis* (also called *recording unit*). This unit of analysis indicates which units are processed and counted. When analysing newspaper reports in quantitative content analysis, for example, the entire newspaper report, a paragraph, sentence, or even an individual word can be selected as a unit, which must then be coded accordingly.

Meaning units can also be chosen as the unit of analysis, but they must be defined beforehand and the text must be segmented accordingly. In one and the same study, analyses can be carried out with different units of analysis, that is, the definition of the unit of analysis and the segments to be coded should be well thought out at the beginning of the content analysis, but the units of analysis can vary during the analysis.

In a QCA of newspaper reports, the analysis can also be carried out at the levels just mentioned, and the same applies to the analysis of interviews. Mostly, however, one will not adopt formal units of analysis here, but work with units of meaning, which do not have to be defined in advance. If coded segments of a category (i.e., the category frequencies) are counted, this can be done per interview or also per group of several interviews if these groups are to be compared with each other. It should be noted, however, that high category frequencies in one interview do not necessarily imply a high importance of the category for this interviewee. If the category 'learn dealing with global problems' was coded many times in an interview, this does not necessarily mean that the person mentioned many different ways of learning, but he or she may have made the same suggestion several times in short statements. *Frequent*, therefore, does not necessarily mean *diverse* and *relevant*. Consequently, group comparisons are usually based on the number of cases in which a category is coded, rather than the number of coded segments. Instead of asking how many times a particular category was assigned per case, one should ask whether the category was assigned to the particular case or not, or to how many cases the category was assigned. A special situation arises in the case of focus groups and group interviews, because here either the entire interview or the individual person can be defined as the unit of analysis, so in a sense another hierarchical level is added.

What else should be considered when quantifying in qualitative content analyses? The primary goal of working with quantifications does not have to be the presentation of frequencies, percentages, and statistics in the research report. Quantitative analyses can also serve as an exploratory tool and provide entry points into more in-depth analyses. Be careful when working with percentages because the presentation of percentages is not useful when the sample is very small. For example, reporting case percentages with five interviewees is considered to be a methodological mistake, because here one case is already equal to 20%. Normally, the calculation of percentages with a sample of less than 20 cases is not very meaningful. Also beware of supposedly increased generalizability through quantification: the inclusion of statistics in the analysis and the presentation of results does not per se guarantee generalizability, because this is primarily a question of sampling and the type of conclusion (cf. Section 9.5).

4.5 Starting the Analysis: Initial Work with the Text, Writing Memos, and Writing Case Summaries

No matter which of the variants of QCA presented in this book is chosen, the start of the analysis is always the same. At the start, you should review the goals and context of your research, asking yourself: Which questions am I interested in and what is my focus? Which concepts and constructs are important to my study? What relationships would I like to examine? What sorts of preliminary assumptions do I have regarding these relationships? For whom or what do the results have a use? Likewise, it is helpful to reflect on your own prior knowledge and assumptions about the object or phenomenon under investigation – preferably in writing (Rädiker & Kuckartz, 2020, pp. 26–28).

Clarifying your objectives in this manner does not violate the principle of openness, which is frequently named as a characteristic of qualitative research. The postulate of openness refers first to the process of data acquisition, as respondents should have the opportunity to express their own views, use their own words instead of being forced to use predetermined categories, and express their individual motives and reasoning. On the part of the researcher, openness in the sense of the principle of 'approaching the project without any research question and without any concept' would not only be mere fiction (because we always operate on the basis of prior knowledge and prejudices and a knowledge of the world that precedes any observation), but also imply ignorance of the scientific community in which one moves. After all, in most situations there is already a long-standing tradition of engagement with the object of research. However, openness on the part of researchers is very much necessary with regard to openness to other perspectives and interpretations as well as openness in the sense of reflecting on one's own prior knowledge and existing 'pre-judgements'.

Initial Work with the Text: Reading and Reflecting

The first step you take in analysing qualitative data should always be hermeneutical or interpretive in nature and should involve reading the text carefully and trying to understand the subjective meaning:

> We cannot analyse our data unless we read it. How well we read it may determine how well we analyse it. ... The aim of reading through our data is to prepare the ground for the analysis. (Dey, 1993, p. 83)

For systematic data exploration taking hermeneutic principles into account, it is helpful to first visualize the context in which the data were generated. In an interview study, one can ask oneself questions such as: What information did interviewees receive in advance? In which settings did the interviews take place? What expectations might the research participants have had of the interview? When starting the analysis, it may also be possible to refer back to the actual raw data in the form of audio and video recordings. This beginning of the first phase of QCA is called *initial work with the text,* whereby – as in literary studies – working through the text is to be understood as intensive exploration of the content and the language of a given text. Starting with the first line, you must read the text sequentially and completely. The goal is to gain a general understanding of the given text on the basis of the research question(s). It is often helpful to outline your research questions and attempt to answer them as you work though the interview data. For example, in a study about individual perceptions of climate change, we were able to answer or address the following points while reading through each of the interviews:

- What does the respondent actually know about climate change?
- How does he or she relate to it?
- How does he or she personally act or behave?
- Does he or she have any demands or expectations for him- or herself?
- Does the respondent discuss the topic with friends or others?

It can also be useful to examine the text formally. How long is the text? Which words are used (particularly noticeable words)? What sort of language does the respondent use? How long are the sentences? What sorts of metaphors are used?

So, what does it mean to systematically read and work through a text? Reading is an everyday skill that we have mastered, and we have developed a variety of individual reading techniques within the sciences. Some people highlight texts with one or more multi-coloured highlighters, some people write notes in the margins using their own abbreviations, and others record their notes on other pieces of paper, index cards, or in a research journal. The list of such individual techniques that have proved effective over time is long; such methods should by no means be considered inappropriate here. However, there is a strict procedure that must be followed in QCA in order to ensure its comparability, understandability, and methodological consistency, and it will be explained in more detail in the steps below. Moreover, it should also be noted that many of the tried and tested methods mentioned above (highlighting, etc.) can also be used in QDA software programs (cf. Chapter 8). In addition to electronic text markers, word-based analysis options are also available which support the initiating text work in a meaningful way and which are almost impossible to use without software. With QDA software, frequently used words and word combinations can be identified, and using a keyword-in-context display, the question of within which formulations selected terms are used can be answered. Results of such analyses can provide initial answers to the research questions or offer valuable suggestions for how to proceed with the analysis. In an analysis of the first 50 transcripts from the multi-award-winning podcast on the Covid pandemic with virologist Christian Drosten (in German), we became aware of the two words 'natürlich' ('of course') and 'vielleicht' ('probably'). Both occur about 650 times and are thus among the 15 most frequent words, if you exclude definite and indefinite articles as well as other typical 'stop words'. In what contexts are these two words used? To what extent do they express a degree of certainty in the statements made? Do they occur with specific topics? Are they used more by the interviewer or by Dr Drosten? With QDA software, these questions can be answered directly and the results recorded. Regardless of this, it can be stated for the further analysis that the degree of certainty with which statements are made in the podcast should be taken into account as an analytical perspective. It may be possible to develop (evaluative) categories for this at a later stage.

Word-based methods can refer to several cases or be applied to individual texts. Although the initial work with the text is primarily focused on the individual case, the perspective on the entire data always remains important, especially in order to be able to assess and situate the individual case in the overall context and to select specific texts for comparison, for example a text in which the word 'maybe' occurs frequently.

When starting the analysis, you should include as much data as possible to get a comprehensive picture and to create a solid foundation for the following analysis phases. With very large amounts of data, a sample may be selected. Normally, a quota-based selection is appropriate for this purpose, in that cases are selected from each group under study. A random selection or a selection based on relevant attributes such as the complexity and linguistic characteristics of cases is also possible. In our example of the Covid podcasts, the date of broadcast also plays a role and it would make sense to select podcasts from the beginning of the pandemic as well as at several later points in time. Whatever the situation, the selection should be made in such a way that the widest possible range of data is achieved with maximum variation.

In qualitative research, there is not a very strict distinction between the phase of data collection and that of data analysis as there is in the classical model of quantitative research. This is also true for QCA. In contrast to statistical analyses of standardized data, you do not have to delay the analysis until all of the data has been collected. Thus, normally, you can start analysing the data you already have while continuing to collect additional data. Even if you do not adhere to the grounded theory, in which data acquisition and analysis are explicitly crossed, it can be beneficial to start analysing the content before all of the data has been collected. Hence, you can start reading and working through the first interview as soon as it has been transcribed.

Let us summarize once again:

Initial work with the text involves:

- Determining the sequence for working with the texts and making a selection if necessary
- Analysing the text in light of the research questions
- Reading the text intently
- Highlighting central terms and concepts
- Marking and making note of important sections
- Marking passages that are difficult to understand
- Analysing arguments and lines of argumentation
- Examining the formal structure (length, etc.)
- Identifying the internal structure (paragraphs, breaks, etc.)
- Directing your attention to the general progression of the text
- Examining frequently used words and phrases and considering selected words in their context.

The above list is not intended to imply that all exploration techniques must be used in every analysis. For example, while it can be very relevant in an analysis of party manifestos how long the sections on taxation are, the length of text passages in interviews may be much less significant. Generally, it is advisable to go through the list of exploration techniques systematically and consider which ones are used in one's own project, with what objective, for what gain in knowledge, and for what reasons other exploration techniques are dispensed with.

After completing the initial work with the text, one should be familiar with the data and especially with the individual cases. Furthermore, the results of this step can be very diverse. Initial text work can provide useful insights for the design of the category system, indications of the relevance of themes and aspects, as well as ideas for further analysis. Furthermore, attention is drawn to important terms, metaphors, and formulations and relevant, possibly particularly striking, text passages are identified. It is also possible to identify salient cases, such as those in which interviewees hold extreme opinions. All in all, the initial work with text brings the research questions closer to the data and triggers insights into how to approach the material in order to answer the research questions. Last but not least, this step of the analysis can also produce surprises and serendipitous findings.

Writing Memos

Whether you work directly on the computer screen or rely on a printed version of the text depends on your own personal work preferences and style. Many people find it helpful to read through a printed version of the text first so that they can make notes in the margins and highlight passages that seem particularly important. If you choose to do so, make sure that the paragraphs or lines are numbered so that it is easier to transfer your markings and comments into the electronic version later. On the screen, you can highlight important or notable passages using an electronic highlighter.

Any peculiarities in the text or ideas that you may have while reading the text should be recorded as memos.

> A memo contains any thoughts, ideas, assumptions, or hypotheses that occur to researchers during the analysis process. Memos can be short notes (like a sticky note) or more reflective comments regarding the content which act as building blocks for the research report. Writing memos should be considered an integral part of the research process.

When writing memos, it is helpful to be aware of what kind of content is being noted down. A distinction can be made between descriptive, interpretive, and analytical memos. Description primarily means the descriptive summary of data, while interpretation goes beyond this and includes the researcher's interpretation (e.g., 'cause could be'). Memos regarding the further analysis process are more organizational in nature and may include decisions and outstanding tasks (e.g., 'Check in other cases too!'). To distinguish the different types of content in a memo, it can be useful to format the content differently, for example, using a particular font colour.

Grounded theory addresses the role that memos play in the research process in detail (Charmaz, 2014; Strauss & Corbin, 1990, pp. 197–223) and differentiates between different types of memos. While memos are not quite as important within the framework of QCA as they are in grounded theory, they are considered helpful resources that can be used throughout the entire research process, just as they can be in grounded theory.

Writing Case Summaries

After working through the text, it is helpful to write a case summary – a systematic, ordered summary of what is characteristic to the given case. A case summary is really just a summarizing case description that focuses on what is important to the research question(s). It should note any characteristics of the individual case that are central to the research question. Unlike memos, case summaries should not contain your own ideas or even hypotheses that you may have developed while working through the text; instead, case summaries are fact-oriented, condensed summaries of the text.

In our study of individual perceptions of climate change that is described in more detail below, we considered the following questions in writing the case summaries: What does the respondent know about climate change? How does he or she relate to it? How does he or she act personally? Does he or she have any demands on or expectations for him- or herself? Does he or she talk with friends or others about the subject? In addition, case summaries should address two questions that include a comparative aspect: How would you characterize this respondent? What makes this person or this perspective unique?

Case summaries are fact-oriented and based on what was said, not on a hermeneutic or psychological interpretation of the story. Any assumptions about the text that seem plausible but cannot be confirmed by the information provided in the text should not be noted or marked as assumptions.

So, what does a case summary look like and how long should it be? For relatively short texts, we recommend simply noting key words. For interviews, it is common to create a headline or motto for each of the case summaries. For example, we created key word summaries of the cases in a qualitative evaluation project (Kuckartz et al. 2008, pp. 34–35), in which the participants in a university lecture course on statistics were asked about their individual study methods and behaviour as well as their overall experiences in the different sections of the course (Figures 4.3 and 4.4).

Interview with Person R1: Positive Attitude without Ambition

- She only found the tutoring sessions in the second half of the semester interesting.
- The tutoring and practice sessions were the best, but they were too full towards the end.
- People attended the tutoring sessions instead of preparing for class and reviewing afterwards on their own.
- The basic structure of the lecture seems fine. It inspires productive learning.
- She did not have her own study group (rather, she studied with a friend).
- She wished she had a small study group.
- Did not read any additional material but finds her own notes good.
- The practice test was good and all she wants is to pass the course.

Figure 4.3 Example of a brief case summary (interview R1)

Interview with Person R2: The Economical Self-Learner
- Rarely went to the lectures but participated in the tutoring sessions more regularly.
- Always liked maths in school and now likes statistics, too.
- Can concentrate better at home, which is why she didn't go to the lectures.
- The lectures were useless because she didn't understand anything.
- Practice exercises with solutions on the internet were her source for learning materials.
- Bought the recommended textbook and worked through it.
- Found the tutoring sessions very good.
- Also attended another, more practical lecture course on statistics.
- Her study methods changed fundamentally in the middle of the course.
- She suggests that there be more time to solve practice problems and more material presented in such a way that the students must take their own notes.
- Feels like she was well prepared for the final exam.

Figure 4.4 Example of a brief case summary (interview R2)

Case summaries can also take the form of a detailed, fluid text. They can be written not only for individual interviews, but also for qualitative studies with groups and organizations using mottos. A motto can focus on a particular aspect of the research question, be based on a statement or quote in the given text, or be creatively formulated by the researchers to fit a given text. However, because mottos are accentuated characterizations, they are highly subject to interpretation. Thus, while a motto can be useful, it may not always be.

The case summary in Figure 4.5 is headed with a concise characterization. It is taken from a study of the graduates of the first two years of the Marburg BA programme in Educational Science. It is an example of a more detailed, fluid text. It is written using the guideline structure and questions, which are highlighted and precede the respective paragraphs.

For interview studies, it is usually advisable to prepare case summaries, whereby a well-reasoned sample should be selected in studies with larger numbers of cases. By preparing case summaries, one gets an overview of the spectrum of cases included in the research, which is of great value especially in studies with larger numbers of cases. According to the criterion of maximum and minimum contrast, one can compare cases that are particularly similar or particularly dissimilar to each other.

How can case summaries be handled for types of data other than interviews? This is highly dependent on the characteristics of the material and the answer to the question of what should be considered a case. If you are studying the role of the father in children's picture books, the case is the individual picture book and the production of case summaries certainly makes sense. In focus groups, there are two possible definitions of what a case is: either the respective focus group as a whole or an individual participant. The more important differentiation by individual participants is for the analysis, the more useful it is to write case summaries for individuals. If a differentiation by participants is not intended, case summaries for the respective focus group are more constructive. In surveys with open-ended questions, on the other hand, where there are usually short answers from a very large number of people, case summaries do not make sense because summarizing the short answers would not bring any analytical benefit.

R3 'Master's student with the aim of social pedagogical counselling'.
Motivation to study: R3 has been interested in counselling since grade 11. She deliberately did not want to study psychology but wanted to become a child and youth therapist after her 'training'. It is interesting that psychology seemed attractive to her as a minor, but not as a major subject. Learning expectations in the BA: She wanted to learn good basic knowledge of education and psychology.
Job title/perceived profession: R3 gives the job title 'pedagogue, not teacher'. She actually thinks that she is not yet a fully qualified educator, but to third parties it is 'easier' to 'circumscribe' her profession as social worker.
Competences: She claims to have acquired counselling, socio-educational and psychological competences as well as rhetoric, interviewing, and research skills during her studies.
Professional qualification: She can imagine entering the job market now. However, she needs time to develop basic pedagogical skills. She sees her current studies as an entry point.
Further studies: She is studying a master's programme in educational science and had already planned this before her BA studies. Reasons were: (a) it is easier to continue studying; (b) improvement of qualifications; (c) better chances on the job market compared to pedagogues with only a bachelor's degree. In favour of Marburg was the fact that she feels comfortable here, has a friend and friendships, and knows the structures and professors, so that she can take more with her in terms of content. In the MA, she wants to deepen and supplement the previous material. She sees the BA as an intermediate exam and not as a real degree.
Career goal: She wants to work in counselling; she has put aside her original wish to become a child and youth therapist.
Practical experience: Before beginning her bachelor's degree, she worked for nine months in a residential home for people with disabilities, she was also a scout group leader. None of the practical activities had a direct influence on her choice of a study programme. During her bachelor's studies, she continued to work in the residential home and completed two internships in counselling centres.
Understanding of practical relevance: R3 understands practical relevance as the internship itself and practical examples in seminars. Would have liked more 'basic tools', 'more the kind of things you learn in educator training', at least 'a hint of it'.
Added value of the university BA: The university degree tends to be at a higher level and promotes individuality.
Rating and final question: Very good with 13 out of 15 points. As minor points of critique, she once again mentions the lack of practical relevance, the university library, and the fact that the grading is mainly done through homework. She pleads for the possibility of starting the master's programme in the summer semester in order to have more time for the BA.

Figure 4.5 Formulated case summary for Interview R3

The same applies to manifestos of political parties, as these have already been written with the aim of providing highly condensed and thematically structured statements.

Case summaries are meaningful for the research process for five main reasons:

1   They provide an overview of the material for larger research teams in which not every team member can systematically work through every text (team aspect).

2   The summaries are a good starting point for creating tabular case overviews for multiple cases (comparative aspect).

3   They highlight the differences between the individual cases (aspect of analytical differentiation).

4   They help to generate hypotheses and categories (inspiring aspect).

5   They represent a first result of a case-based approach and can give the readers of your research report a useful insight into the respective case, possibly in a form enhanced by the later analysis (aspect of transparency and presentation).

4.6 **Summary and Concluding Remarks**

There are numerous variants of QCA. Some scholars, such as Schreier, suggest a modular system, whereby, depending on the research question and the type of data, an appropriate QCA is assembled from different elements. In our view, Schreier's proposal is worth considering, but it provides little guidance to researchers on the rules they should follow to design such an optimal form of analysis for their approach and data. We would compare this to cooking a soup: describing the ingredients does not make a good soup. To stay with this comparison, our preference is to describe not only the ingredients but also their preparation, which in this book means describing three different strategies of QCA and their steps in detail. These are: structuring QCA, because it is the one that is used very often in research; evaluative QCA as an analysis strategy, which works with the evaluations of the researchers and is particularly suitable for theory-oriented research; and type-building QCA, since research projects often have the goal of developing a typology, for example, in order to determine target groups in marketing, to identify learning types in pedagogy, or to determine group-specific effects in intervention programmes.

The three types of QCA described are based on a general process model that begins with the initial work with the text, a step oriented towards hermeneutic principles. It is important to first gain an understanding of the data through intensive reading, to mark important points, and to record comments and initial ideas. While structuring QCA is usually used to structure the material according to topics and themes, the evaluative strategy allows the researcher to assess segments of the data that are relevant to specific research questions. Structuring and evaluative QCA can also be combined; for example, in a structuring QCA, selected topics can also be assessed with evaluative categories.

Type-building QCA builds on previous structuring or evaluative QCA or requires that appropriate coding of the data has already been done.

We see all three strategies as primarily qualitative methods and not as preparation for ultimately quantitative-statistical analyses. Quantification can play a role in QCA and can provide a lot of interesting information, but in our opinion it should not replace the actual qualitative analysis. We emphasize in this chapter that, in qualitative content analyses, researchers should always adopt a complementary case-oriented perspective in addition to the category-oriented perspective. What is considered a case depends on the focus of the research: for example, a person, a family, a group, a company, or an institution. Depending on the research question and the approach chosen, the relation of case-oriented and category-oriented analysis can be different. For example, case orientation usually plays a greater role in small samples such as in interview studies than in large samples when analysing social media data.

5

STRUCTURING QUALITATIVE CONTENT ANALYSIS

Chapter objectives

In this chapter you will learn about:

- The characteristics of structuring QCA and its seven steps
- Creating main categories
- The first coding cycle: applying the main categories
- The second coding cycle: mainly using data-based inductive development of sub-categories
- Analysing the coded data in various ways
- Writing case-related thematic summaries
- Possible ways to prepare and present your results.

5.1 Characteristics of Structuring QCA

Structuring qualitative content analysis has been proven and tested in numerous research projects and described in the methods literature in various forms, for example in two special issues of the online journal *FQS* on QCA (Janssen et al., 2019; Stamann et al., 2020). A wide range of procedures can be found, regarding ways to construct the categories, with which structuring QCA can be conducted; these range from creating the categories inductively using the data to creating the categories deductively based on an underlying theory from the field or the research question.

The extremes of the spectrum of ways to construct the categories – completely inductively or completely deductively – are rarely found in research practice, and in most cases, a multi-stage process of developing categories and coding is used. In the first stage of the analysis, the data are coded rather roughly using main categories, which, for example, originate from the guidelines used in data collection. The number of categories in this first phase is relatively small and manageable; it does not usually include more than about 10–20 main categories. In the next phase, the categories are further developed and differentiated based on the data. The entire data set is then coded with the detailed coding system, analysed based on this coding, and prepared for the research report. The more elaborate category structure may provide a basic framework for the research report. By comparing and contrasting subgroups of interest, the category-based analysis gains sophistication, complexity, and explanatory power.

In principle, this process allows for the thematic analysis of guideline-oriented, problem-centred, focused, as well as many other types of interviews, such as focus groups, episodic, and narrative interviews (see Flick, 2007, pp. 268–278). Modifications would have to be made for each different type. For example, with a narrative interview, the analysis will focus on passages that actually contain narratives and will ignore other parts. The structuring analysis method is also frequently used in the analysis of media articles and documents, such as party programmes, image brochures, training regulations, academic literature, school books, and children's books. The procedure presented below can easily be adapted to such types of data, but it is important to bear in mind that not all parts of a work are always included in the detailed analysis, although in the hermeneutic sense the work is considered in its entirety.

5.2 The Example Study

In many of the examples throughout Chapters 5–7, in which the three basic methods of qualitative content analysis are described in detail, we will refer to data collected within the framework of our research project, 'Individual Perception of Climate Change – The Discrepancy between Knowledge and Behaviour'.[1] The central research question of this study was: 'To what extent do people's fundamental assessments, as seen in their world-views, their perceptions of

---

[1]The study was conducted by students within the 'Environmental Education and Communication' seminar in the winter semester 2008/2009.

others, and their own positioning in a "global society", cause a discrepancy between knowledge and behaviour when it comes to protecting the climate?' (Kuckartz, 2010b).

The sample consisted of 30 participants who were divided into two age groups: 15–25 years of age ('network kids') and 46–65 years of age ('baby boomers'). The data consisted of two parts: a qualitative, open survey in the form of an interview; and a standardized questionnaire that collected respondents' social and demographic characteristics as well as their general assessment of climate change using scales. We started with a problem-centred interview (Witzel & Reiter, 2012), which followed the interview guide shown in Figure 5.1.

For interviewers: World view

In your opinion, what are the biggest problems facing the world in the 21st century? How can we address these problems? Who or what has an impact on them, if at all? Consider climate change and the necessary CO_2 reductions. Can changing consumption habits in developed countries have a positive effect on such issues?

For interviewers: View of others

People often talk about a discrepancy between attitudes and behaviours, such as when a person says one thing, but does another. What do you think causes this sort of behaviour?

For interviewers: View of oneself

How do global developments affect you? How do you think you can impact them? What sort of behaviour impacts them? Do you actually do that? Would you like to do more? Do you feel a sense of responsibility to wrestle with the problems of the 21st century?

For interviewers: Closing

Do you think that people can learn how to address these problems? If yes, how? Where?

Figure 5.1 Excerpt from the interview guide of the example study

The accompanying four-page standardized questionnaire contained questions regarding the personal relevance of environmental protection, people's assessment of the risks associated with different environmental problems (global warming, nuclear power, etc.), climate change and its causes, as well as covering personal attitudes towards the environment, communication about the environment, and the individual's level of commitment. In addition, socio-demographic data such as gender, age, level of education, and income were collected.

The qualitative interviews were transcribed verbatim and the data from the standardized questionnaires were entered directly into the software used for qualitative data analysis. Both parts of the study were then compiled and analysed with the help of this software. The project serves as a good example for this book because the research question is quite focused and the data from the qualitative interviews are manageable in size.

5.3 Structuring QCA: Step by Step

Figure 5.2 shows the seven phases of structuring QCA, starting with the research questions.

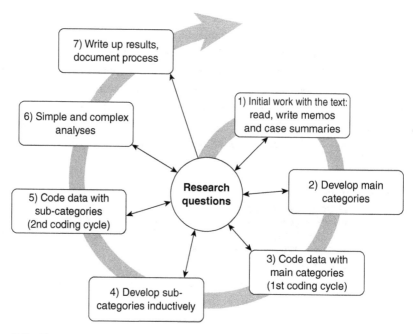

Figure 5.2 The seven phases of structuring QCA

Phase 1: Initial Work with the Text: Read, Write Memos and Case Summaries

As with all forms of QCA, the first analysis steps consist of initial text work, writing memos and preliminary case summaries. How this is done has already been described in Section 4.5, so only a brief summary is given here. The beginning of the structuring QCA process is marked by an engaged, careful reading of the text and the selection of particularly important text passages to highlight. You can note comments and observations in the margins and create memos to record things that strike you as particularly interesting or relevant as well as any ideas you may have regarding the analysis. At the end of this first phase of working through the text, you can write an initial, short case summary.

Phase 2: Develop Main Categories

In structuring QCA, categories and sub-categories are used to structure the content of the data. Very often, topics and sub-topics serve as categories in this process. Where do these topics come from? How do you find the 'right' topics and sub-topics for the analysis? How many topics should be included for analytical differentiation?

The main topics can usually be derived directly from the research question and have often already impacted the way in which data were collected. Since respondents in our example study were asked in an open interview what they view as the biggest problems in the world, it is logical that 'biggest problems in the world' serves as a main category for our analysis. The same is true for the topic 'personal behaviour towards climate change': because this point is central to the entire research project, it is included in the research question and serves as one of the main topics for the analysis. It is possible that researchers may discover new, unexpected topics through their careful reading of the text. It is best to approach working with the text as you would approach open coding in a grounded theory approach: by writing notes regarding the new topics in the margins and/or memos. As a rule, you should note anything that seems relevant or peculiar at first; as you work through the data, you will gain a better sense of how to distinguish between random topics and topics that could be significant for the given analysis.

Whether you develop the categories and sub-categories – according to the procedures described in Chapter 3 – directly using the data or deductively based on the theoretical framework of the research questions or the interview guide, you should first process some of the data in order to check if your categories and sub-categories and their definitions can actually be applied to the empirical data. How much of the material should be included in such a test depends on the size of the entire data set and the complexity of the category system. The more complex the data and the greater the number of categories, the more material should be included in the trial run. In general, 10–25% of the data should suffice for the initial test of the applicability of the topics and categories. The trial run should facilitate a smooth transition to the next phase, and the coding already performed initiates the first coding cycle of the entire material.

Phase 3: Coding Data with Main Categories (First Coding Cycle)

The *first coding process* can be carried out in a straightforward sequential manner, meaning that researchers work through each text, section by section and line by line, from beginning to end, assigning text passages to categories. Thus, researchers must determine which topics are being addressed in a given passage of text and assign it to the appropriate category. Passages that do not contain information pertaining to the predetermined topics and sub-topics are irrelevant for the research question and should remain uncoded.

As a rule, categories should be assigned with due regard to the overall assessment of the text, especially where researchers are uncertain. Hermeneutically speaking, in order to understand a text as a whole, you have to understand its individual parts. Because one text passage can include multiple topics, it is possible to assign it to multiple categories.

> In structuring QCA, one text passage can refer to different main and sub-topics. Thus, one passage can be assigned to multiple categories. As a result, some of the coded passages will overlap and intertwine with each other.

The demand for precisely defined categories in classical content analysis is often misunderstood to imply that a text passage can only be assigned to one category. This is only true for category systems that are designed in such a way that sub-categories exclude each other (see the first example of deductive category development in Chapter 3). In thematic coding, it is assumed that a given text passage can refer to multiple topics and thus be assigned to multiple categories.

In our example project, we developed categories using the general thematic structure of the interviews (Figure 5.3).

Abbreviation	Main thematic category
WP	Biggest problems in the world
IP	Impact on world problems
CC	Consumption and global climate change
CD	Causes for discrepancy
PR	Personal relation to global developments
PB	Personal behaviour
SR	Sense of responsibility
LE	Learnability

Figure 5.3 List of main thematic categories

In addition to the general quality standards for good category systems from Section 2.4, the following rules apply to the category system used in the first coding process. The category system should:

- Be established in close connection to the research question and goals of the given project
- Not be too detailed or too broad
- Contain precise, detailed descriptions of the categories
- Be formulated with the report of results in mind – for example, categories should be selected that are suited to give structure to the research report at the end of the analysis process
- Be tested on a section of the data.

The entire data set is coded during the first coding cycle. Of course, this raises questions about the scope of the segments to be coded: you must bear in mind their size. The following excerpt from an interview illustrates this issue.

> **I:** In your opinion, what are the biggest problems in the world in the 21st century?
>
> **R1:** Well, that's a totally broad question ... I would definitely say that religious and cultural conflicts are some of the most difficult, and of course the environment and natural conflicts, because, well, I believe you can't really rate them because all the conflicts are affecting the world and they are very deeply rooted ... From conflicts about water to religious conflicts, there are many, many conflicts! But I think the environment and cultural and religious conflicts are currently the most serious.

The passage clearly falls under the category of 'WP – biggest problems in the world'. A coded segment should be large enough that it can still be understood when it is taken out of its original context. If the answers to a guideline-oriented interview are relatively short, they can be coded quickly when the entire answer to a given question is coded as a unit. The whole section pertaining to a given topic, which could contain multiple paragraphs, should be assigned the relevant code, here 'WP – biggest problems in the world'. This approach prevents the same category from being assigned to the same section or paragraph of text repeatedly. It is possible that other topics and categories could be mentioned in the middle of this section, in which case those individual sentences would also be assigned to a second category.

The following rules for coding – how to assign text passages to categories – can be formulated:

> 1. The scope of a segment is not defined by formal criteria, but by semantic boundaries. Thus, these units of meaning should always be complete thoughts and are mostly full sentences.
> 2. If the meaning unit comprises several sentences or paragraphs, these are coded as one coherent segment.
> 3. If interview questions or clarifications are essential for understanding the respondent's statement, they are included in the coding.
> 4. When assigning categories, it is important to develop a good sense of how much text surrounding the relevant information should be coded. The most important criterion for this is that the given passage can still be understood when taken out of context.

Ensure the Quality of the Coding Cycle

In the practice of qualitative text analysis, an important issue is whether a text should be coded by one single coder or by multiple (at least two) coders. Hopf and Schmidt (1993) recommend a cooperative approach called consensual coding. This is a technique in which two or more members of a research team code interviews independently. This requires a category system where the categories and sub-categories are well described and explained with examples. Consensual coding improves the quality of the research project and the reliability of the coding.

In the first step, two or more coders code the data independently. Then, in the second step, the coders sit together, sort through the codes and coded segments, and check for similarities and differences. After discussing their reasoning, they should aim to find a consensus regarding the most appropriate coding. By doing so, researchers can often fine-tune their category definitions and codings, using the disputed text passages as prime examples.

If they are unable to reach a consensus, they should call in more members of the research team or discuss the disputed passages with the entire team. This process makes differences in coding and analysis visible and can lead to constructive discussions within the research team. Unlike any issues with coding agreement that may arise in the course of a quantitative text analysis, where the main concern is to achieve a satisfactory coefficient of intercoder reliability, the focus here is on clarifying any discrepancies as a group and coming to a consensus. Consensual coding requires at least two different researchers who are, ideally, involved in the coding process from the very beginning.

Thus, it is generally advisable to work with two or more coders who code the material independently of each other. The category definitions will almost automatically become more precise and the text assignments to categories more reliable, if the data are coded by multiple researchers. However, it will not always be possible to work with multiple coders – for example, if you are writing a master's thesis or dissertation you often do not have others to support you. If this is the case, researchers should carefully look to improve explicit category definitions and prototypical examples where necessary. There is little doubt that coding by only one person is sub-optimal and should be avoided. There may be an exception if the coding scheme contains only a few well-described main categories, as is the case with a transcript of a strictly structured interview. Here the coder would not have to make any real decisions regarding the correct assignment of categories since the answers always belong to the corresponding question in the interview guide which is the basis for the coding scheme in the first coding cycle.

Phase 4: Inductively Form Sub-Categories

As a rule, following the first coding cycle, the next step should be to create sub-categories within the relatively general main categories. This applies at least to the categories that are of central importance for the study. This process generally includes:

- Selecting the category that you would like to differentiate, that is, the category for which you would like to create (new) sub-categories.

- Compiling all of the coded text segments that belong to this category into a list or table. This is called *text retrieval*.
- Creating sub-categories based on the data according to the procedures described in Section 3.2 on inductive category development. Add the new sub-categories to a list, which is initially not ordered. When working in a team, each researcher can be responsible for suggesting sub-categories for parts of the data. If you are in a team of four and have conducted, for instance, 20 interviews, then each researcher can work through five cases and make suggestions.
- Systematizing and ordering the list of sub-categories, identifying the relevant dimensions, and, if necessary, grouping the sub-categories into more general and more abstract sub-categories.
- Formulating definitions for the sub-categories and illustrating these using prototypical quotes from the material.

First Example: Developing Sub-Categories for the Category 'Biggest Problems in the World'

In our example project, we created sub-categories for the category 'WP – biggest problems in the world' based on the data material. We initially collected everyone's proposals for the sub-categories during a team meeting. Next, we systematized and grouped all of the global problems that were named.

How does one convert such a large list into a solution that is suitable for further analysis? In general, you must take the goal of the analysis into account. You have to ask yourself: What would I like to report on this subject later in my research report? How detailed can I and should I be at this point? Do I need the sub-categories to establish relationships between the categories? What degree of differentiation is useful and necessary?

In this example, as a research team, we assumed that what the respondents mentioned as the world's most important current problems are closely related to their personal attitudes and, therefore, influence people's actions in everyday life. With respect to the main topic of the study, namely the individual's perception of climate change, we also wanted to investigate whether mentioning global climate change as one of the biggest problems in the world has an impact on the individual's everyday actions. Categories should be clear and concise, as simple as possible, and as sophisticated as necessary. The greater the number of sub-categories, the more precise their definitions must be; the greater the susceptibility to incorrect coding, the more difficult it is to achieve intercoder agreements. Generally, for the sake of completeness, all categories should also include an extra sub-category; in our example we had 'other problems'.

In the example project, our final list of sub-categories was as shown in Table 5.1.

Table 5.1 Definition of the sub-categories within the main category 'biggest problems in the world'

Sub-category	Definition	Examples from the data
Environment	Includes changes and conditions that affect the environment in terms of natural environment	Climate change Environmental pollution
Conflicts	Includes all non-violent and violent conflicts between states and different social, political, ethnic, or religious groups	War Terrorism Religious conflicts
Problems in society	Includes social changes and problems at different levels of society	Social change Egotism Moral deterioration of society Migration
Disease	Includes extensive problems that are caused by illness	Epidemics
Technology	Includes technical changes today that affect our lives forever	Changes in technology
Scarcity of resources	Includes any shortage of goods that are necessary for survival or for maintaining certain social standards	Starvation Water shortages Raw material shortages Energy shortages
Poverty	Identifies poverty conditions in a global context as well as within the context of their own culture	Child poverty
Social injustice	Does not focus on aspects of poverty, but rather emphasizes the unjust distribution of wealth or the gap between rich and poor. Can also relate to equal opportunities, such as educational opportunities	Gap between rich and poor Inequality: First, Second, Third World
Other problems		

Second Example: Developing Sub-Categories for the Main Category 'PB – Personal Behaviour (Regarding Climate Change)'

Our second example of how to identify dimensions and create thematic sub-categories is slightly more difficult. This time, we will process the main category 'PB – personal behaviour (regarding climate change)'. We began by closely reading the text passages that were coded during the initial coding process. Then we coded the concepts and themes using open coding before figuring out how to systematize these and identify their dimensions. We noted a long list of initial open codes including:

- Drive a fuel-efficient car
- Separate trash/recycle
- Buy energy-saving light bulbs
- Solar panels on roof
- Industry should be a role model
- We could certainly do more
- No time
- No money to buy organic
- Individuals cannot really do anything
- Buy energy-efficient appliances
- Only technology can really make a difference
- Political correctness
- Save energy
- Not the environmentally-conscious type
- Too comfortable/easy to fall into old routines
- Developing morals is more important than the environment.

Systematizing and summarizing such a seemingly endless list of useful sub-categories requires some skill and practice, but most importantly, these should pertain to the research questions, bear the final product of the study in mind, which, in most cases, is the research report, and be appropriate for the given recipient or audience. The classification system should be plausible, easy to communicate, include current theoretical considerations, and push for further theoretical differentiations. The latter in no way means a call to fall back on differentiations and categorizations already existing in the literature, it only means a plea to avoid punishing existing concepts with ignorance, and to replace them, if necessary, with appropriate justification by other better differentiations and systematizations.

Within the main category 'PB – personal behaviour (regarding climate change)' we identified four thematic dimensions, which were adopted as sub-categories and further subdivided:

1   **Current behaviour.** The areas in which respondents indicated actively aiming to protect the environment were defined as sub-categories. These included: 'save energy', 'separate trash/recycle', 'buy energy-efficient appliances', 'use environmentally-friendly modes of transportation', 'commitment to environmental conservation groups', 'drive fuel-efficient cars', and a residual category 'other'.

2   **Willingness to change behaviour.** In principle, nearly all of the respondents were willing to do more to protect the climate; however, most formulated their own readiness by saying 'Yes, but' and listing excuses for not following through. Their arguments and obstacles were defined as sub-categories, including 'not enough time', 'too comfortable (in my old ways)', 'one person is not enough', 'industry and

government should be role models', 'everyday routines get in the way', 'too expensive', 'public infrastructure is insufficient', and a residual category 'other'.

3 **Philosophy of behaviour.** This dimension refers to the general attitude conveyed by many respondents regarding personal behaviour and/or changing personal behaviour. Personal action occurs amidst the tension between two central points. On the one hand, 'ecological correctness' exerts pressure to act and is perceived as such by almost all respondents. On the other hand, people experience a desire to maintain their own habits, particularly in self-defined core areas. This tension led many respondents to make statements regarding their own personal behaviour based on their principles. As a result, we defined sub-categories that represent mottos and mentalities, such as 'Managers and political leaders should be role models', 'Start slowly by taking little steps', 'If others do not change, I will not either', 'Technology does not bring substantial change', 'I do not think about stuff like that', and 'We must all behave properly'.

4 **Associated areas of behaviour.** The fourth dimension was defined by the areas of behaviour that the respondents named. This dimension partially overlaps with the first dimension, 'current behaviour'. The purpose for defining an independent dimension was to establish which areas of behaviour were mentioned within the context of climate behaviour, regardless of whether one is currently doing something or would be willing to act (change one's behaviour) in this area in the future. The manner in which such sub-categories were formed here is similar to the course of action outlined for the 'biggest problems in the world'. The sub-categories are consistent with the sub-categories of the current behaviour dimension; a precise definition was formulated for each sub-category.

Phase 5: Code Data with Sub-Categories (Second Coding Cycle)

After successfully defining sub-categories and dimensions, you can proceed to the second coding cycle, in which you assign the coded text passages within each main category to the newly defined sub-categories. This is a systematic step of the analysis that requires you to go through the data again. Now you will discover why it is important to ensure that a sufficient amount of data was used to differentiate the main topics and define new sub-categories in phase 4. When researchers create the categories on the basis of a small selection of the data, they often find it necessary to extend and redefine the sub-categories later in the analysis process. While it is easy to summarize and to merge sub-categories later in the process, defining new sub-categories later proves to be more problematic since it would require you to go through and code all of the data again. This, of course, is detrimental since it would require significantly more time and effort.

Be pragmatic and take the size of your data set into consideration when determining how many dimensions or sub-categories are suitable for your project. For example, it would make little sense to establish a large number of sub-categories or characteristics for a project containing relatively few respondents. This is especially true if you plan to create and analyse types following the structuring analysis, as the focus of type building is on the similarities and differences between respondents. The defined characteristics should be found in several of the sample cases, not unique to individual cases.

In most research projects one will not develop sub-categories for all main categories but focus on one or more categories. Phases 4 and 5 are run through in several cycles: after developing the sub-categories for one main category, these are first applied to all the cases before moving on to the next main category.

If the analysis process in the project is so far advanced that the sub-categories have already been formed, phase 3 'Coding data with main categories' can be skipped for newly collected data (e.g., further interviews). In this situation, text passages can be assigned directly to the sub-categories and no coding with the main categories need be carried out.

After the coding has been completed, it may be useful to revise the case summaries written in phase 1, taking into account the categories and sub-categories formed during the subsequent analysis, especially if they are to be integrated into the later report. For this purpose, categories that are very important to the research questions can be selected, which then serve as an outline for the case summaries, so that all summaries have a uniform structure. Below, we describe an optional intermediate step in which selected topics are summarized on a case-by-case basis after coding. If you choose such an intermediate step, it makes sense to then revise the case summaries and to incorporate the work done into the revision.

Write Case-Related Thematic Summaries (Optional Intermediate Step)

After completing the second coding cycle, you have essentially structured and systematized the data and you can begin the next phase of the QCA. It can be useful to add an intermediate step in which you create thematic summaries of the data that have been structured in the previous phases of the qualitative text analysis. This approach is especially helpful when you are dealing with an extensive amount of data or when the text passages assigned to any given topic (such as 'personal behaviour') are scattered throughout the entire interview.

Creating case-related thematic summaries, especially for the purpose of comparative tabular summaries, is an approach that is common in qualitative analysis and is well represented in the methods literature (e.g., Miles & Huberman, 1994; Miles et al., 2020). Ritchie and Spencer (1994) and Ritchie et al. (2003) present a detailed form of this approach within the realm of applied political research, which they refer to as 'framework analysis'.

A thematic matrix serves as a starting point and is virtually transformed by the systematic process into a thematic matrix whose cells no longer contain passages from the original material, but analytical summaries written by researchers (Figure 5.4). Through this step of systematic thematic summarizing, the material is compressed and reduced to what is really relevant for the research question. The necessary process is described next.

Step 1: Create a Thematic Matrix

Systematic coding produces a thematic grid or matrix (Figure 4.2). Each cell of this matrix represents a node to which segments from the original material are assigned. The text segments may be found scattered throughout the entire interview. The previous phases of the content analysis process have produced a reorganized form, or permutation, of the interviews within the categorical framework of the researchers. The more complex and elaborate the category system is, the more difficult it is to present it in a (printable) thematic matrix.

	Biggest world problems	**Personal behaviour**	...
Person 1	*Person 1's text passages on biggest world problems*	*Person 1's text passages on personal behaviour*	...
Person 2	*Person 2's text passages on biggest world problems*	*Person 1's text passages on personal behaviour*	...
...	...	...	...

⇩

	Biggest world problems	**Personal behaviour**	...
Person 1	**Summary of** *Person 1's text passages on biggest world problems*	**Summary of** *Person 1's text passages on personal behaviour*	...
Person 2	**Summary of** *Person 2's text passages on biggest world problems*	**Summary of** *Person 2's text passages on personal behaviour*	...
...	...	...	...

Figure 5.4 Thematic cases-by-categories matrix as a starting point (top) for thematic case summaries (bottom)

Step 2: Write Case-Related Thematic Summaries

In this step, researchers create summaries for the topics and sub-topics. The summaries should be paraphrases of the text using the researchers' words, not direct quotes from the text. This requires more effort on the part of the research team; however, it aids in the analysis process since it forces you to reduce one person's actual statements to their core and summarize them in light of the research question.

Paragraph	Text passage
26	Yes, as I said, I would just live more energy-efficiently; I think that's the only way. Or just that the big energy companies rely more on nuclear power, of course, but the general public doesn't really approve of that. (...) Otherwise, yes, just as I said regarding driving – to use more public transportation or ride a bike for short distances (...) Yes.
27–28	I: Do you actually do that or not really? R2: No, I personally do not. I have to say that I'm pretty easy-going and live quite comfortably and like I said, I am not really sure that we are responsible for the drastic changes in the climate in the first place.

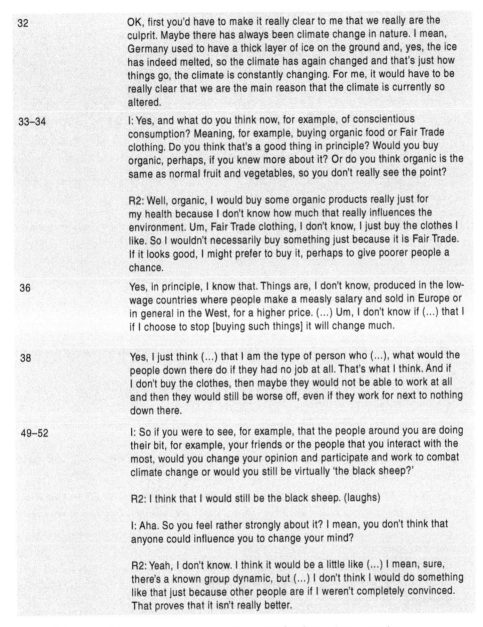

32	OK, first you'd have to make it really clear to me that we really are the culprit. Maybe there has always been climate change in nature. I mean, Germany used to have a thick layer of ice on the ground and, yes, the ice has indeed melted, so the climate has again changed and that's just how things go, the climate is constantly changing. For me, it would have to be really clear that we are the main reason that the climate is currently so altered.
33–34	I: Yes, and what do you think now, for example, of conscientious consumption? Meaning, for example, buying organic food or Fair Trade clothing. Do you think that's a good thing in principle? Would you buy organic, perhaps, if you knew more about it? Or do you think organic is the same as normal fruit and vegetables, so you don't really see the point?
	R2: Well, organic, I would buy some organic products really just for my health because I don't know how much that really influences the environment. Um, Fair Trade clothing, I don't know, I just buy the clothes I like. So I wouldn't necessarily buy something just because it is Fair Trade. If it looks good, I might prefer to buy it, perhaps to give poorer people a chance.
36	Yes, in principle, I know that. Things are, I don't know, produced in the low-wage countries where people make a measly salary and sold in Europe or in general in the West, for a higher price. (…) Um, I don't know if (…) that I if I choose to stop [buying such things] it will change much.
38	Yes, I just think (…) that I am the type of person who (…), what would the people down there do if they had no job at all. That's what I think. And if I don't buy the clothes, then maybe they would not be able to work at all and then they would still be worse off, even if they work for next to nothing down there.
49–52	I: So if you were to see, for example, that the people around you are doing their bit, for example, your friends or the people that you interact with the most, would you change your opinion and participate and work to combat climate change or would you still be virtually 'the black sheep?'
	R2: I think that I would still be the black sheep. (laughs)
	I: Aha. So you feel rather strongly about it? I mean, you don't think that anyone could influence you to change your mind?
	R2: Yeah, I don't know. I think it would be a little like (…) I mean, sure, there's a known group dynamic, but (…) I don't think I would do something like that just because other people are if I weren't completely convinced. That proves that it isn't really better.

Figure 5.5 Coded text passages as a starting point for thematic summaries

Let us look at an example in the thematic matrix in Figure 5.4: the 'personal behaviour' column for Person 2. This cell of the matrix is filled with the coded statements from seven passages within the interview. The coded passages are presented in Figure 5.5, in which the numbers of the first and last paragraphs pertaining to each statement are listed in the first two columns. These statements were summarized as follows:

Person R2 makes no effort to consider the connection between his personal behaviour and protecting the climate. The reasons he gives for this are that it is questionable whether climate change is driven by human activities and it is also questionable whether one can really change anything by, for example, buying Fair Trade products. Moreover, his own convenience and comfort are the deciding factors. Even if many of the people around R2 are environmentally conscious, he would see no reason to change his behaviour. Potential areas for behavioural change are identified in the subjunctive: save electricity, use public transportation, ride a bike, and buy organic products (but only for health reasons).

It is not necessary to create case-related thematic summaries for every single topic and sub-topic. You might certainly focus on the topics that you find especially relevant and for which you would like to create comparative case overviews later in the analysis process.

This approach to writing case-related thematic summaries has many advantages:

- It is systematic, not anecdotal, since all cases are handled in the same manner.
- The summaries are based on original statements; thus, they are literally *grounded in empirical data.*
- The analysis covers all areas, because all of the data that pertain to a given topic are included in the analysis.
- The analysis is flexible and dynamic; researchers can add, expand, or edit the summaries at any point during the analysis process.
- The analysis is well documented and it is easy for other researchers to understand which original statements led to which summaries.
- The thematically oriented summaries are a very good preparation for subsequent forms of analysis, such as a detailed individual interpretation ('within-case analysis') and a cross-case analysis ('between-case analysis') as well as for type-building analysis.
- If the analysis is carried out using QDA software, connections are established within the thematic structure between summaries and original data, which allows quick access to both.

Phase 6: Simple and Complex Analyses

The second coding process, or the intermediate step of creating case and topic-related summaries, is followed by simple and complex analyses of the coded data. In structuring QCA, the focus is, understandably, on the topics and sub-topics. There are different types of analysis, arranged clockwise in Figure 5.6.

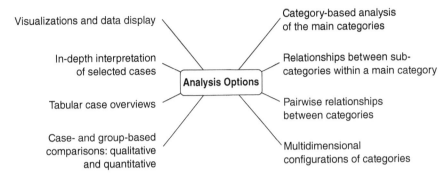

Figure 5.6 Analysis options after completion of coding in structuring QCA

It is important to emphasize that the types of analysis listed in the figure and explained below are *options for* analysis; it is neither necessary nor mandatory to apply all of them in a project. Although the 'category-based analysis of the main categories' placed at 1 o'clock forms the prelude to the analysis in almost all studies, this is followed by different forms of analysis depending on the project. While in one study the focus is more on the cross-case, category-based analysis, in another the case-based approach to the analysis may dominate and in a third both are treated equally. Visualizations have a special function, because on the one hand they represent an independent form of analysis, but on the other hand they are also used in many other types of analysis, for example, in the form of tabular case overviews.

It can be helpful to first draw up an analysis plan that shows which research questions are to be answered with which types of analysis. Usually, it is desirable to arrange a smooth transition between the current phase and the subsequent writing in phase 7, because the results and findings provide the basis of the presentation. Therefore, it is advisable to record all important results during this stage in memos or as preliminary text blocks in the results report. Accordingly, in the following presentation of the types of analysis, we also include considerations about writing up the results.

Category-Based Analysis of the Main Categories

The initial results for each main category (i.e., for the columns of the profile matrix presented in Figures 4.2 and 5.4) should be reported in the first part of the research report. It may be helpful to ask: What do respondents have to say about this topic? What do they leave out or only mention briefly? During this descriptive step of the analysis process, the categories should be ordered in a reasonable manner that the reader can follow, not simply in the order that they appear in the category system or in alphabetical order.

If thematic sub-categories were created, such as for the major categories 'biggest problems in the world' and 'personal behaviour (regarding climate change)' in the above example, the sub-categories should also be reported. Important or interesting numbers from the research should be included. For example, it may be important for readers to know whether 3 or 29 out of 39 respondents consider 'environmental and climate problems' to be some of the biggest problems in the world today. Instead of merely listing the frequencies with which topics and sub-topics are mentioned in the interviews, the report should present content in a qualitative manner, which can also include assumptions and interpretations on the part of the research team. For example, while it is important to know that nine respondents consider 'economic and financial problems' to be some of the biggest problems facing the world today, it is even more important to know which economic problems were named and the words respondents used to describe them. It can be seen in our study, for example, that economic and financial problems are only referred to very generally; respondents mention the 'financial crisis' or the 'economic system'. What could be the reasons for this? This should be addressed in the report.

In order to be able to write the draft of this part of the report, the segments of each sub-category should be read, looked through for similarities, differences and salient features. Prototypical quotes should be included in the results report.

Relationships between the Sub-Categories within a Main Category

The relationships between thematic categories and sub-categories can be analysed and described in two different ways: within the main categories and/or between them. When analysing within the main categories, you can examine the relationships between their sub-categories. This involves naming the sub-categories that identify which problems in the world are named most frequently and which ones are seldom or never mentioned. How do the respondents formulate their answers? Do they mention other sub-categories within their answers? For example, do they mention poverty or other specific topics in statements about 'social inequality'? Can you identify patterns (i.e., clusters of themes) in their answers?

Pairwise Relationships between Categories

The main categories can then be searched for relationships on a larger scale. First of all, the connection between two main categories or their sub-categories can be examined (e.g., between the world problems mentioned and one's own sense of responsibility). What is meant by 'connection' in this context? As indicated in the previous form of analysis, it is, on the one hand, a matter of *categorical* connections, for example, considering in which interviews both a certain sub-category of world problems and the category 'sense of responsibility' were coded, or whether many codings of world problems arise together with many codings regarding a sense of responsibility. On the other hand, it is a question of *content-related* relationships, for example, if the interviewees refer to world problems within their answers on their sense of responsibility. It is then not only a question of whether two categories are related, but above all, in what relationship they stand.

Multidimensional Configurations of Categories

In addition to the pairwise relationship of two categories, there can also be a focus on the complex relationship of multiple categories. How often do certain combinations of (three or more) categories occur in the data? In contrast to the previous form of analysis, which looks for relationships between two categories each time, it is also possible to research multidimensional correlations between categories and sub-categories, for example, between the biggest world problems mentioned, the assessment of influence over these problems, and personal behaviour.

Case-Based and Group-Based Comparisons: Qualitative and Quantitative

Qualitative and quantitative cross-tabulations can be used to examine correlations between characteristics, such as socio-demographics and coded thematic statements. For example, you could use a table to compare how men and women indicate a sense of responsibility or to compare respondents with a higher and with a lower level of education or income. 'Qualitative' tables present the verbal, qualitative data in a systematic manner. In the columns, either the full coded segments of each respective group can be listed or the case-related thematic summaries. The latter are much clearer and more economical for the analysis, since the comparison is based on the already condensed and 'pre-analysed' information. Because crosstabs can also display numbers and percentages, they can also indicate how often specific groups of respondents named specific categories or sub-categories. For example, using a 'quantitative' table, you can figure out how often the sub-category 'biggest problems in the world' was coded to compare specific subgroups.

Tabular Case Overviews

In order to compare individual cases synoptically in relation to selected categories, they can be compiled in a so-called tabular case overview. Typically, the cases form the rows and the categories the columns of the table, following the pattern of a profile matrix or thematic matrix as we have seen in Figures 4.2 and 5.4. In the cells of the table, the summaries written in an intermediate step before phase 6 are presented. Standardized case characteristics can also be added in further columns. Table 5.2 shows an example of an extract from a tabular case overview with two cases in the rows and two categories in the columns as well as three selected standardized case characteristics (membership in an environmental non-governmental organization (NGO), gender, occupation) in the first column.

Table 5.2 Tabular case overview (excerpt)

Case	Impact on world problems	Learnability
R01 – Membership – environmental NGO: no – Gender: male – Occupation: no	Problems have existed for a very long time and are therefore not so easy to solve. No belief in climate change because humans don't have that much influence. Nevertheless, we have to conserve resources because of environmental protection.	Parents are the most important authority. They have to set an example. Media can also play a role, but one should be critical.

(Continued)

Table 5.2 (Continued)

Case	Impact on world problems	Learnability
R05 – Membership environmental NGO: yes – Gender: male – Occupation: yes	Conflicts of faith have existed since the Crusades, there's not much you can do about it. The same applies to capitalism, the greed for power is part of human nature. It's different with climate change, which can perhaps be influenced.	In early childhood, children should already develop an awareness of nature, e.g., through environmental projects in kindergarten. But it's not easy if the parents don't get involved. You have to get them on board.

Miles and Huberman (1994, pp. 172–206), Schmidt (2010, pp. 481–482), Hopf and Schmidt (1993, p. 16), and Kuckartz et al. (2008, pp. 52–53) present instructive explanations of how to create case overviews. A case overview is very similar to a thematic matrix; however, it only includes selected topics or categories. Usually, tabular case overviews compare a selection of cases, or in the case of relatively small samples ($n < 15$) all the cases, studied together with regard to characteristics that are considered particularly relevant to the research questions.

Case overviews provide a good basis for an analysis. Thus, Hopf and Schmidt recommend:

> preparing case summaries, which represent an important initial step in the analysis of individual cases because they facilitate the comparative analysis based on selected cases. They aid in selecting which individual cases to further analyse (according to the principles of theoretical sampling). They also aid in the controlled, disciplined, comprehensive interpretation of results by preventing distortive or theoretically coherent but presumptive summaries. Case overviews enable researchers to test their hypotheses on the bases of multiple individual cases. (Hopf & Schmidt, 1993, p. 15)

The rows of a case overview can be arranged to suit the given analysis. For example, you can arrange it so that individuals with similar characteristics appear next to each other in the table. It may also be useful to indicate numbers and frequencies, for they reveal even more information about the data, including whether a phenomenon or collection of phenomena occur frequently or should be considered as unique cases. It must be noted that the numbers here are fundamentally different from the numbers you would use within the framework of statistical tests in studies with representative samples where the goal is to identify standard, universal statements. However, scientific knowledge about relationships does not require representative samples. If it did, a good deal of medical and pharmaceutical research would be meaningless.

Overall, it can be stated that creating thematic summaries as described above in the 'Write Case-Related Thematic Summaries (Optional Intermediate Step)' section can be an analytically very effective step, which enables the displays of results in a different manner, because now not only original quotations, but also their condensed analytical processing can be compared. Case summaries and comparisons are made possible by this step in the analysis, especially because it would be impossible to create such overviews using original quotations and passages from the text due to space limitations. Moreover, the comprised and more abstract overviews have more analytical power and evidence. The compilation of the summaries in tabular case overviews can also be used as a starting point for further condensations and summaries. Maksutova (2021) gives an instructive example of how the case-by-case summaries of a category can be aggregated for groups of interviewees.

In-Depth Interpretation of Selected Cases

Case overviews arranged like spreadsheets are a good starting point or backdrop for individual case studies because they give you a sense of how each person compares to the others and where they each fall on a spectrum. Particularly interesting individuals can be included in the research report in the form of in-depth interpretations (Schmidt, 2010). How can special cases be recognized? As a rule, these are either cases that embody a recognized pattern or phenomenon in a particularly typical way or – exactly the opposite – that deviate furthest from these patterns. Various criteria can be used to identify special cases (Rädiker & Kuckartz, 2020, pp. 98–99). Some of these criteria can be derived from the case overviews, but some only from the original data:

- Formal features (e.g., particularly long or short texts)
- Linguistic features (e.g., unusual words used)
- Content-related features (e.g., extreme viewpoints and opinions)
- Frequency and amount of content (e.g., repeated emphasis on one aspect) or
- Standardized characteristics (e.g., extremely high or low test scores).

To create an in-depth interpretation of an individual case, you have to reread their transcript carefully, concentrating on a specific topic or question:

> At the end, responses are compiled that refer to this individual case. Depending on the question at hand, these responses can consist of detailed or concise descriptions, contextual evidence of relationships, or theoretical conclusions. In-depth interpretations can be used to verify existing hypotheses or assumptions, to come to new theoretical conclusions, or to question, extend, or modify the theoretical framework. The technique used depends on the interpretation of the question and the respective tradition to which the researchers feel connected, e.g., the hermeneutic or the psychoanalytic. (Schmidt, 2010, pp. 482–483)

Usually, it is only a detailed analysis of one or a few selected cases and not a step of analysis to be carried out for all research participants. The rules for in-depth interpretation of individual cases are not as strict as those for tabular summaries and interpretations presented in the previous steps. Here, researchers are free to choose between different models of interpretation such as hermeneutic or psychoanalytic-oriented techniques (as noted above).

Visualizations and Data Display

Visualizations play a central role in all analyses of the coded data. They help to identify patterns in the material, to recognize connections and relationships, and to check assumptions. At the same time, they are suitable for presenting the findings and can therefore also be used later in the results report, posters, and presentation slides. In many of the types of analysis explained above, visualizations can be used for exploration and presentation; actually, many of the analyses are hardly conceivable or meaningful without supporting visualizations.

In principle, two types of visualizations can be distinguished. On the one hand, there are *tabular overviews* in which coded text passages, their summaries, or category/case frequencies are shown in the cells. Individual cells, rows or columns can be highlighted in colour to emphasize special statements, cases, or other salient features or to indicate group affiliations. On the other hand, there are *graphics and diagrams* that either follow a standardized, systematic structure, as is the case with a mind map, or are designed in a more flexible manner and in which, for example, connections between categories, theoretical aspects, and individual or several cases are illustrated by arrows and other symbols.

Diagrams can be used to gain overviews of sub-categories. For example, you could present all of the behaviours that the respondents name as environmentally-friendly behaviours in a diagram or a mind map. If you are interested in the specific numbers and distributions of such behaviours, you can create a bar graph or a pie chart. Similarly, the reasons that prevent one from changing one's own behaviour could be grouped and presented in the form of a concept map. A concept map visualizes the relationships between concepts – in this case between categories and sub-categories – in the form of shapes, arrows, and labels (similar to the concept map used in Figure 3.7). Graphs can even be used to compare selected individuals or groups with each other.

Phase 7: Write Up Results and Document Procedures

Writing up Results

At the end of the analysis, the results found, the insights gained, and the answers to the research questions examined must now be written up in a report. Of course, this involves going back to the preparatory work done in the previous phases and combining the memos, the text fragments, and analytical texts already written in draft form. The graphics, tables, and concept maps created earlier are brought in for illustration or serve as a starting point for explanatory descriptions of connections, patterns, similarities, and differences that were identified.

We highly recommend that you start writing down important findings at an early stage, not only in the present phase. During the initiating work through the text in phase 1, but especially in the analysis phase 6, drafts and completed text sections on the results can emerge, especially if you worked intensively with individual topics and aspects for which sub-categories are developed and applied in phases 4 and 5. Generally, you should consider phases 6 and 7 as an iterative process, because they may be run through several times in succession for different topics: analysing and writing results for topic 1, and again analysing and writing results for topic 2.

In category-based analysis, retrieving the texts that correspond to a given category or sub-categories serves as the starting point for the writing process (see also Chapter 8 on software support for this task). Take, for instance, the category 'biggest problems in the world' in our example project. Let us examine the issues that the respondents indicated as the biggest problems in the world today (which we defined as sub-categories). Which problems are named frequently? Which are seldom named? Which problems are frequently named in association with other problems? Which groups of respondents named which problems? Examining a thematic category in detail often leads to the development of additional sub-categories or dimensions. You do not always have to go through the entire data set again in order to differentiate between these different dimensions and recode the relevant text passages. You can also organize the answers in a simple, systemized manner and prepare them for the research report.

When it comes to the research report, it is important that you define your framework and determine how you would like to report the results of the analysis and how long you would like your research report to be. For instance, it may be suitable to allot 60 pages to the results section of a dissertation, but you would only be allotted 5–10 pages for an article in a journal or book.

Developing a storyline is quite useful. Starting with the research questions that serve as the basis for the research, you can develop the story by introducing the categories that you wish to write about in such a way that they pique the reader's interest. If the study was theory- or hypothesis-oriented, the corresponding categories and concepts should of course be considered first when developing the structure. Once you have conceptualized the general structure of the research report, you can adjust the number of pages allocated as necessary, but it is helpful to know what you are aiming for as you begin writing about your analysis of the first category.

At the end of each report on the results, the original research questions should be addressed once again. Could these questions be fully answered by the study? Were any assumptions and hypotheses confirmed or refuted? Which questions could not be answered with the data collected? Where can (knowledge) gaps be identified? What new questions arose during the research process?

Documenting the Analysis Process

The entire analysis process should be documented in the report. To do so, researchers must illustrate the steps of the analysis process, explain how categories were constructed, and describe the extent to which the categories and sub-categories were based on the data. The category system should not be withheld from the reader. If it is too large to include directly in the report, it should be included in the appendix at the end of the report. Coding rules and prototypical examples should also be documented in the appendix, perhaps via a QR code containing a link to a website. Examples of coding rules and prototypical examples for some of the categories can be included in the methods section to illustrate the methodological approach. Further notes on documenting the procedure and writing the results report can be found in Section 9.6.

5.4 Summary and Concluding Remarks

With the help of structuring qualitative content analysis, a very broad spectrum of research questions can be processed, ranging from very explorative and descriptive to theory-oriented research. As a typical qualitative method, it is precisely the open, rather explorative research projects for which this method can work particularly well. Structuring QCA can be used equally well in theory-oriented projects, and even theory-testing projects, which work primarily with deductive category development.

In this chapter, we have described the individual phases of the method in detail. We have paid special attention to the analysis process after coding. Under no circumstances should the analysis process end with the analysis of frequencies of categories and subcategories. We have described various options for analysis beyond statistics: for instance, statements by members of particular subgroups can be compared with each other, simple and complex relationships between categories can be identified and explored. It is also recommended to visualize such relationships and present them, for example, in the form of concept maps. Above all, constant comparisons and contrasts within the coded data make it possible to gain deeper insights into the interrelationships. In addition to the category-based analysis, which (as a cross-case analysis) represents the core of QCA, we advocate taking a complementary case-oriented perspective (within-case analysis). For both cross-case and within-case analyses, condensing coded segments into thematic summaries for each case is an effective procedure, allowing movement from the data level to a more analytical level.

A case analysis can contribute important insights to both thick description and theory building, for example when complex case summaries are formulated.

Structuring QCA can be carried out very effectively with the support of special computer software. How this is done is described in detail in Chapter 8.

6

EVALUATIVE QUALITATIVE CONTENT ANALYSIS

━━━━━━ Chapter objectives ━━━━━━

In this chapter you will learn about:

- The characteristics of evaluative QCA and its seven steps
- Developing and applying levels of evaluative categories
- Possible ways of preparing and presenting your results
- The differences compared to structuring QCA.

6.1 Characteristics of Evaluative QCA

Evaluative QCA is a second type of qualitative content analysis. It is used in many projects in empirical research and is well represented in the methods literature. Unlike in structuring QCA, which focuses on identifying, systematizing, and analysing topics and sub-topics and how they are related, evaluative qualitative analysis involves *assessing, classifying, and evaluating content*. Researchers or coders assess the data and build categories, whose characteristics are usually set as ordinal numbers or levels. In an interview study on climate change, for example, one might analyse to what extent the statements of the interviewees express a low, medium, or high sense of responsibility with regard to global climate change.

Instead of ordinal scales, as here with the category 'sense of responsibility', in some cases, nominal scales that are not ranked, or interval scales, such as rating scales for assessments, can also be used in conjunction with evaluative content analysis, as this type of analysis does not strictly require characteristics to be defined by ordinal scales or levels. After the evaluative coding process, you can use the categories to explore assumptions regarding correlations as well as test any initial hypotheses on the data, such as by use of crosstabs. Evaluative QCA is similar to classical quantitative content analysis, which is not word-based like its nowadays widespread computer-assisted variant (Früh, 2017, pp. 272–279; Rössler, 2017, pp. 195–200) but evaluates units of analysis (cases) on the basis of human understanding. As with the structuring QCA variant, in evaluative QCA the coders' language and interpretation skills are important. To a certain extent, Osgood's 1940s content analysis model (Krippendorff, 2018, pp. 183–185; Merten, 1995, pp. 193–199) served as a precursor to evaluative QCA; however, in practice, Osgood's very formal and detailed approach, which he called *evaluative assertion analysis*, is very different from the type of evaluative qualitative analysis practised by researchers today.

Mayring's approach of a scaling and structured analysis also demonstrates a more quantitative orientation, for it strictly transforms text into numbers and ultimately leads to a statistical analysis (Mayring, 2015, p. 114). In contrast, Hopf and Schmidt focus on a detailed interpretation of the text rather than on a statistical analysis (Schmidt, 2010). The evaluative QCA presented in this chapter is open to both objectives and allows one to conduct both qualitative evaluations, for example, by creating case overviews and in-depth individual case analyses, and quantitative evaluations.

Formally speaking, evaluative QCA contains the same main phases as structuring QCA, including:

- Working with the text
- Developing categories
- Coding
- Simple and complex analyses
- Presenting results.

In structuring QCA, categories are created using topics and sub-topics, which impacts the following phases of the analysis. Evaluative qualitative analysis is different, as can be seen in Figure 6.1, which presents the typical evaluative analysis process for a single evaluative category. When analysing multiple categories, simply proceed through phases 2–5 for each category.

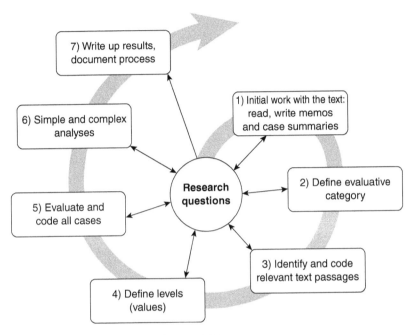

Figure 6.1 The seven phases of evaluative QCA

6.2 Evaluative QCA: Step by Step

The individual phases of the evaluative QCA are described in detail in this section.

Phase 1: Initial Work with the Text: Read, Write Memos and Case Summaries

As with all three types of QCA, the evaluative analysis begins with the task of familiarizing oneself with the material – initial work with the text, writing memos, and writing case summaries, as described in detail in Section 4.5. The material is read carefully and commented on, and important findings are recorded in memos. If it is already clear at the beginning of the analysis that evaluative categories are to be developed, then attention can be paid to the relevant aspects: Which topics or themes would be suitable for an evaluative analysis? Which cases can be characterized as special, possibly extreme cases regarding selected features? And when writing case summaries, any evaluative assessments already made can be included in the summaries.

If the evaluative analysis is based on a previously conducted structuring QCA, then this initial analysis has already been conducted. This phase can then be skipped or at least shortened by examining the results of the structuring analysis in a focused way, for example, by identifying suitable categories for an evaluative analysis or by concentrating the initial work with the text on relevant text passages that have already been identified.

Phase 2: Define an Evaluative Category

The second phase of the analysis involves deciding which categories are suitable for the evaluative analysis. Where do the categories come from? Why do you wish to evaluate or assess these categories rather than simply including them as thematic categories? First of all, we refer to the explanations given in Chapters 2 and 3 on types of categories and the development of categories. Whatever the approach may be, there must be strong connections between the categories or types of categories and the research question. For example, one particular category may already have played an important role when you formulated the research question and collected the data. Take, for instance, the category 'sense of responsibility' in our example project. As you can imagine, researchers examining individual and societal perceptions of global climate change often encounter people's 'responsibilities' or 'sense of responsibility'. It would be quite difficult to discuss such a topic without addressing personal or societal responsibility; a researcher in this field will rarely be able to attend a relevant conference where the topic of 'responsibility' does not play a role. Thus, it would be foolish to act as though you have discovered the category for the first time when you analyse the data. Such a category is supported by the data, but it was not discovered or developed within this research project. Of course, researchers may discover other suitable categories during the analysis process, which would then represent new discoveries.

In order to decide whether the category 'sense of responsibility' should be used as an *evaluative* category, you could consider the fact that it is believed that expressing one's sense of responsibility is an important factor influencing behaviour and that it may be worthwhile to compare it to other thematic categories over the course of the project, such as 'personal behaviour towards protecting the climate'.

Because it requires a good deal of time and effort to create and code an evaluative category, you should carefully consider your reasons for conducting an evaluative coding of a selected category. Moreover, you must ensure that the data enable you to conduct this assessment for all respondents (possibly with just a few exceptions). Select only those categories for evaluative coding that are particularly important to the research question.

Phase 3: Identify and Code Relevant Text Passages

The entire data set is processed in this phase. Every text passage that contains information pertaining to the chosen category – such as to the interviewee's sense of responsibility – must be coded. Concerning the question of how to determine the size of a text segment to code, the same considerations apply as in structuring QCA (see p. 103–105). If a category has already been coded thematically, you can build on previous codings and save time by skipping this phase. One evaluative category could conceivably integrate multiple existing thematic categories.

Phase 4: Develop Levels (Values)

In this phase, all coded segments of the selected category are first compiled on a case-by-case basis. In our example study on climate awareness, for example, all segments coded with the evaluative category 'sense of responsibility' can be listed one after the other, case by case, so that all thematically relevant passages of an interview can be considered. This compilation by category and case serves as the starting point for the analytical work that now follows.

In order to determine a category's characteristics, the range of sub-codes needed to express your evaluations of the relevant data segments, you have to read a sufficient number of text passages and decide how detailed you would like to make the category distinctions. At the very least, you should differentiate between two values ('feature is present' and 'feature is not present/not identifiable'). As a rule, however, at least three characteristics should be distinguished:

- Highly characteristic of the category (high level)
- Relatively uncharacteristic of the category (low level)
- Unable to classify, meaning the information available is not sufficient to assign a case reliably to one of the defined values.

The third characteristic ('unable to classify') is almost always necessary in evaluative QCA since the data collected in qualitative research often do not contain sufficient information about every thematic aspect for every case in the sample. It can also happen that a case cannot be classified beyond doubt, because the information is ambiguous and could reasonably be attached to two characteristics.

During this phase of the analysis, you should also decide whether you would like to evaluate the case's text as a whole or the individual text passages separately. In the end, the goal of evaluative QCA is usually to evaluate the case's entire text. If the number of passages is manageable, we recommend making an overall assessment for each respective text.

Phases 4 and 5 comprise a process that may have to be repeated and refined through several cycles, because the characteristics should be defined and then applied to a sample of the data to test their practicability and applicability. If necessary, changes can be made to the definitions and differentiations between characteristics. It can be difficult to prescribe hard and fast rules regarding how much data is required to determine and test characteristics. If you are dealing with a large number of cases, a selection of 10–25% of the cases should be sufficient. However, you should be careful not to select respondents or groups of respondents systematically, that is, do not select only men or interviewees belonging to a specific socio-demographic group. The more heterogeneous and the more difficult the data set is to evaluate, the more cases must be included.

If your data set is composed of distinct groups (such as the age groups 15–25 and 45–55), you should include a representative selection from each group, such as five from the younger group and five from the older group. In most other cases, a random selection would be better.

Constructing an Evaluative Category in the Example Project

One of the main research questions in our 'Perception of climate change' project addressed the extent to which an individual's sense of responsibility influences his or her actions or behaviour in protecting the environment as well as his or her assessment of other people's actions. Thus, the category 'sense of responsibility' was selected for evaluative analysis. It should be noted that in our study, one's sense of responsibility refers to one's willingness to take responsibility at some point in the near future, not one's accountability in a legal sense.

Several variations on how to define characteristics were developed and tested in our project. Two of the variations, which include three and five characteristics respectively, are presented in Tables 6.1 and 6.2.

Table 6.1 Category 'sense of responsibility' with three characteristics

C1: Sense of responsibility exists	
Definition	Subjective conviction to take responsibility for the problems connected with global climate change.
Notes for coders	The majority of the statements indicate a sense of responsibility, which is articulated in the first person ('I', 'me').
C2: No sense of responsibility	
Definition	No subjective conviction to take responsibility for the problems connected with global climate change.
Notes for coders	The majority of the statements indicate little or no sense of responsibility. Impersonal language (e.g. 'people', 'you') is used.
C3: Unable to classify sense of responsibility	
Definition	The topic 'responsibility' is mentioned, but the individual's personal attitudes towards it are unclear or are not articulated.
Notes for coders	The individual's sense of responsibility cannot be determined using the coded text passages.

In essence, the first way of defining evaluative categories consists of the dichotomous characteristics 'sense of responsibility exists' and 'no sense of responsibility'. The third characteristic is allotted for ambiguous or unclassifiable cases or respondents. The advantage of using this minimalistic variation with only three characteristics is that there is only one differentiation that has to be made, which can be articulated by precise definitions and fitting prototypical examples. The disadvantage is that the less differentiated assessment of the data will lead to limitations in subsequent phases of the analysis. In contrast, selecting five different characteristics produces a more detailed assessment (Table 6.2).

Table 6.2 Category 'sense of responsibility' with five characteristics

C1: High sense of responsibility	
Definition	Subjective conviction to take responsibility for the problems connected with global climate change.
*Prototypical examples**	No prototypical example
Notes for coders	All coded statements indicate a sense of responsibility, which is usually articulated in the first person ('I', 'me').

C2: Moderate sense of responsibility	
Definition	Some or varied subjective conviction to take responsibility for the problems connected with global climate change.
Prototypical examples	No prototypical example
Notes for coders	Many, but not all, of the coded statements indicate a sense of responsibility.

C3: Low sense of responsibility	
Definition	Little subjective conviction to take responsibility for the problems connected with global climate change.
Prototypical examples	'I only feel somewhat responsible because I don't have kids and I don't plan to .... I am sure I would think differently if I had kids, but otherwise, I think it doesn't really matter to nature whether there are people or not.'
Notes for coders	The majority of the coded statements indicate little sense of responsibility. Impersonal language (e.g., 'people', 'you') is used.

C4: No sense of responsibility	
Definition	Subjective conviction not to take responsibility for the problems connected with global climate change.
Prototypical examples	'No, I personally do not.'
Notes for coders	All of the coded statements indicate no or very little sense of responsibility.

C5: Unable to classify sense of responsibility	
Definition	While the topic is addressed, the individual's personal attitudes remain unclear.
Prototypical examples	'If I think about it yeah, but if I just live my life, I know that the responsibility is there, but I don't really feel it directly ....'
Notes for coders	Contradictory or ambiguous statements.

*This table and Table 6.3 only contain a few selected citations as examples. For space reasons, we have omitted further source information regarding the prototypical examples here.

While testing the applicability of these characteristics on our data, it became evident that 'high sense of responsibility' was never assigned because the coding rules were so strict. The same is true for the fourth characteristic, 'no sense of responsibility', which was never assigned since it could only be coded if a person specifically indicated feeling 'no sense of responsibility'.

Given the relatively small number of interviews to analyse ($n = 30$), we pragmatically decided to distinguish only between three characteristics plus the characteristic 'unable to classify sense of responsibility' if there is insufficient information. The characteristics were then defined as shown in Table 6.3 and provided with prototypical examples.

Table 6.3 Final category 'sense of responsibility' with four characteristics

C1: High sense of responsibility

Definition	Subjective conviction to take responsibility for the problems connected with global climate change.
	• Person clearly states: 'I feel responsible' and reflects on his or her own involvement.
	• Reference to behaviour: Conviction to contribute something to improve the problems connected with global climate change.
	• Names specific actions and behaviours, which do not merely refer to small-scale efforts such as picking up litter or cigarette butts off the street.
Prototypical examples	'Definitely. The problems of the 21st century, that's a huge concept, a huge thing and I clearly feel a responsibility. First, I feel responsible for my immediate environment because that's where I can act. If I feel responsible for some huge flooding disasters that are increasing in the world in the 21st century, I wouldn't really know where to start or what to do. But when I see that our soil is eroding, then I definitely feel a responsibility to do something to prevent it. If I buy something, then I buy it from people who are working to preserve the land from which we obtain our food.'
Notes for coders	All three aspects within the definition must rate predominately high.
	It must be recognizable that the person is referring to him- or herself (indicator: using 'I' and 'me' instead of 'people' or passive constructions).

C2: Moderate sense of responsibility

Definition	Some or varied subjective conviction to take responsibility for the problems connected with global climate change. Recognizes the need for acting responsibly in principle; however, sometimes he or she feels responsible and acts accordingly and sometimes he or she does not. Responsibility is often transferred to others (e.g., politicians).
Prototypical examples	'Yes, like I said, if I think about it yeah, but if I just live my life, I know that the responsibility is there, but I don't really feel it directly that it is connected to certain behaviours.'
	'I think we as citizens can't do as much as perhaps more responsible people, such as politicians or the government or perhaps the European Union, which would probably know better and could do more to address the problems anyway.'
Notes for coders	Include context if the reference to behaviour is unclear.

Table 6.3 (Continued)

C3: Low sense of responsibility	
Definition	Little or no subjective conviction to take responsibility for the problems connected with global climate change.
	Only somewhat aware of the problem. The language is rather defensive. Little awareness of actions. Often expresses conviction that he or she cannot do much to help solve the problems.
Prototypical examples	'I only feel somewhat responsible because I don't have kids and I don't plan to …. I am sure I would think differently if I had kids, but otherwise, I think it doesn't really matter to nature whether there are people or not.'
	'No, I don't feel responsible. I am just not receptive to that. It's all about …. I mean, I don't feel an inner desire to get more involved, especially in terms of environmental matters.'
	'No, I personally do not. I have to say that I live comfortably and I don't really know if we are the ones who are responsible for the drastic climate changes.'
Notes for coders	Pay attention to avoidance of first person ('I' and 'me').

C4: Unable to classify sense of responsibility	
Definition	The individual's personal attitudes remain unclear or are so contradictory that they are impossible to characterize as high, moderate, or low.
Prototypical Examples	–
Notes for Coders	In case of inconsistency, include context where necessary.

Phase 5: Evaluate and Code All Cases

This phase includes the final category-based assessment and evaluative coding of the entire data set. Two different strategies can be applied when coding the data. Either all relevant text passages of a case can be evaluated in their entirety and the entire case is coded with the relevant characteristic. This results in one assignment to a characteristic per case. Alternatively, each text passage can be coded individually, whereby ambivalences in the case can be recorded and made clear. This strategy results in one or more characteristics assigned to a single case. In our example project, we used the first strategy: all passages on the sense of responsibility of an interviewee were assessed and recorded together in their entirety and only one characteristic was coded per respondent.

If you are uncertain how to characterize a given case, make note of why the person could be characterized one way and not another. It is easy to do this using memos, which you can assign to specific text passages. As before, this phase of the analysis does not merely involve mechanical coding; rather, coders should stay alert and look for especially relevant passages or examples to include in the research report. It is not uncommon to discover that the definitions of the characteristics should be more precise or illustrated using additional examples. Any uncertain cases should be discussed with other researchers (e.g., in your working group or in a colloquium for junior researchers).

Reminder: if there is more than one evaluative category, go through phases 2–5 for each of them.

Phase 6: Simple and Complex Analyses

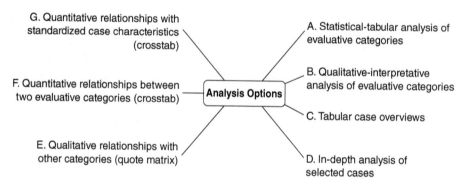

Figure 6.2 Analysis options after completion of coding in an evaluative QCA

Different forms of analyses can be distinguished, as shown in Figure 6.2. Especially in this analysis phase, the motto of constant writing, the continuous recording of important findings, should be taken to heart. Most of the results produced in this phase can be transferred verbatim into the results report and form an important basis for writing up the results in phase 7.

Simple Qualitative and Quantitative Analyses of the Evaluative Categories

Typically, the analysis process begins with simple analyses of the evaluative categories after the coding is completed. The first steps of the analysis are primarily descriptive, whereby the description refers to both quantitative and qualitative aspects. The starting point is the documentation of the previous procedure: a presentation of the categories developed, their theoretical reference, and a summary of the process of category development.

In the following step, the categories, selected characteristics, and their content are described. In the above example, this would mean that the first three levels of sense of responsibility are presented with examples (see Table 6.3).

Each evaluative category's results can then be presented in two ways: statistical-tabular and qualitative-interpretive.

A. Statistical-Tabular Analysis of Individual Evaluative Categories
The following analyses can be carried out:

- How frequently the characteristics of an evaluative category appear, in absolute frequencies and percentages, that is, how many people demonstrate a high, moderate, or low sense of responsibility.

- Presentation of the frequencies of characteristics as a graph, such as in the form of pie charts or bar graphs.
- Overview tables with the cases listed in the columns, in which a characteristic is noted for each person. The table can be sorted by the characteristics.

B. Qualitative-Interpretive Analysis of Individual Evaluative Categories

The qualitative analysis focuses on the *how* with respect to the individual evaluative categories. This includes:

- Presentation of what was said in what way and using which arguments (e.g., regarding the topic of responsibility), sorted by characteristic.
- Presentation of general and extraordinary statements, the latter of which are usually found in marginal characteristics. For example, the person who is completely ignorant regarding climate change is in the group 'People with little or no sense of responsibility'.

Complex Qualitative and Quantitative Analyses of the Evaluative Categories

The descriptive analysis of individual evaluative categories can be followed by various forms of complex analyses that go beyond the individual categories. In this phase, too, both qualitative and quantitative analyses can be carried out. Overview tables (analysis option C) and in-depth individual case analyses based on them (option D) are suitable as qualitative procedures. An investigation of the relationships between the evaluative categories and other categories (e.g., thematic or theoretical categories) connects evaluative and structuring QCA (option E). The spectrum of quantitative analyses ranges from the investigation of bivariate correlations between the evaluative categories (option F) to the analysis of correlations between evaluative categories and socio-demographic characteristics (option G).

Beyond the seven forms of analysis described in detail here, there are no limits to creativity for the selection (and development) of further qualitative and quantitative methods. There is still scope for innovation here, especially if the QCA is carried out within the framework of a mixed methods approach. For example, so-called 'joint displays' offer numerous possibilities for linking qualitative and quantitative data and results (Guetterman, Creswell, & Kuckartz, 2015; Kuckartz, 2014b; Kuckartz & Rädiker, 2021).

Visualizations play an important role in most forms of analysis. On the one hand, they serve to explore connections between the evaluative categories and to develop and test hypotheses. On the other hand, subsequently, they are suitable for presenting the findings, whether in the results report, on posters, or in a lecture. For example, in a study on urban development, Gugushvili and Salukvadze (2021) developed three evaluative categories and arranged their respective values on a concept map around four thematic categories to illustrate the relationships with the four themes.

C. Tabular Case Overviews with Evaluative Categories and Standardized Characteristics

Overview tables, which organize the data in a cases-by-categories matrix (e.g., respondents' answers by categories or socio-demographic variables) can be used to identify constellations of characteristics at a glance. Such tables serve as the basis for identifying patterns and enable researchers to gain an overview of selected topics within the greater research project. The case overview presented in

Table 6.4 in which the respondents comprise the rows, shows whether or not each respondent considers natural and environmental problems to be some of the biggest problems in the world today (thematic sub-category), to which age group the person belongs (socio-demographic variable), how the person was classified in terms of his or her sense of responsibility (evaluative category), and gives a characteristic statement regarding his or her personal behaviour (thematic category) in the form of a quote directly taken from his or her interview.

Table 6.4 Tabular case overview

Case	Biggest WP: nature and environment	Age group	Sense of responsibility	Statements regarding personal behaviour
Person 1	no	15–25	low	'Yeah, basically, I know that. … I don't think much will change if I stop.'
Person 2	yes	46–65	low	'I think I should be fine for the rest of my time on this planet …. Otherwise, I think it doesn't really matter to nature whether there are people or not.'
Person 3	yes	15–25	high	Intentionally environmentally conscious. However, 'sometimes my hands are tied for financial reasons.'
Person 4	no	15–25	low	Throws little trash away (i.e., recycles); does not drive a 'gas-guzzler'.

D. In-Depth Interpretation of Individual Cases

As with structuring QCA, in-depth interpretations of selected cases represent a reasonable end point for the analysis work within evaluative analysis, for example based on tabular case overviews. After summarizing and condensing the data in the previous phases of the analysis, you can now turn your attention back to the individual cases. On the one hand, you can interpret their statements and meanings and explore their particularities. On the other hand, the individual case can also be examined as an exemplary 'case of …' for analysing patterns (Schmidt, 2010).

E. Qualitative Relationships with Other Categories (Quote Matrix)

The relationships between evaluative categories and other categories (e.g., thematic categories) can be presented in matrix form. If one is only interested in numerical relations, crosstabs such as those described in Tables 6.6 and 6.7 can be created. In this matrix one only takes into consideration whether or not the given thematic category or sub-category was coded. For example, the matrix indicates whether respondents currently consider 'natural and environmental problems' to be some of the biggest problems in the world or not.

You can also create another, more detailed matrix called a quote matrix, which is presented in Table 6.5. The goal here is not to aggregate all possible interactions in numerical form, rather to examine the original text passages that have been coded with the thematic category.

Table 6.5 Quote matrix for the relationship between an evaluative and a thematic category

	Sense of responsibility		
	High	Moderate	Low
Food/diet	Text passages pertaining to the eating habits of people with a high sense of responsibility	Text passages pertaining to the eating habits of people with a moderate sense of responsibility	Text passages pertaining to the eating habits of people with a low sense of responsibility
Transportation	Text passages pertaining to the modes of transportation that people with a high sense of responsibility use	Text passages pertaining to the modes of transportation that people with a moderate sense of responsibility use	Text passages pertaining to the modes of transportation that people with a low sense of responsibility use

F. Quantitative Relationships between Two Evaluative Categories (Crosstab)

Traditional crosstabs, such as those used by statistical analysis programs, can be used to investigate the correlations with other evaluative categories. The result is an arrangement of two evaluative categories in the manner presented in Table 6.6. The cells of the table can contain the absolute frequencies, meaning the number of respondents, as well as percentages. Such a table contains valuable descriptive information, even if there are only a limited number of cases. If there are a large number of cases in all and each cell contains a sufficient number of cases, you can also calculate statistical coefficients (chi-squared calculations) and measures of association.

Table 6.6 Crosstab for the relationship between two evaluative categories

| Personal behaviour to protect environment | Sense of responsibility | | | |
	High	*Moderate*	*Low*	*Total*
Yes	Number of people with *positive* personal behaviours and a *high* sense of responsibility	Number of people with *positive* personal behaviours and a *moderate* sense of responsibility	Number of people with *positive* personal behaviours and a *low* sense of responsibility	Total number of people with *positive* personal behaviours
No	Number of people with *negative* personal behaviours and a *high* sense of responsibility	Number of people with *negative* personal behaviours and a *moderate* sense of responsibility	Number of people with *negative* personal behaviours and a *low* sense of responsibility	Total number of people with *negative* personal behaviours
Total	Total number of people with a *high* sense of responsibility	Total number of people with a *moderate* sense of responsibility	Total number of people with a *low* sense of responsibility	

G. Quantitative Relationships with Standardized Case Characteristics (Crosstab)

The associations between evaluative categories and standardized case characteristics, such as socio-demographic data in interviews, can be presented in a cross-tabulation in a similar fashion to the correlations between two evaluative categories. The socio-demographic variable simply takes the place of the second evaluative category. Crosstabs could be used to answer questions such as 'Are there gender differences evident in people's sense of responsibility?' or 'Does an individual's level of education, social status, or other social characteristic influence their sense of responsibility?'

These questions can be answered using statistical tables and methods in which the correlations are presented in crosstabs. In Table 6.7, the relationship between sense of responsibility and gender is presented. Again, if there are enough cases included, you may compute statistical coefficients and parameters.

Table 6.7 Crosstab for the relationship between an evaluative category and a socio-demographic variable

| Sense of responsibility | Gender | | |
	Male	*Female*	*Total*
High	Number of males with a high sense of responsibility	Number of females with a high sense of responsibility	Total number of people with a high sense of responsibility

Table 6.7 (Continued)

	Gender		
Sense of responsibility	Male	Female	Total
Moderate	Number of males with a moderate sense of responsibility	Number of females with a moderate sense of responsibility	Total number of people with a moderate sense of responsibility
Low	Number of males with a low sense of responsibility	Number of females with a low sense of responsibility	Total number of people with a low sense of responsibility
Total	Total number of males	Total number of females	

Phase 7: Write Up Results and Document Process

In evaluative QCA, the results report typically begins with a description of the evaluative categories and their characteristics (values). How are the individual characteristics defined and what criteria were used to assign them? How many and which cases were assigned to which values? These questions must first be answered for the readers before the results of analyses of relationships with other categories, socio-demographic, and other standardized background variables can be reported. Usually, the necessary descriptions of the categories and values have already been created in phase 6 and can be transferred verbatim into the results report. The results are recorded in the same way as in structuring QCA. All the text parts already written during the analysis process, the findings recorded in memos, as well as the illustrations, overviews, and tables created are brought together in the results report, in which quotations from the material can also be included.

When documenting the process, it is necessary to explain how the evaluative categories and especially their characteristics (values) have been developed. If there was any ambiguity in the assignment of cases to the values of an evaluative category, it should be explained how these were dealt with and what decisions were made for what reasons in the final assignment. If the category definitions have not already been included in the results section, they should be integrated into an appendix.

We have compiled general information on writing up the results and documenting the process in Section 9.6.

6.3 Differences between Evaluative and Structuring QCA

Evaluative QCA appears more hermeneutic-interpretive than structuring QCA. Assessments are conducted at the case level; thus, this kind of analysis is more holistic because it generally analyses the case as a whole rather than assessing individual passages. However, you can also code using more detail by evaluating and coding each of the individual relevant passages before integrating them into the overall analysis, which gives the cases an overall score. It is questionable if this is more effective in practice, for researchers often like to (or must) include broader context in order to evaluate text passages correctly. From a hermeneutical standpoint, it would be difficult to justify not taking the entire text into consideration and simply focusing on the statements directly surrounding the given text passage. However, by including the broader context, you can assess the entire text in relation to the given category.

In general, the categories in the evaluative analysis are more holistic than the categories or sub-categories in a content-structuring QCA. The classifications and assessments to be made in evaluative QCA demand more of the coders than in structuring analysis. It is hard to imagine that multiple coders could reach agreement without having specialized knowledge in the field of research. Coders must understand what they are doing and be able to justify their codings using the data. We recommend having at least two coders working independently in evaluative analysis. Of course, there may be situations in which analysts must work alone, such as when writing a thesis or dissertation; however, even then it can be beneficial to think about when a second person should be brought in to assist you or double-check your work.

The evaluative approach is especially suitable for theory-oriented research. This does not necessarily mean that you must have profound theoretical knowledge regarding the research question and seek to investigate explicit hypotheses, as it is quite conceivable that an interest in the formulation of hypotheses and theories only develops during the course of the project. However, evaluative qualitative analysis is especially suitable for theory-oriented research; if the primary aim is description, the method of structuring content analysis is usually more appropriate.

Of course, it is also possible to combine evaluative QCA with structuring analysis and define evaluative categories only for particularly interesting themes or topics. In some cases, the evaluative categories could build on the content-structuring coding and make use of the work already done on the text. Evaluative QCA is a method that clearly demonstrates that the frequently expressed characterizations of qualitative research as mainly explorative, for generating theories, and not suitable for testing theories, are too restrictive. Those characterizations describe the mainstream of qualitative research, but they are not always true without exception. Hopf et al. (1995) argue that standardized questionnaires with predetermined answers are often inadequate in social research because they cannot express the complexity of the research question. So, in theory-testing research too, it may be useful to let respondents answer in their own words with whatever nuances they may express and then analyse their responses as a research team and try to reconstruct the levels of the evaluative category or categories. This approach often yields more valid information and data than standardized tests and instruments.

Also in evaluative qualitative analysis, the analysts can follow the case-oriented perspective in the form of in-depth interpretations of individual cases. In addition, crosstabs may present an overview of the data using thematic as well as evaluative categories; however, they cannot be compared with those based on a large number of representative studies.

6.4 **Summary and Concluding Remarks**

Unlike structuring content analysis, which aims to open up and break down the data to structure them thematically, evaluative QCA works with the researchers' assessments of content. Accordingly, this QCA strategy works primarily with evaluative categories. Researchers usually assess relevant text content on a nominal or ordinal scale with appropriate levels. With a nominal scale, it is recorded whether a certain characteristic, a certain attitude, a certain opinion, etc. is present or not (e.g., whether interviewees perceive themselves as environmentally conscious or not). With ordinal ratings, researchers assess the extent to which a certain phenomenon, characteristic, or attitude is present in the text (such as a person's climate-protective behaviour in their everyday life).

Evaluative QCA is usually more case-oriented than structuring QCA, because the aim is to evaluate each case in its entirety and not just individual passages of text. Evaluative QCA requires more skills from the coders. In projects involving several coders, intercoder agreement should be checked and ensured by suitable procedures (such as consensual coding).

Evaluative QCA is particularly well suited for theory-oriented research and projects in which the researchers have a profound knowledge of the topic at the outset. In such projects, the evaluative categories and their levels are often formed deductively, based on the current state of research or on theoretical approaches.

In evaluative QCA, a variety of analyses, both qualitative and quantitative, can be carried out after the material has been coded. For quantitative analyses, various statistical methods such as correlation statistics and factor analysis methods can be applied. Evaluative and structuring QCA can be linked very well with each other: for example, the response texts coded with thematic categories, generated by structuring QCA, can be compared with each other at different levels of evaluative categories (such as the person's climate-protective behaviour in their everyday life).

7

TYPE-BUILDING QUALITATIVE CONTENT ANALYSIS

Chapter objectives

In this chapter you will learn about:

- The tradition of type building in social research
- The concept and role of attribute space
- The characteristics of type-building QCA and its nine steps
- Deciding on the kind of type-building method
- Constructing typologies
- Possible ways of preparing and presenting your results.

The type-building QCA presented in this chapter shows a way to progress from structuring QCA and/or evaluative QCA to the construction of typologies.

According to many qualitative methodologists, creating types and developing a typology are the main goal of qualitative data analysis (Creswell & Plano Clark, 2011, pp. 212–238; Kluge, 1999; Lamnek & Krell, 2016, pp. 218–227; Schmidt, 2000). Type building is an excellent method for analysing target groups and makes it possible to identify and analyse multidimensional patterns in the data. Metaphorically speaking, it is a matter of systematizing and analysing the cases-by-categories matrix (as shown, for example, in Figure 4.2), as a systematization and meaningful ordering of the cases in their entirety. With the help of qualitative content analysis, the developing of types is possible in a methodically controlled form. Compared to structuring and evaluative QCA, type-building analysis is more complex and methodologically more demanding. For this reason, the characterization of the procedure in this chapter starts with a discussion of its methodological foundations.

The real core of type building involves searching for multidimensional patterns and models that enable researchers to understand a complex subject or field. Type-building analysis often builds on the preliminary work done in structuring or evaluative QCA.

7.1 The Tradition of Type Building in Social Research

Type-building methods are used in many qualitative studies[1] and there are numerous suggestions in the social research methods literature for how to analyse qualitative data using systematic, empirical approaches to building types.

Constructing typologies and thinking in terms of types were already important to the classical social psychology research of the 1930s. Widely known is the field research project about an Austrian municipality, 'Marienthal: The Sociography of an Unemployed Community'.[2] This study used a variety of methods to collect data – including observation, interviews, time sheets, and more (Jahoda et al., 1933/2002) – and create detailed descriptions of each of the 100 families who participated in the study. Many factors were taken into consideration, which emerge as a framework for describing the families in the sample:

- Family (composition of the family, age, income, property)
- Home visit protocol (description of the apartment and furnishings and their condition; impression of children)

---

[1]Approaches to building types can often be found in biography research, in youth research, in lifestyle research, and in interdisciplinary research fields such as public health and environmental awareness and attitudes.

[2]This study was conducted towards the beginning of the 1930s by the Research Unit for Economic Psychology at the University of Vienna under the direction of Paul Lazarsfeld and Marie Jahoda. See http://agso.uni-graz.at/marienthal/e/pictures/15_marienthal_study.htm (accessed 20 March 2022).

- Husband's life story (biography, education, occupation/career, position, political orientation, hobbies)
- Wife's life story (biography, education, occupation)
- Interviews (attitudes, basic orientations, political views, future perspectives)
- Observations (behaviour of individual family members, daily life/structure, visit to restaurant, activities).

By constantly comparing and contrasting the individual cases according to the above criteria, researchers were able to identify four different mindsets for dealing with unemployment and responding to the deprivation it caused (Jahoda et al., 1933/2002, pp. 64–82):

- The *unbroken* continue their daily life and household, search for a new job, and stay active and happy.
- The *resigned* maintain their daily life and household but do as little as possible and refrain from making future plans.
- People *in despair* have lost hope and are moving backwards; they make little effort to improve their situation and do not even bother to look for work.
- The *apathetic* have lost the energy to take care of their home and their children; they are like passive bystanders to what is happening to them and do not even try to change their situation.

These mindsets were precisely based on the data and their characteristic features were named explicitly, as can be seen in the following excerpt from the description of the 'resigned':

> If we were to single out from this description the criteria which lead us to categorize a family as resigned and summarize them epigrammatically, we would say: no plans, no relation to the future, no hopes, extreme restriction of all needs beyond the bare necessities, yet at the same time maintenance of the household, care of the children, and an overall feeling of relative well-being. (Jahoda et al., 1933/2002, p. 53)

Looking back at the history and development of empirical social research, we find not only practical applications for building types, but also works that reflect on the methodical foundations of type building, such as Weber (1964), Hempel and Oppenheim (1936), Lazarsfeld (1972), Schutz (1962), Kluge (1999), Kelle und Kluge (2010), Bailey (1973, 1994), and Kuckartz (1991). Schutz examined everyday life and concluded that 'the individual's common-sense knowledge of the world is a system of constructs of its typicality' (Schutz, 1962, p. 7). According to Schutz, all of the knowledge that comes with experience is organized in the form of typical experiences. We do not experience our surroundings and environment 'as an arrangement of individual unique objects, dispersed in space and time, but as "mountains", "trees", "animals", "fellow-men"' (Schutz, 1962, pp. 8–9). Types are often constructed in anthropology, though the basic aim there is to understand types in a psychological sense of understanding individuals' inner lives. In social science research, the goal of analysis is simply to understand what is typical. Schutz follows the tradition of Max Weber, who declared that constructing comprehensive types was the main goal of empirical social science research. Types as analytic devices link hermeneutic methodology, the aim of which is to understand individual cases, with social science statistics, the aim of which is to find standard inter-relationships and correlations (Kuckartz, 2006; Lazarsfeld, 1972).

7.2 Characterization of the Type-Building Approach

A general definition of type building is as follows. Elements are grouped by type (cluster) according to how similar they are in terms of selected attributes and characteristics. The elements of each type – in social research these are usually persons – should be as similar as possible and the types should be as unalike and heterogeneous as possible.

Thus, within empirical research, type building refers to grouping cases into patterns or groups that differ from the other groups or patterns around them. A type always contains several (individual) cases that are similar to each other. The set of types that are used to describe a given phenomenon is called a *typology*. Therefore, according to its definition, a typology always contains several types and structures them according to their similarities and differences.

Types are the result of comparing and contrasting cases; thus, they are different from inductive conclusions based on individual cases. Characteristically, type-building aims to differentiate rather than develop a general theory. It is based on cases, not variables or characteristics, meaning that cases are examined and grouped according to their similarities. The objects to be analysed and grouped do not have to be people; for example, you could also analyse institutions or organizations, or even group arguments according to typical patterns of thought.

7.3 The Concept of Attribute Space and the General Procedure of Type Building

Defining an 'attribute space' is fundamental to type building. Typologies are based on several ($n \geq 2$) characteristics or attributes, which constitute an n-dimensional attribute space (Barton, 1955).

To illustrate this, one can imagine the simplest case, namely a two-dimensional attribute space, for example in the form of a chart of 'environmental awareness' by 'environmental behaviour', in which a certain number of research participants are represented as data points of the measured values on the two scales. In such a representation, it may be easy to form types.

The social milieus in lifestyle research, such as the prototypical milieus used by the SINUS Institute,[3] are good examples of a complex, four-dimensional attribute space. There, one of

---

[3]See www.sinus-institut.de/en (accessed 20 March 2022).

10 social milieus can be selected for a given household. Regardless of the method used, each type is – implicitly or explicitly – based on the notion of an attribute space.

In both qualitative and quantitative research, the process for building empirical types contains five phases (Figure 7.1):

1   *Determine the attribute space.* In this phase of the analysis, researchers must define the attribute space (i.e., select the categories/attributes by which all cases are to be compared) that serves as the basis for type building.
2   *Group individual cases and build typology.* In this phase, typologies are constructed, that is, cases are grouped into clusters (types). After comparing and contrasting the typologies, you can decide which typology is best suited to the data. This phase is thus an experimental phase. Several solutions for grouping the individual cases are tested and compared.
3   *Describe typology.* The constructed typology and the individual types that have been created are described in greater detail.
4   *Explicitly assign individual cases to the types created.* This phase shifts the focus from the groupings back to the individual elements. Here, individual cases (usually respondents) are assigned finally to the created types.
5   *Analyse relationships.* In the final phase, the typology and the different types within it are presented according to their characteristics and the relationships between the types and secondary variables are analysed.

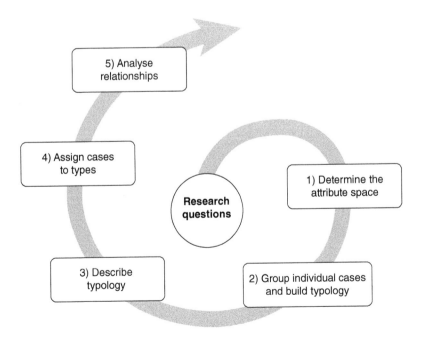

Figure 7.1   Five phases of empirical type-building

The first phase of building types involves deciding which attributes are relevant for the desired typology and determining what information is available in the data that have been collected. In the above example of mindsets from the Marienthal study, all of the attributes that were used to describe the families were relevant to the typologies. The number of attributes you can include in your type building depends on the construction of the typology. There are three main approaches to constructing typologies:

Building Types with Homogeneous Attributes ('Monothetic Types')

This is a typology in which all elements of a type have identical characteristics. A simple example of such a typology is a four-field table based on two dichotomous attributes, such as Table 7.1, the idea for which comes from a research paper by Peter Preisendörfer (1999, pp. 94–103).

Table 7.1 Simple typology of environmental awareness and behaviour according to Preisendörfer (1999, p. 98)

		Environmental behaviour	
		positive	negative
Environmental awareness	high	Type 1: Consequent protector	Type 2: Environmental rhetorician
	low	Type 3: Uncommitted protector	Type 4: Ignorant to environment

Assigning a particular participant to a particular type, such as type 2 'Environmental rhetorician', is only appropriate if both attributes are indicated at the appropriate levels. Thus, since type 2 is defined by a high level of 'environmental awareness' and negative 'environmental behaviour', all of the respondents assigned to this type must indicate high awareness and negative behaviour towards the environment. All four types of the typology show no variance; internally, they are perfectly homogeneous. The disadvantage of this kind of homogeneous attribute typology is that it only allows researchers to work with relatively few attributes and characteristics. Even using just three attributes with four characteristics each would produce as many as $4 \times 4 \times 4 = 64$ homogeneous attribute types.

Building Types by Reducing the Diversity

A large number of homogeneous attribute types can be pragmatically reduced to a manageable number using a method described by Lazarsfeld. Table 7.2 illustrates just how to do this. Here, all possible combinations of parental level of education are presented in a 4×4 table with 16 cells. The 16 different combinations are not only difficult to grasp, it would also be difficult to work with them in an empirical study, such as to explore how educational background impacts the environmental awareness of teenagers. It makes sense to reduce the diversity of the 16 cells to a more manageable number of types. To do so, you must order the combination of attributes and reduce the number of combinations by merging so that the typology of parental educational level, for example, only contains five types, which are illustrated in Table 7.2.

Table 7.2 Building types by reduction

Mother's level of education	Father's level of education			
	No school-leaving certificate	Middle school	High school	College
No school-leaving certificate	Type 5	Type 4	Type 3	Type 2
Middle school	Type 4	Type 4	Type 3	Type 2
High school	Type 3	Type 3	Type 3	Type 2
College	Type 2	Type 2	Type 2	Type 1

The five types can be summarized as follows:

- Type 1: Both parents graduated from college.
- Type 2: Only one parent graduated from college.
- Type 3: At least one parent graduated from high school.
- Type 4: At least one parent graduated from middle school.
- Type 5: Neither parent finished school.

Two of the types created, specifically types 1 and 5, are homogeneous in terms of attributes, meaning that both parents of all of the respondents within the type have the same level of education. In the case of type 1, both parents graduated from college; in the case of type 5, neither parent finished school. The other types created via reduction (types 2, 3, and 4) show variance, for they contain respondents with different attributes, in this case different levels of parental education. For example, five different attributes can be assigned to type 3. The determining factor is that one parent graduated from high school; the other parent could have graduated from high school, middle school, or never have finished school.

Building Types with Heterogeneous Attributes ('Polythetic Types')

The first two forms of type building are referred to as 'artificial types' because they are constructed without direct reference to the empirical data; they are *constructed* by combining attributes and characteristics. Some combinations may not even exist in reality (such as 'Mother graduated from college' and 'Father did not finish school'). 'Natural types', on the other hand, are built directly using the empirical data, meaning that respondents are grouped according to types which are as homogeneous as possible internally and as heterogeneous as possible externally. Such types are almost always polythetic; the individuals that belong to a type are not absolutely the same in terms of the attributes within the attribute space, but they are quite similar.

Natural typologies can be ordered according to systematic, intellectual structures as well as using statistical algorithms. Cluster analysis methods are especially suitable for the latter (Kuckartz, 2010a, pp. 227–246). A good way to build complex polythetic types without such formal algorithms is to systematically process and group case summaries, as presented in the five phases shown in Figure 7.2.

Phase	Task
1	Define attribute space and create a case summary for each respondent that is focused on these attributes
2	Sort, order, and group case summaries according to similarity
3	Decide on a reasonable number of types to be built
4	Formulate creative names for each type that poignantly express the main characteristics of each type
5	Assign each respondent to a type; order the respondents according to their similarity to the central type

Figure 7.2 Type building: from case summaries to typologies

In research practice, you can implement this method by writing each case summary on a note card and asking the research team to arrange these cards (which represent respondents) on a large bulletin board. To do so, proceed as follows:

Preparing for team meeting

1 Distribute the case summaries evenly among members of the research team.
2 Each researcher must now closely review the cases that have been assigned to him or her, checking the case summary and revising it as necessary before writing it on the note card.

Working as a group

1 As a group, determine the nature and scope of your typology.
2 Each researcher should then present his or her cases to the group and pin them to the bulletin board according to how well they correspond or relate to the cases that have already been pinned on the board.
3 Eventually, arranging and rearranging the cards in this manner will make clusters evident.
4 Once all of the cards have been placed on the board, discuss any remaining uncertainties within the group.

5   Assign each cluster a fitting title and colour.
6   For the cases that could not be assigned initially, check again whether an
     assignment is possible.

Constructing, arranging, and assigning an order to types in this way represents a creative act and will not produce a precise, canonized description. Here are a few helpful
tips. It is often useful to work through this type of categorizing and typifying task as a
group. The technique described of writing case summaries on note cards and grouping
them together has proven successful in research practice, but this does not mean that
successful type building is only possible in a team. Even when working alone, it can be
useful to proceed in a similarly methodologically controlled way.

7.4 Type-Building QCA: Step by Step

The type-building qualitative text analysis process differs in many respects from structuring and evaluative analysis. The type-building process begins with considerations
regarding the aim and purpose of building types. Several different typologies could be
constructed within one project. For example, one typology could demonstrate how
information is handled regarding the risks of atomic energy and another could demonstrate how atomic energy risks were communicated regarding the Fukushima
disaster. As a rule, the attribute space is constructed using categories and variables that
have already been established; if a desired typology requires the creation of new categories, they will have to be coded first. If this is the case, the structuring and/or
evaluative analysis methods described above can be implemented.

   If you plan to create a typology at the beginning of the research project, it is also
worth considering asking the research participants themselves which types they
might see in the respective field. In the later analysis, this enables a comparison
between the types formed by the content analysis and the typology of the research
participants. Of course, *member checking* is also possible (Bazeley, 2021, pp. 499–501)
by reflecting the typology back to the respondents after the analysis phase has been
completed, in order to find out whether the types formed are also seen as plausible in
the field itself.

   Figure 7.3 shows the detailed process of type-building qualitative content analysis,
which basically follows the process of social scientific type-building mentioned above.
The start of the analysis, in the form of initial work with the text, writing memos and
writing case summaries, has already taken place in the preceding structuring and/or
evaluative analyses. If type building has been determined as the goal at the beginning
of the research project, the analysis can focus on the relevant features and the case summaries can be written at the very beginning, focusing on the central features of the
planned type building.

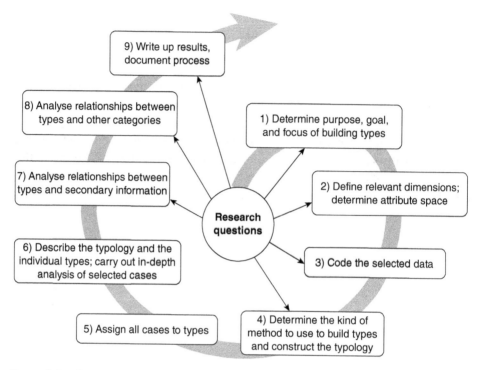

Figure 7.3 The nine phases of type-building QCA

Phase 1: Determine Purpose, Goal, and Focus of Building Types

The first step in type-building is to determine what exactly you would like to accomplish by building types. You must also determine how complex the typology should be and how many differentiations are necessary within it. In addition, you should consider how important primary and secondary attributes and characteristics are to your own research interests as well as the research question. Attributes that are essential for building types and form the basis of the attribute space are considered primary attributes; other characteristics that are influenced by or related to the typology are secondary attributes. If, for instance, you would like to create a typology for environmental awareness and examine the impact of an individual's personal behaviour towards the environment, behavioural dimensions should not be included in the typology because that would result in a tautological analysis of the impact of behaviours on behaviours, so here the behavioural categories would be secondary attributes.

Typologies can be constructed to be quite complex or quite simple: you can select a large or small number of attributes for the attribute space, which determines the complexity of the typology. For example, an 'environmental awareness' typology would demand a complex attribute space, while a 'personal behaviour to protect the climate' typology would only include a smaller attribute space.

Phase 2: Define Relevant Dimensions and Determine Attribute Space

The next step in type building involves deciding which of the attributes that are empirically based on the data are seen as relevant to the typology. Selecting the relevant attributes should be based on the project's theoretical framework and/or be focused on the research question. In the Marienthal study, attributes were selected according to their potential relevance for a typology of mindsets. After a few visits to the field (i.e., the village of Marienthal), the researchers developed a feeling for factors that influence how people cope with unemployment. Those attributes that were essential to the mindsets (types) were selected. These included: manage household, take care of children, search for a new job, active lifestyle, future perspectives, etc.

To determine the attribute space, you can rely on the existing thematic and/or evaluative codings or use the other information available about the respondents (such as socio-demographical or biographical data). It is recommended to limit the selected attributes to those that pertain to a sufficient number of respondents. The attributes and characteristics will be used to differentiate the types; thus, it makes little sense to select an attribute that only applies to 2 out of 40 respondents, since that means that 38 of 40 respondents are identical. The concept of attribute space requires a manageable number of attributes, assuming you would like to create a pure typology or a typology based on a reduced number of attributes. A larger number of attributes is only suitable if you would like to create a polythetic typology by grouping the case summaries together or using an automatic method of classification (such as cluster analysis).

Qualitative interviews are characterized by the fact that not all interviews include information regarding potentially relevant attributes, especially if the interviews are conducted without a structured guide. In such situations, it is advisable to select a less complex attribute space that contains fewer attributes because researchers may have difficulty grouping the available information reliably into types. If, for instance, the data only contains information about household management for a few of the respondents, it makes little sense to select such an attribute as a primary attribute for constructing the typology, even if it is theoretically considered significant. In some situations, such as field studies, it may be possible to ask further questions and gather the missing information.

This second phase of building types is closely associated with the first. Here, you must re-examine the data at hand to determine if and in what form the desired information is available. Thus, you must determine if you can rely on existing thematic and/or evaluative categories or need to create new categories based on sections of the material which will be coded in the next phase.

If you have collected socio-demographical attributes for the respondents (such as information about their biography, age, educational level, career, etc.), perhaps using a survey, you can use these attributes and characteristics to create the types.

Phase 3: Code Selected Data

In most cases, type-building analysis builds on a previously conducted thematic or evaluative coding. If this is the case, type-building analysis is quite easy to perform since you can build on the existing thematic and/or evaluative categories. If you have not conducted a previous analysis of the data, you must begin by coding the data to your selected attributes and characteristics according to the processes and rules described in thematic and evaluative coding. It is particularly helpful for the subsequent phases of type-building analyses if the coded text sections are summarized on a case-by-case basis for individual or all selected categories. Then the most important information for each case is available in condensed form and it is easier to identify multidimensional patterns in the data.

In some cases, it might be necessary to add an intermediate step to this phase of the analysis. For example, assuming that the texts have been coded thematically and all of the passages that refer to household management have been assigned to an appropriate category, you may now wish to further classify the attribute 'household management' according to a three-level scale: (1) manages household as usual; (2) partially manages household; and (3) neglects household. To do this, you now need to review each case and assign the correct values before you can continue constructing the typology.

Even if evaluative categories already exist, an intermediate step may still be necessary, because for type building it is sometimes helpful to standardize the scaling for some categories or to reduce the number of values in a category. If, for example, job search is to be included in the type building in addition to household management, but job search was assessed very finely with five values, then the cases could be recoded for the type-building analysis with a reduced number of values. It would even be possible to work with dichotomous values, 'job search available' versus 'not available'.

Phase 4: Determine the Kind of Method to Use to Build Types and Construct the Typology

Before you begin the actual process of grouping and creating types, you should think about the number of types that would be suitable for your research questions and data. First, consider whether any natural groups exist in the field. Then consider the number of respondents included in the study. If you are dealing with a relatively large number of respondents, such as in the case of the Marienthal study with over 100 families, you can use a greater degree of differentiation (i.e., more types) than in a smaller sample of, say, 20 respondents. Other important factors to consider are the practical relevance of your study and how well you will be able to communicate your typology within the scientific community. When building types and selecting a suitable number of types, you should always keep your audience in mind: readers, reviewers, and recipients. Of course, it is not imperative to determine the final number of types *before* constructing your typology; you can and should try two or three alternative groupings, such as typologies with various differentiations including maybe four, five, and six types. In the

Marienthal study, the mindset typology is especially strong because the distinction between the four types is clear, plausible, and comprehensible. If the researchers had attempted to differentiate between eight or more types, the unions and politicians – the main recipients of the study – would likely have had more trouble understanding the results. Conversely, merely including four social milieus in a lifestyle research project would likely be perceived as too simple because current lifestyle models, such as the Sinus Milieus, include 10 or more different types.[4]

In order to determine how to build your types, you must consider your sample size and the dimensionality of your desired attribute space:

- *Monothetic homogeneous attribute types* can be created using two or three attributes with relatively few characteristics.
- *Building types by reduction* is much more flexible and can include more features and more characteristics.
- *Polythetic type-building*, however, makes it possible to integrate numerous characteristics and define a truly multidimensional attribute space.

Unlike the homogeneous attribute typology, which is virtually self-explanatory, the other two forms of typologies require that the types are described in terms of their position in the attribute space. For typologies that were formed by reduction, creating a list of the attributes that have been combined is usually sufficient, just as we did in the example typology of parental level of education. Characterizing complex polythetic typologies, however, is a little more difficult.

Phase 5: Assign all Cases to Types

An integral part of constructing a typology involves assigning respondents to the selected types. They must be clearly assigned – one respondent cannot be assigned to two or more types simultaneously. After all, it would not make much sense to assign a family in the Marienthal study to both the 'apathetic' and the 'unbroken' mindsets. So, after you have compared different typologies in the previous step of the analysis and decided which one fits best with the data, you have to focus again on the individual cases. Now you must decide to which cluster (type) each individual case belongs.

Following the construction of a typology, there are a variety of further analyses you may wish to conduct. For example, you could examine the options arranged clockwise in Figure 7.4 and described below. First, in the section on phase 6, the options for describing the typology and individual types are presented, as well as more advanced options such as the formation of ideal types. The section on phase 7 deals with the analysis of relationships between types and secondary information, and the section on phase 8 with the analysis of relationships between types and other categories.

---

[4]The last version of the Sinus Milieus was developed in 2022 and differentiates between 10 significant clusters (milieus). See www.sinus-institut.de/en/ (accessed 20 March 2022).

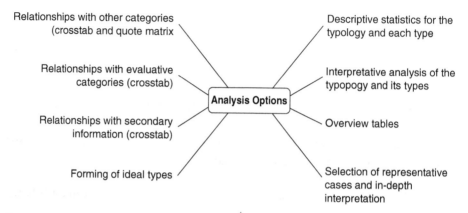

Figure 7.4 Analysis options after creating a typology

Phase 6: Describe the Typology and the Individual Types; In-Depth Analysis of Selected Cases

The first step deals with the typology and its types and describes them quantitatively (e.g., the number of persons belonging to each type). Then *interpretive analysis of the typology and its types* is useful. Here the different types are described in words: what makes each type unique, what are the key differences, etc.

Overview tables compare the types and their characteristics in a tabular format. The contents of the tables may be qualitative (verbal description) or quantitative (the distribution of characteristics in numbers and percentages). Thus, in the Marienthal project, the four different mindset types are presented in as much detail as possible. Particularly meaningful and exemplary statements can be taken from the data.

Then comes the possibility of an *in-depth analysis of individual cases*. The typology provides the backdrop and framework for organizing and interpreting the individual cases. The overviews that display the numerical distributions of types and attributes as well as cases do not speak for themselves and alone are not sufficient; the types and constellations gain meaning and significance when you refer back to and interpret the individual cases.

What criteria should you use to select the cases for such an in-depth analysis? Because not all of the cases within a qualitative study can be presented in detail in the research report, you have to select a sample of the cases to analyse in more detail. There are two strategies for doing so.

The first option involves creating a *representative case interpretation* based on one single prototypical case per type, which is then presented in detail and deemed representative for all of the respondents that belong to that given type. If you have used a formal method, such as the statistical method of cluster analysis, it will include information about the proximity of each respondent to the centre, which serves as a formal criterion for selecting the most suitable cases for in-depth analysis. If you have not used such a formal method, you will have to re-examine the text segments that form the basis of the typology and from these identify the most suitable case or cases for in-depth analysis. Computer-assisted analysis techniques, such as text retrieval, are very effective aids in this part of the analysis process. In the Marienthal study, this strategy of *representative case interpretation* would mean selecting a person who is the best example of the 'unbroken' type. This person and his or her characteristics would then be presented and interpreted. The same would be done for the other three types, the 'resigned', those 'in despair', and the 'apathetic'. Select the most representative persons and describe them in detail. The result is that four – real – people are shown as examples to produce a better understanding of the constructed typology.

The second option for selecting which cases to study with in-depth analysis involves *constructing a model case* based on a synopsis or montage of the most suitable text segments. This approach is less focused on the individual cases and in many ways is similar to Weber's approach of building ideal types (Kuckartz, 1991). However, because the polythetic types and their position in the attribute space have already been determined via the typological interpretation of the text, they are real, not ideal types, and they represent real individual respondents from the sample. By reviewing relevant text passages, you can determine which cases would be suitable for the given type and include them in the synopsis.

Phase 7: Analyse Relationships between Types and Secondary Information

After evaluating and presenting the characteristics of the types formed, it is also of interest to examine the relationships between the types and secondary information. Secondary information means socio-demographic characteristics, and also any other information about whole cases that was not part of the attribute space during type building. Secondary does not mean that these characteristics are less important in relation to your research questions, but only that they were not included in the attribute space when the typology was created.

The first point of interest is the relationship between the typology and socio-demographic variables, such as gender, age, level of education, and income. Since socio-demographic data are usually standardized data, statistical correlation analyses are possible and useful here; one may not be content with calculating percentages of characteristic values per type but can also test for statistical significance. For example, for each type of the typology, the average age and average household income of the respective members can be calculated. By means of a suitable statistical analysis (e.g., analysis of variance for a random sample), it is possible to test whether the groups differ significantly. The same applies to categorical variables: for example, the percentage of women per cluster can be found, and a correlation coefficient (such as Cramér's V) can be calculated and tested for significance.

Phase 8: Analyse Relationships between Types and Other Categories

What are the relationships between belonging to a certain type and other topics in the study? In this phase of the analysis, the goal is to disaggregate the empirical data according to the types formed and to explore complex interrelationships. Which analyses can be carried out depends, of course, on whether other qualitative data were collected and coded in addition to the typology (e.g., with thematic or evaluative categories). If this did not happen, then this phase is omitted.

If parts of the material have been structured with the use of further categories (thematic or other categories), then connections to these categories can now be analysed. For the cases assigned to a type, the segments coded to specific thematic categories can be compiled and compared with those for other types. Similarly to the evaluative categories described in Section 6.2, a quote matrix can be created for comparison. Statistical analyses of the correlations are also possible: using cross-tabulations, it can be shown whether and how often certain topics were coded for each type or for how many members of a type.

Formally, the identification of a type is similar to an evaluative category as described in Chapter 6. For each individual, the type to which he or she belongs is stored. In this respect, all kinds of complex analyses described above for evaluative content analysis are also possible for a typology, for example the analysis of *relationships to other evaluative categories*. Since evaluative categories are a classification on the one hand, and are based on specific text passages on the other, relationships can be analysed both qualitatively and quantitatively. This means that both simple and complex statistical analyses can be calculated, and the corresponding text segments or thematic summaries can be compiled for the groups formed.

Phase 9: Write up Results and Document Process

Arranging the types in a two-dimensional coordinate system makes it easier to understand a typology, though it is more difficult to do so if the typology contains more than two dimensions. The following example stems from a study on identity and life plans of young German-Indonesian women conducted by Wenzler-Cremer (2005, p. 336). The typology is arranged in a coordinate system in which the *y*-axis represents 'belonging to a culture' and the *x*-axis 'use of bicultural resources' (Figure 7.5).

Besides employing a suitable form of visualization, how can the results of a type-building QCA be presented? What should be reported? Information about the type-building process should be as comprehensive as possible, the constructed typology and the individual types should be described, and the results of the interrelation analyses should be reported. The presentation of the results of type-building includes in detail:

- Description of the objective of type building
- Presentation of the attribute space and the underlying data (which categories are referred to, how were they developed, etc.)
- Presentation of the typology construction process
- Detailed description of the typology, the individual types and their mutual proximity
- Information on the number of cases for each type in the sample
- Results of the analyses, such as the distribution of socio-demographic characteristics by type
- Considerations regarding the possibility of generalizing the results.

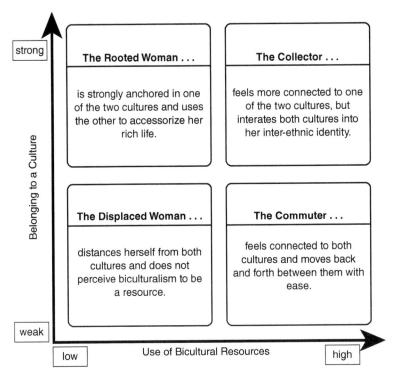

Figure 7.5   Two-dimensional representation of four types (Wenzler-Cremer, 2005, p. 336)

7.5 Summary and Concluding Remarks

The formation of groups based on certain characteristics is often a goal of research projects. In marketing, target groups are formed for efficient marketing activities; in education, groups are identified for interventions (e.g., for early intervention programmes among young children in kindergartens); and in social work interventions are carried out on certain groups (e.g., prevention of tobacco consumption among young people).

In this chapter, we use the terms 'typology' and 'type' in this context. We could also have written about clusters, groups, or patterns. Why did we prefer the terms 'typology and type'? One important reason was that these terms have a tradition in social research and therefore many aspects, such as the concept of the attribute space (Hempel and Oppenheim; Lazarsfeld) or the concept of the ideal type (Max Weber), have already been developed and discussed. Equally important is that 'type' and 'typology' are in principle generalizing terms that can cover many ways of grouping or clustering. In psychology, the term 'type' is often associated with personality psychology and type theory, so it has a very specific meaning, a meaning that has nothing to do with the method of forming analytical types described in this chapter. Of course, the strategy of type-building QCA can also be used if you do not call the groups that are formed in your research project 'types', but instead 'target groups', 'clusters', or simply 'groups'.

8

USING SOFTWARE

━━━━━ Chapter objectives ━━━━━

In this chapter you will learn about:

- Transcribing audio and video data using specialized computer software
- Connecting transcripts with audio and video files
- Preparing and anonymizing the data for computer-assisted analysis
- Performing structuring, evaluative, and type-building QCA using QDA software
- Using additional analysis options available in QDA software, such as links and memos
- Visualizing relationships and dependencies using diagrams, charts, timelines, concept maps, etc.
- Using word-based features such as word frequencies, keyword-in-context lists, and dictionary-based automatic coding.

Under the name 'QDA software', a special type of computer program is available that is now popularly used in qualitative research. For over three decades, the field of computer-assisted analysis of qualitative data has been considered one of the most innovative fields of social science methodology development. QDA software programs do not prescribe one specific method of analysis but can be used for many types of data and in a variety of methodological approaches (Kuckartz & Rädiker, 2019; Silver & Lewins, 2014). For example, Creswell and Poth (2018, pp. 207–218) describe how QDA software can be used in five different research traditions, including biographical life history, phenomenology, grounded theory, ethnography, and case study.

In this chapter, the capabilities of QDA software are presented, focusing on qualitative content analysis. The aim of this chapter is to give an overview of the different possibilities for analysis. Since software quickly becomes outdated and new versions are usually accompanied by new interfaces and changed menu navigation, this presentation focuses on the general procedures and does without specific instructions in the sense of 'select menu item XY', 'click here', and 'double-click there'. Detailed overviews of QDA software's options and features can be found in Silver and Lewins (2014), Friese (2019), Jackson and Bazeley (2019), and Kuckartz and Rädiker (2019).

At the beginning of any kind of QCA, questions arise regarding how best to manage and organize the data. How should we format the data? How can the data be analysed using QDA software? How should we organize, save, and store files and folders? How can we organize and coordinate the work within a research team?

8.1 Transcribing and Rules for Transcription

If you and your research team have collected the data yourselves, for example by means of qualitative interviews or focus groups with audio recording, the data must be transcribed first before you start the analysis. The first question, then, is how to transcribe the data. Within social science research, transcription was for a long time a fairly complicated and time-consuming matter, but recently a number of possibilities for automatic transcription have been created that considerably reduce the effort involved. But even if a very accurate transcription is not required, the research team must agree on certain rules for transcription.

The procedure from data collection to importing the data into the software involves the following seven steps:

1   Determine a set of transcription rules or choose an established transcription system that is suitable for the planned analysis.
2   Transcribe the texts (or relevant parts of the texts) on the computer or using a tool for automatic transcription.
3   Proof-read, edit, and modify the transcriptions, if necessary.
4   Make the transcriptions anonymous and pseudonymize the transcriptions, if necessary.

5 Format the transcriptions in such a way that the QDA program can be used optimally.

6 Save and archive the transcriptions as RTF or DOC/X files.

7 Import these files into the QDA software.

The first three steps are of course only necessary if new data material has been collected and must be transcribed. If the text data has already been digitalized, proceed with step 4 to anonymize, format, and import the existing data into the QDA software.

If possible, when working with qualitative interviews, group discussions, focus groups, and similar forms of data collection, you should work with audio recordings rather than with manuscript notes to jog your memory.

Table 8.1 Advantages and disadvantages of audio recordings

Advantages of audio recordings	Disadvantages of audio recordings
• Accuracy	• Respondents may feel uncomfortable that everything is being recorded, which may lead to uncertainties or distort the interview
• Direct quotations in research report possible	
• Immediacy, no distortion via retrospective memory	• Respondents may be less spontaneous because more attention is given to the choice of words
• Relaxed interview setting because there is no need to record notes, keywords, etc.	• Interaction can be disturbed by the recording
• Easier to analyse	*Note*:
• Critical reflection of the interview techniques and the course of the interview possible	The potential adverse effects of the audio recording may weaken as the respondents grow accustomed to the situation as well as the recording devices.
• Better documentation and controllability, which lead to increased reputation in the scientific community	

Table 8.1 presents the advantages and disadvantages of using audio recordings. The advantages of audio recording are obvious, unless you are dealing with particularly sensitive issues which require a very confidential interview setting that would be disturbed by simultaneous audio recording. Writing an exact transcription is only possible using an audio or video recording, meaning that such recordings are the only way to ensure that you can use direct quotations in later steps of the analysis as well as in the research report.

Audio recordings are best carried out with digital recording devices; usually a smartphone offers quite sufficient quality for face-to-face interviews.

The same is true for video recordings, though researchers usually focus on the audio recording of the interview. Modern smartphones, digital recorders or video cameras, and transcription software make recording and transcribing much easier than in the past. The rules for transcription presented below apply to both audio and video recordings.

Determining Rules for Transcription

Rules for transcription determine how spoken language is converted into written form. Some information is always lost in this transmission; thus, the aims of the planned analysis must determine which losses are acceptable and which are not. There are many different transcription systems available (Dittmar, 2009; Dresing et al., 2015; Höld, 2009; Kowal & O'Connell, 2014), most of which differ only in whether and how various features are to be included in the transcription, such as intonation and emphasis, volume, drawl, pauses, overlaps between the utterances of different speakers, accents, gestures, facial expressions, and non-verbal expressions such as laughing, coughing, and groaning. Furthermore, some characteristics of the interview setting could be relevant for the analysis, such as if someone enters or exits the room or a telephone rings. Whether or not researchers actually transcribe all of these details depends on a study's budget, too, since transcription is very time-consuming and thus involves considerable expense. Even simple transcription takes approximately five times longer than the time taken by the interview itself. Documenting the intonation, dialects, and overlaps of different speakers within a group interview or focus group setting would further increase the cost. However, the cost should not be the only determining factor; it is much more important to determine the degree of accuracy necessary or desired for later steps in the analysis process. Sometimes, transcribing too precisely can hinder the overall analysis, such as when the text is difficult to read as a result of too many details pertaining to dialect or other features having been transcribed. A relatively simple transcription system is sufficient for most research projects in social research. Within the framework of an evaluation project, we have created a set of easy-to-learn transcription rules.[1] These rules have been developed based on personal experience as well as suggestions from Dresing et al. (2015), and are presented in Figure 8.1. The second column of the figure contains information on the extent to which the rules are implemented by software tools for automatic transcription: A '+' means that the rule is usually implemented, a '–' stands for 'no or only conditional implementation', a '+/–' stands for 'partial implementation'. We will discuss automatic transcription separately below.

Dresing et al. (2015) supplement these rules with instructions for uniform spelling which are especially useful within the framework of a research group where multiple researchers are involved in transcribing interviews.

The transcription rules presented in Figure 8.1 allow for a sufficiently accurate transcription for the application of qualitative content analysis. In the contexts of linguistic analysis and conversation research, there are much more complex transcription systems such as GAT, HIAT and CHAT (Dittmar, 2009; Rehbein et al., 2004). Moreover, EXMARaLDA (www.exmaralda.org) is a software program for more complex transcriptions.

---

[1]Further references to more complex transcription rules can be found in Kuckartz (2010a), pp. 38–47).

Transcription rules	Automatic transcription
1. Each contribution to the conversation should be transcribed into its own paragraph. This applies also to short interjections by other persons, such as 'Yes', 'No', 'Exactly'. Changes in speaker are denoted by an empty line (double space) to improve the readability of the transcription.	+/– (short interjections are usually not recognized)
2. Paragraphs belonging to the interviewer or moderator should begin with an 'I:' or 'M:' while those belonging to the respondent are denoted by a unique abbreviation such as 'R:'. To distinguish between several persons in one recording, the abbreviations should be supplemented by numbers, such as 'M1:', 'M2:', 'R1:', 'R2:'. Names or pseudonyms can be used as an alternative to abbreviations. The identifiers of the speakers should be set in bold to make them easier to recognize.	+
3. Transcription should be verbatim, not based on sounds or simply contain summaries. Any components of dialects should be translated into the standard language.	+/– (no automatic translation into standard language)
4. Language and punctuation should be smoothed slightly to accommodate written standards.	+/– (no approximation to written language)
5. Long, clear pauses should be marked by three full stops in brackets '(…)'.	– (recognizable by time stamps, if applicable)
6. Any terms that a person emphasized should be underlined.	–
7. Anything a person says loudly should be capitalized.	–
8. The approving or affirming vocalizations on the part of the interviewer ('mhm', 'aha', etc.) should not be transcribed as long as they do not interrupt the person's flow of speech or can be interpreted as direct answers to a question.	–
9. Fillers such as 'um' are only transcribed if they are meaningful in terms of content.	–
10. Any disruptions should be listed in double parentheses indicating the cause, e.g., '((telephone rings))'.	–
11. Any of the respondent's or interviewer's vocalizations that support or clarify a statement should be noted in simple parentheses, e.g., '(laughs)', '(sighs)'.	–
12. Like vocalizations, non-verbal activities in video recordings of interviews and focus groups should be noted in simple parentheses, e.g., '(opens the window)', '(turns away)'.	–
13. Unintelligible or unclear words should be noted as '(unclear)'. Words and passages where the wording is only suspected are bracketed and marked with a question mark at the end, e.g., '(kobold?)'.	+/– (only limited)
14. Time stamps are inserted at the end of each conversational contribution; if necessary, time stamps are also inserted in cases of incomprehensible passages in a longer paragraph.	+/– (rarely time stamps in incomprehensible places)

Figure 8.1 Transcription rules for computer-assisted analysis and notes on their implementation in automatic transcription software

Non-Automatic Transcription

For the 'manual' transcription of audio and video files on the computer, a number of specialized programs such as the following software tools are available, some of which are even free of charge:

- EasyTranscript (www.e-werkzeug.eu/index.php/en/)
- ExpressScribe (www.nch.com.au/scribe/)
- f4/f5transcript (www.audiotranskription.de/en/)
- HyperTRANSCRIBE (www.researchware.com)
- InqScribe (www.inqscribe.com)
- Transcriber (https://sourceforge.net/projects/trans)

It is also possible to transcribe directly with QDA software such as MAXQDA, ATLAS.ti, or NVivo. Most transcription programs are easy to use and contain all of the functions normally required for transcribing interviews within social research. As with most media players, you can play, stop, pause, restart, rewind, and fast-forward as desired. In addition, you can adjust the playback speed as well as the return interval, that is, the time in seconds that the recording rewinds and resets upon stopping. A footswitch or pedal is useful for stopping and starting the recording while transcribing.

The transcription software can insert a time stamp into the transcript, for instance at the beginning or end of a paragraph (when you press the Enter key). This makes it possible to synchronize the text and audio recording within the QDA software so that you can click on a given time stamp when reading the text in order to play that exact excerpt from the audio recording. The transcription rules described above can thus be implemented without any problems.

Figure 8.2 shows an excerpt from a transcript that was created in accordance with the rules presented above (excluding time stamps).

R7: My boyfriend and I have a study group. I mean, I explain everything to him two times and then I understand it better myself. (...) And, yeah, I studied with one of the other students from my statistics group one time, too.

zI: And how do you feel when you are studying? Do you have a positive or negative attitude or feeling towards statistics?

R7: I like it a lot. I didn't think that would be the case, but I always liked maths, so I think that's why I think it's OK.

I: And did that change at all over the course of the semester?

R7: <u>Yes</u>.

I: And how?

Figure 8.2 Excerpt from a transcript (interview with participant R7)

Automatic Transcription

Recently, there has been great progress in the field of automatic transcription. What seemed a long way off a few years ago is now state-of-the-art: if audio and video files are available in good recording quality and the recorded voices are as dialect-free as possible, they can be automatically converted into a transcript with the help of artificial intelligence. In the process, time stamps are also inserted into the text, the speakers are identified, and their conversational contributions are marked accordingly in the transcript. In this way, even transcripts of focus groups with different speakers can be created automatically.

Even though the market of providers and the functionality offered are subject to fast change, we would like to mention here some providers that have become better known, and we have also added the location of the company as a first clue regarding data protection: AmberScript (Netherlands), f4x (Germany), HappyScribe (Ireland), Otter.ai (USA), TEMI (USA), Trint (UK), Sonix (USA). Some of these software programs allow you to edit the reference dictionary to increase the recognition rate. The biggest difference between the providers, however, concerns the languages that are supported. While some companies offer only English, others allow you to choose from more than ten different languages. In the meantime, Microsoft Teams, Zoom.us, Cisco WebEx, and other tools for conducting video conferences also offer the possibility of transcribing conversations live and inserting live subtitles. After an interview carried out with these tools, in addition to the audio and video recording, a transcript can be downloaded that then can be imported into QDA software.

Although the quality of automatically generated transcripts is steadily improving, one should not expect the technology to work error-free. Automatically created transcripts always need to be checked and corrected manually. Instead of 5–10 hours for manual transcription, only about 3–6 hours are necessary to check and correct the transcript of a one-hour interview. In addition to the time saved, there is also an analytical gain: if the transcript is checked directly in the QDA software, the initiating work with the text can also be started during the process of checking the transcription.

With all the possibilities offered by automatic transcription, however, two points should not be ignored. Firstly, it is important to pay attention to the aspect of data protection and privacy because, although typically confidential, the audio and video recordings usually have to be uploaded to the providers' servers. Therefore, the server locations especially, as well as the possibility of concluding contracts for commissioned data processing, have to be checked before choosing a transcription service provider. Secondly, it should be taken into account that most providers do not specialize in social science transcripts and the automatic techniques may only capture some of the analytically relevant information. Even the simplest information, such as pauses in the flow of speech, is rarely represented, which is why, in our proposed transcription rules in Figure 8.1, we have pointed out corresponding limitations in automatic transcription. It must be decided, having regard to the research questions, whether the limited accuracy of automatic transcription is acceptable for a proposed research project.

Regardless of whether manual or automatic transcription is used, and regardless of which transcription system and software is used, the transcripts should be formatted in such a way that they are easy to read on the computer screen in later steps of the analysis process and that they can utilize various functions within the QDA software programs, particularly the lexical or word-based search options. For example, it is important that the terms used to identify either the speaker, a specific question from the interview guide, or a particular section of the survey are used consistently throughout the entire text. You should choose how you would like to abbreviate each speaker's name and use the same abbreviation throughout the entire work, such as 'I' or 'INT', and not interchangeably 'I', 'INT', and even 'Interviewer'. Uniform spelling and referencing are absolutely imperative if you plan to use the lexical search options in QDA software later.

After the transcription is finished, the entire text should be proof-read again; errors should be corrected if necessary. It is recommended that interviewers take the time to compare the transcript with the audio recording one last time.

In qualitative research, the analysis of the interview begins with or even before the transcription. Researchers develop ideas and perhaps even hypotheses during the interview and while listening to the audio recordings. They keep the interview situation and any particularities in mind, and may discuss them with the research team. All of these thoughts deserve to be recorded, though not within the transcript itself. Such ideas should be documented in the form of notes and memos that can be saved together with the text and linked to the corresponding passages. In many cases, it has also proved useful to prepare interview documentation, sometimes called a postscript, as soon as possible after the interview (Witzel & Reiter, 2012). This postscript should include everything relevant: location, time, contact information and everything the researcher noticed during the interview, such as communication behaviour, the course of the interview, information on the interview situation, and external influences, should be documented (Helfferich, 2011, pp. 193, 201).

8.2 Making the Data Anonymous

Qualitative data usually contain sensitive information that could be used to directly identify respondents; therefore, it must be made anonymous. Depending on the type of data, it can be made anonymous either during the transcription phase or upon completion of the transcription. If the data set contains a large number of details that need to be made anonymous, it is usually recommended to wait until the transcription is complete. Even if the transcription is done by a typing service or by office assistants who were not involved in obtaining the data, making the data anonymous during the transcription process is not recommended because the extra work could overwhelm the transcribers.

When making the data anonymous, all of the sensitive data in the form of names, places, dates, and the like must be replaced by pseudonyms or abbreviations. They must be changed so that the respondents cannot be directly identified based on the information contained in the transcript. Care should be taken here that the pseudonym is chosen in such a way that essential characteristics (e.g., gender, age cohort) remain recognizable. A Japanese exchange student should not be renamed 'Horst', for example. 'For all names, an attempt is made to retain the cultural context from which a name

originates, for example, Mehmet can become Kamil or Nadine can become Juliette'
(Przyborski & Wohlrab-Sahr, 2014, p. 170). Frivolous names such as 'Donald Duck'
should also be avoided.

Place names, calendar dates, and the like should also be changed in such a way that
direct conclusions about research participants are no longer possible. Places can be
replaced by more general references such as 'small town' or 'village' and dates can be
changed to indicate general time frames, such as 'summer' or 'last winter'. A table should
be created to summarize the changes and provide information for decrypting the
anonymization, which, of course, must be stored separately from the data in order to
maintain privacy and confidentiality. The storage of this information as well as the data
set itself must comply with the appropriate data protection regulations. The open-source
software QualiAnon, provided by the Qualiservice of the University of Bremen, Germany
(www.qualiservice.org), has been specially developed for anonymizing interview data and
allows the sometimes time-consuming process to be systematized and simplified.

After the data have been edited, formatted, and made anonymous, they should be
saved as an RTF or DOCX file and additionally backed up in a second location (e.g., in
the cloud). This is the only way to effectively protect against data loss, because a copy
on the same hard disk is of little help in the event of a disk crash.

8.3 Organizing Data and Planning Teamwork

Qualitative data are usually quite extensive and can contain hundreds or even thousands
of pages of text, in the form of transcribed interviews, field notes, observation protocols,
documents, and more. Before beginning the actual analysis, you should ponder how to
organize all of the data. Ask yourself: What data are available for analysis? How large is
the data set? Can I divide it into meaningful groups? Next, determine which options
your selected QDA software offers for optimal organizing and structuring the data.

In the case of our example project on climate awareness, in which we interviewed
individuals from two different age groups, it makes sense to organize the data into two
document groups or folders. This makes it easier to perform separate analyses on the
two groups later. Each of the interviews should be treated as an individual text; normally, it is not recommended to merge all interviews together into one file.

Moreover, you must also determine whether your audio files should be archived and
made available for occasional use or readily available for frequent use. In addition,
researchers must adhere to laws and standards regarding data protection.

Any standardized data (such as socio-demographic data) that you collected along
with your qualitative data should be available throughout the QCA process so that you
can, for example, analyse a specific group of the respondents. It is advantageous to enter
these data directly into the QDA software so that they are available from the outset in
combination with the qualitative data. Alternatively, it is also possible to import the
standardized data in tabular form (e.g., as an Excel or SPSS file).

Ideas that you noted during your first reading of the material or during the transcription process must also be organized. You must decide if you would like to label them as a special kind of text that you can link to the interviews or organize them as memos that belong to a given text or text passage. The latter is advantageous because such memos are always directly associated with the text that they reference and so are easily accessible. The same considerations apply to the documents made by the interviewers about the interview process ('postscript'). These should be set up as memos attached to the related transcript documents and not organized as separate documents; this way they always remain associated with the interview and are easily accessible. Some researchers prefer to have the documentation accompanying the interview (such as postscript, interview transcript, etc.) available within the transcription as well. This is also possible, but the argument against this is that then an analysis of the word frequencies of an interview is distorted or additional selections are necessary.

The question of whether to subdivide the text into text units or units of meaning goes back to the transcription phase but can only be answered later in the analysis process. If you plan to code the data according to syntactic or semantic aspects in subsequent codings, now is the time to split up the data into logical paragraphs. It is useful to begin a new paragraph for each meaningful unit of text. In primarily interpretive analyses, defining different groups in advance may seem unnecessary; however, the more elements of QCA you plan to integrate into your analysis, the more useful these sorts of subdivisions can be.

When different members of a research team are involved in analysing the data, it is important to think about how to organize and coordinate your work as a team. Consider the following questions:

- How will we work together?
- Should all of the team members be able to work on the same text at the same time?
- Should we assign certain texts to the team members so that each researcher is responsible for specific texts?
- Should all of the team members have the same rights to modify or delete data, codings, memos, and analysis work?
- Does the selected QDA software support our form of teamwork? Are there multiple alternatives for working in teams? If so, which is the most appropriate for the current analysis?

8.4 Importing Data into the QDA Software

Importing qualitative data into the QDA software is usually a simple process. Depending on the software, importing files may require little more than simply using the mouse to drag and drop the desired files into the chosen program. The standard format of Microsoft Word (DOCX) and also the RTF format used by some transcription programs are accepted by most QDA programs. The PDF format cannot be processed by all QDA programs in the original layout. When analysing studies based on interviews, DOCX or RTF formats are more suitable than PDF, because they allow you to add and edit text at any point in the analysis process. This might, for example, be necessary in order to anonymize the text later. Moreover, only DOCX or RTF formats allow you to use a synchronous time stamp in the transcription to access the audio and video files.

Some types of text (e.g., as transcriptions of focus groups, answers to open questions in online surveys, and texts that stem from internet forums) can be imported into QDA software in a pre-structured format. The software then automatically assigns text passages to categories and sub-categories or, in the case of group discussions or focus groups, to different speakers during the import (Kuckartz, 2010a, pp. 49–55; Kuckartz & Rädiker, 2019).

8.5 Tools for Working through the Text: Comments, Memos, Highlighting Passages

QDA software programs offer useful support in the initial phase of working with the text which takes place at the beginning of every qualitative data analysis. This begins with numbering the paragraphs or lines of a respondent's statement and printing out the interview, which can serve as a basis for joint discussion in the research team. Moreover, QDA software allows you to search the entire data set for interesting words or phrases and view all of the relevant passages with just a few clicks. You can also highlight or change the colour of text passages that you deem especially interesting or important and add your own comments. All of this is possible before the actual analysis begins, that is, before you develop categories, code the text, and start the category-based analysis.

Thus, qualitative data analysis begins in fact before the first formal coding process. If you consider the researchers to be active subjects involved in the research instead of just agents for collecting data, it is easier to understand the entire qualitative research process as a process of data analysis in which, unlike in survey research, there is no strict separation between collecting and analysing the data. If the researchers themselves conduct the interviews, they intuitively analyse certain statements even during the interview according to their background and their own prior knowledge as well as the research questions. Glaser and Strauss refer to this as coding because researchers 'code' what they hear, arrange it in their minds, and ponder it while considering their own ideas and forming hypotheses regarding the relationships (Glaser & Strauss, 1998, pp. 107–121). All of this occurs at every stage of the research process, including the early phases of data collection; thus, you should record such ideas and hypotheses immediately, preferably in the form of memos (cf. Section 4.5). The way that categories, codes, and coding schemes are used in QCA differs from the style of analysis that is often used in grounded theory, where the analytical work is very focused on the development of codes and key codes. Nevertheless, in QCA it is also recommended that you record your ideas, theoretical considerations, and hypotheses from the start of the analysis process.

The term 'memo' for such notes, comments, and recordings is used in particular in the context of grounded theory, in which memos play a central role. According to the grounded theory approach, you should differentiate between different types of memos, including memos that are theoretically oriented ('theory memos'), memos that contain the definitions of the categories and their characteristics or attributes ('code memos'), memos that refer to specific features of the language ('linguistic memos'), and memos that contain case summaries ('document memos'). The latter can also be used for organizational purposes, for example to record the analysis status of an interview text.

In QDA software, memos can be linked to any kind of object, such as whole texts, text passages, categories, and sub-categories. It is recommended that you use different symbols to represent different types of memos. Over the course of the analysis process, you can combine individual memos to form larger, integrated memos that serve as building blocks for the research report.

8.6 Developing Categories Deductively

If categories and sub-categories are defined before coding process begins, they can also be defined in the QDA software before the first data are imported. It should be noted that most QDA programs do not use the term 'category', but rather the term 'code'; thus to create a category, you have to click on a function called 'Create new code' or similar.

The definitions of the categories should each be recorded as code memos so that they are always available to the coders during the work (incidentally, the logic that codes and categories of any kind are consistently called 'codes' in QDA software also applies to the term 'code memos'). The definitions are best designed according to a uniform scheme, as described in Section 2.5.

Category systems that are deductively developed in this way are usually hierarchical, such as the category 'environmental behaviour' in our example study:

Category	Sub-categories
Environmental behaviour	• Travelling
	• Recycling
	• Energy
	• Consumption
	• Other

In principle, a category system can have any number of tiers: not only sub-categories, but also sub-sub-categories and more levels are possible. Most QDA programs support such a hierarchical organization of categories. However, it is usually recommended to work with no more than three or four different levels. In the case of the category 'environmental behaviour' above, a third level would be necessary if valences were to be taken into account when coding. This would result, for example, in the categories 'environmental behaviour → travelling → positive' and 'environmental behaviour → travelling → negative'.

In quantitative content analysis, the categories are often numbered consecutively, for example as follows:

10   Environmental behaviour
11   Travelling
12   Recycling
13   Energy
14   Consumption
15   Other

Such numbering is not actually necessary in QCA, yet it is often practised; however, it is problematic when new categories are developed and inserted into the category system in the course of the coding process.

8.7 Developing Categories Inductively Using the Data

QDA software can be very useful for inductively developing codes and categories directly based on the data. Codes and concepts are recorded following to the techniques described in Section 3.2: by proceeding through the text line by line, you can open up and break down the text (Strauss & Corbin, 1996, p. 45). Much like when working with a pen and paper, you can highlight text passages and assign them a new or an already existing code.

The main advantage of QDA software, in contrast to working with pen(s) and paper, is that the codes created in this way not only stand next to the text but are also automatically recorded in a code system. Later, the codes can be sorted, systemized, and summarized. The codes remain linked with the individual text passages as if by an invisible ribbon, so that with one click one can jump back and forth between the analysis and the actual data on which it is based.

Comments, theoretical aspects, and ideas regarding different dimensions of the codes can be recorded in the form of code memos, which contain descriptions of categories. In this way, a category manual (code book) gradually emerges in which the categories are described in detail and illustrated by examples.

Figure 8.3 shows an excerpt from an open-coded interview in which the open codes are displayed to the left of the text. Notice that a memo has been linked to Paragraph 22, in which the switch from first-person to third-person language is evident: when asked about his or her own behaviour, the respondent answers 'Sure, I'd like to' but then switches to the less obligatory third person and says less concretely, 'One looks for an occasion to do so'.

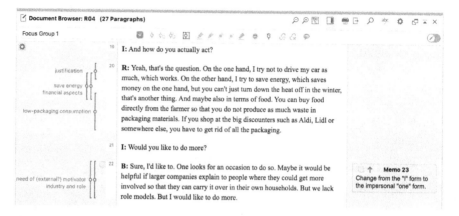

Figure 8.3 Interview excerpt with open codes displayed on the left

Qualitative methods characteristically claim to allow the respondents to speak for themselves – to let them express things in their own words and not simply choose their answers from a number of standard responses. Therefore, their words, concepts, and metaphors are extremely important. QDA software helps you keep track of the respondents' original wording using a feature called 'in vivo coding', in which the respondents' actual words are highlighted and coded and simultaneously recorded as codes within the category system. For example, one of the respondents in our 'Individual Perception of Climate Change' study referred to what he or she called a 'We Save the World Association' (Figure 8.4). This term was highlighted and used directly as a category name.

I: And would you like to do more than what you are already doing?
R29: Theoretically, yes, but the question is how. And I don't know if I would feel comfortable in some (...) We Save the World Association.
I: Do you feel a responsibility to address the problems of the 21st century?
R29: Personally yes, but not globally.
I: Can you clarify what you mean by that?

Figure 8.4 Excerpt from interview R29, paragraphs 33–37

The development of categories is a lengthy process which requires that you go through the data or parts of the data repeatedly. An alternative way of developing categories directly from the text is the technique of category development via focused summaries, which is described in Section 3.2. This procedure is close to the text in that the text passages that are important for their content are first abstracted and paraphrased in a process that may involve several stages. The procedure is quite time-consuming, but proves quite helpful, especially for beginners. In a first step, QDA software allows paraphrases to be recorded directly next to the text, as in Figure 8.5. In a second step, all written paraphrases can be compiled in a table in order to systematize them and to arrive at suitable categories based on them.

8 **R:** I simply believe that climate change, as it is predicted everywhere or painted in black, will not happen. I mean, there are also physicists or meteorologists, I don't know, climate researchers, who are not of the opinion that climate change will happen. But they are not listened to in the media because the catastrophe report simply seems much, much more important or is simply more attractive for the media. But that doesn't change the fact that everyone should live in an environmentally conscious way. And

Doom-mongering about climate change is everywhere. CC will not happen.

There are scientific counter-opinions that are being ignored.

The media do not publish critical positions.

News about disaster is more attractive for the media.

Figure 8.5 Paraphrases next to the text

In an approach to open coding based on grounded theory, codes are formed from the outset with the intention of moving away from the data towards the goal of developing a theory. What Strauss, Glaser, and Corbin refer to as *coding* refers to the theoretical classification of the data, not simply the assignment to codes (Strauss & Corbin, 1996, pp. 43–55). This involves two steps. First anything interesting in the text is coded, meaning that it is given an abstract label. Then you move to the code level to group the codes and examine the relationships between them.

Using QDA software programs to construct categories for qualitative data analysis has many advantages compared to traditional, manual methods using pen and paper. This is true for both methods presented, for the technique of working via summarization as well as for the more abstract and theory-oriented approach of grounded theory. When using QDA software, you stay connected to the original data and are not forced to page through hundreds of sheets of text searching for specific text passages. You can easily gain an overview of how frequently certain codes, concepts, and categories appear in the data, and you can find them, summarize them, and create categories for them that can be used in your analysis. Likewise, you can easily find typical examples to help define the given categories.

For documentation purposes, you can always demonstrate on which text passages a given category is based. Moreover, you can document the different stages of building categories. You can also determine a category's semantic context because all of the text passages that are linked to a given category are summarized in a list.

If you do not wish to assign codes to relevant text passages when you deal with the text for the first time, we recommend that you work with the QDA software programs in two phases. First, you mark important paragraphs and then code them. For instance, MAXQDA allows you to highlight text electronically in different colours. Like when highlighting on paper, you can start by simply highlighting text passages that are important for your research question. Then you can go back through the data a second time to assign codes to those important passages and create categories.

8.8 Using Software for Structuring QCA

A very important capability of QDA software in structuring QCA is to compile all text passages coded with the same category, a process also called 'text retrieval'.

> In computer-assisted QCA, text retrieval is the category-related compilation of previously coded text passages. The text passages compiled by the QDA software usually contain an indication of origin: information about which text they come from and where they can be found there. The compiled list of coded segments can be displayed on the screen, printed out, or exported as a file.

The assistance that can be provided by QDA software in structuring QCA is manifold and considerable at each stage of the analysis process. Table 8.2, which follows the sequence of the phases of structuring QCA, shows the support provided by QDA software for each phase.

Table 8.2 shows that QDA software can be integrated into every phase of thematic text analysis to assist in the analysis very effectively, and it is by no means a complete list of the capabilities that QDA software programs offer. Rädiker and Kuckartz (2020) provide further detailed information on computer support for the analysis of guided interviews; their presentation essentially follows the approach of structuring QCA.

QDA software can be particularly useful for condensing and summarizing coded texts. Such techniques are described in detail in Chapter 5. The so-called 'Summary Grid' of the software MAXQDA allows a systematic form of category-based summaries. Figure 8.6 illustrates working with the Summary Grid. In the left-hand panel you will find the thematic matrix, as described in Chapter 3. The columns of the matrix are formed by the various interviews, and the rows represent the categories. Once you click on a cell in the thematic matrix, the associated coded segments of the person and the category are displayed in the middle pane. In the right-hand panel, the researchers can then write a summary of the coded segments.

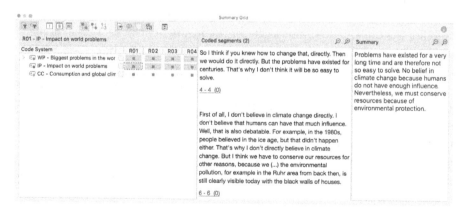

Figure 8.6 Summarizing coded segments using the Summary Grid

Table 8.2 Using QDA software for structuring QCA

Phases and respective computer support

---

1 *Initial work with the text: read, write memos and case summaries*

You can select important text passages and highlight or even code them. You also can automatically search for certain words or phrases. You may write memos and comments and link them to text passages, to the entire text, or to categories. Text passages can be linked together, for example if they are similar or contradictory. You may also link text passages with external documents to provide a broader context for the analysis.

Supplementary (standardized) background information such as the socio-demographic data in interviews can be recorded as case variables.

You can compose initial case summaries and save them as memos linked to the text. For interviews, the postscript with important information about the interview can be saved as a document memo.

2 *Develop main categories*

Categories (codes) can be developed deductively or inductively directly from the data. A hierarchical category system with several levels can be created. Alternatively, category networks can be defined.

Categories and sub-categories can be grouped and combined into more abstract categories. Descriptions and definitions of categories may be recorded in code memos.

3 *Code data with main categories (1st coding cycle)*

You should sequentially work through each text line by line and assign your main categories to relevant text passages. The full list of categories or codes is always available on screen, with definitions and examples just a click away.

Coding is done by selecting text passages with the mouse and assigning them to an existing or new code.

4 *Develop sub-categories inductively*

Using the text retrieval function, all of the text passages that have been assigned to a given main category can be compiled into a list that may be printed or saved as a DOCX file or spreadsheet. Standardized data (such as socio-demographic characteristics and other variables collected in an accompanying questionnaire) can be used for selecting, grouping, and contrasting.

In a deductive-inductive approach, you can develop sub-categories for each of the main categories directly based on the data. For this purpose, functions are available for the visual grouping of codes into categories, for merging via drag-and-drop as well as for differentiating categories.

As before, you should record the definitions of sub-categories as code memos and add typical examples to the category descriptions. All code memos can be compiled into a coding guide for the entire, now complete, category system.

5 *Code data with sub-categories (2nd coding cycle)*

You should now go back through all of the text passages that have been coded with the main categories in order to assign them to the constructed sub-categories.

(Continued)

Table 8.2 (Continued)

Phases and respective computer support

You can modify the case summaries written in the first phase of the analysis according to the categories and sub-categories formed. Among other options, functions for writing case-related thematic summaries, text retrieval, and comment functions are available for this purpose.

Intermediate step: Writing case-related thematic summaries

For important categories, the coded text passages may be listed on a case-by-case basis and summarized in terms of content.

6 *Simple and complex analyses*

The text retrieval function allows you to compile the text passages that have been assigned to a category or sub-category and determine the frequency with which each sub-category appears.

Correlations between sub-categories within a main category and between main categories can be analysed qualitatively and quantitatively.

A list of the occurring configurations of categories and sub-categories (i.e., their combinations in the material) helps to identify patterns.

Selective text retrievals enable the qualitative comparison of subgroups based on socio-demographic and other characteristics. Cross-tabulations present category frequencies differentiated by groups (e.g., the text passages coded on a topic broken down by selected socio-demographic characteristics).

Case overviews structured according to categories allow comparisons of individual cases and groups. In doing so, it is possible to go back to the summaries formed in an intermediate step.

Visual representations show the presence and, if desired, the frequency of the categories broken down by cases.

Diagrams present the proximity of categories and sub-categories (and any overlaps between them).

The thematic progression of an interview can be displayed as a 'codeline'. In the case of focus groups, the sequence in which the speakers talked and the topics of each of their contributions are displayed.

Concept maps and diagrams visualize the relationships between the categories and present the hypotheses and theories developed during the analysis (e.g., in the form of causal models).

7 *Write up results and document process*

Memos written during the analysis process can be integrated into the corresponding parts or chapters of the research report.

The analyses and visualizations created in phase 6 can be included in the report.

A category book with the code memos can be created automatically to document the category system.

Report functions can be used to create a report of the coded text passages structured according to selected topics.

8.9 Using Software for Evaluative QCA

Evaluative qualitative content analysis can be carried out independently as well as based on the coding previously carried out within the framework of the structuring QCA. In the latter case, you have already identified all of the text passages that pertain to important topics, you only have to read, classify, and evaluate these passages. If you have not yet identified and coded such relevant passages, you will have to go back through the text and do so. Otherwise, your analysis will not be linked to the original data and it will be difficult to trace it back to the data.

The ways in which QDA software can assist in the seven phases of evaluative QCA are presented in Table 8.3.

Table 8.3 Using QDA software for evaluative QCA

Phases and respective computer support
1 *Initial work with the text: read, write memos and case summaries*
You can select important text passages and highlight or even code them. You can also automatically search for certain words or phrases. You may write memos and comments and link them to text passages, to the entire text, or to categories. Text passages can be linked together, for example if they are similar or contradictory. You may also link text passages with external documents to provide a broader context for the analysis.
Supplementary (standardized) background information such as the socio-demographic data in interviews can be recorded as case variables.
You can compose initial case summaries and save them as memos linked to the text. For interviews, the postscript with important information about the interview can be saved as a document memo.
2 *Define evaluative category*
In this phase, based on the research question, the category is defined for which evaluations will be made across all cases.
Search and retrieval functions make it easy to gain an overview of the data and determine if they are suitable for evaluative QCA.
3 *Identify and code relevant text passages*
In this phase, all text passages that refer to the relevant category are identified and coded.
QDA software codes the data quickly and efficiently. You can also compare the codings completed by different coders.
Code memos allow you to record and modify category definitions and typical examples.
4 *Develop levels (values)*
In this phase, the coded segments of the selected category are compiled and read on a case-by-case basis. Levels (values) are defined and segments are assigned; the number of different levels is chosen on a trial basis and code definitions are written.

(Continued)

Table 8.3 (Continued)

Phases and respective computer support

With the help of a text retrieval, all text passages belonging to a category are compiled. The results of the retrieval can be displayed as a table and printed out.

Case-related summaries of the relevant text passages can be written as a basis for developing the values and compiled in overview tables.

If the entire case is to be coded, the assignments to the values can be recorded in a case variable.

If each individual text passage is coded, the values can be defined as sub-categories. The assignment of the appropriate sub-category is done by simply dragging and dropping the text passage from a table of relevant text passages.

Changes can be made to the definitions of the values and examples using the memo functionality.

If the number of values of a category is changed, targeted compilation of the codes already made and new assignments of the coded segments or the case to the changed category scheme are facilitated.

5   *Evaluate and code all cases*

In this phase, categories are applied to all cases that have not yet been evaluated and, in cases of doubt, records are kept of the reasons for the decisions made.

Using the drag-and-drop function, you can assign text passages case by case to the appropriate sub-category.

If uncertain how to code a given passage, use the memo function to document your reasoning.

Comparisons of coding by independent coders should be made.

6   *Simple and complex analyses*

Quantitative analysis: the absolute and relative frequency for each value of the evaluative categories can be presented as a table or diagram.

Qualitative analysis: text retrievals are used to compile the text passages for each value of the evaluative category.

Cases-by-categories tables provide an overview, allowing comparisons and contrasts to be made.

For certain combinations of characteristics, the verbal data of the respective individuals can be used for in-depth individual case analyses.

Cross-tabulations allow quantitative comparisons and the quote matrix allows qualitative comparisons of the thematic statements by groups; these can be formed, for example, by evaluative categories or by socio-demographic characteristics.

Overlaps and the co-occurrence of categories and sub-categories can be analysed and visualized.

The conversion of evaluative categories into variables enables statistical analyses (e.g., cross-tabulations, correlations, and complex statistical procedures).

An analysis of the configurations of categories and sub-categories helps to identify patterns.

As with structuring QCA, many visualizations are available: visual representations of the presence and, if applicable, also the frequencies of the evaluative categories broken down by case; progression graphs, concept maps, and causal models.

Table 8.3 (Continued)

Phases and respective computer support
7   *Write up results and document process*
Memos written during the analysis process can be integrated into the corresponding parts or chapters of the research report.
The analyses and visualizations performed in phase 6 may also be included in the report.
To document the meaning of the different levels (values), a category book with all of the code memos can be generated automatically.

As described in Chapter 6, there are two different ways to evaluate cases, such as persons, families, or institutions. Either you can decide from the start to analyse the cases based on the categories, which requires you to read through the collection of relevant text passages (phases 4 and 5), determine adequate characteristics based on the definition of each evaluative category, and assign the given respondent an assessment variable or level (e.g., sense of responsibility → high level). Or you can decide to conduct detailed evaluations of every relevant text passage (e.g., meaning that you evaluate the level of responsibility expressed in each of the text passages). For this, the levels 'high', 'moderate', 'low', and 'not to be classified' can be defined as sub-categories for the code 'sense of responsibility' and assigned to the appropriate text passages.

If you coded by smaller sections and defined the characteristics of the evaluative categories as sub-categories, you will have to aggregate your codings at the case level. You may have evaluated several relevant text passages with different values for a given participant. For instance, some text passages show that a person feels very responsible towards climate change, other text passages show only moderate responsibility. In some QDA programs, these evaluations can be automatically converted into categorical variables. Then a variable with the name 'sense of responsibility' is created, and automatically populated with the value of the most frequently assigned characteristic or level for each respondent. The most frequently assigned characteristic or level may be unclear because two or more sub-categories have the same frequency, in which case the value is set to 'undecided'. As a result, the coders must re-examine the given text passages and assign an appropriate value manually.

Some QDA programs allow two or more analysts to code independently. In MAXQDA, for example, this works as follows. Two coders code independently of each other. After all coding has been done, the software compares the codings, and calculates a coefficient of agreement per category as well as the intercoder agreement in the form of percentage agreement and the coefficient kappa (Kuckartz & Rädiker, 2019). A detailed table of agreements per code then shows where differences exist between coders. The analysts take a closer look at the problematic passages and try to find a consensual solution. At times, the definitions in the coding guidelines must be modified or made more precise. If the coders cannot reach an agreement, they can record their arguments in the form of a memo, which can be discussed later with the research group or project management.

After the entire data set has been coded with the evaluative categories in phase 5, QDA software offers a variety of qualitative and quantitative analysis possibilities.

As *quantitative analyses*, frequency analyses can first be carried out for each evaluative category, that is, an overview is obtained of how many of the interviewed persons were classified as 'sense of responsibility → high' or as 'sense of responsibility → low'. Corresponding graphical representations can also be created such as pie charts or bar charts.

Furthermore, statistical correlation analyses between the different evaluative categories are possible. For this purpose, the matrix of the codings made can be transferred to a statistical analysis program. Some QDA software packages, such as QDAMiner and MAXQDA, also offer statistical functions, so that no transfer is necessary and the calculations can be made directly in the QDA software. Questions can then be answered such as 'What influence does a person's sense of responsibility have?' or 'With which other categories does sense of responsibility correlate?'. Since the assessment categories usually have an ordinal scale level, rank correlation methods such as Spearman's rho (Kuckartz et al., 2013, pp. 216–219) are appropriate here. Correlations to socio-demographic characteristics can also be examined by means of cross-tabulation analysis: Cross-tabulations can be created, for example between sense of responsibility and level of education.

The spectrum of conceivable *qualitative analyses* is not much smaller than that of the quantitative analyses. The statements (coded segments) for each value of an evaluative category can be compiled and compared with each other in a matrix representation. For example, for all persons with a low sense of responsibility, their definitions of the biggest world problems can be compiled and compared with those of persons with a high sense of responsibility. Furthermore, the different values can serve as selection criteria for accessing statements on other thematic categories. For example, what do persons with a high, moderate, or low sense of responsibility say about their sources of information on the topic of 'learnability'? Finally, the evaluative categories can also be included in visualizations and concept maps.

8.10 Using Software for Type-Building QCA

Type-building QCA can also be very well supported by QDA software. In fact, QDA software has even made it possible for the first time to construct types and typologies for qualitative data analysis in a methodical manner, so that the process of constructing type is totally transparent.

Table 8.4 gives an overview of computer support in the various phases of type-building qualitative content analysis.

It is very easy to construct typologies based on the combinations of attributes and to construct ideal types using QDA software because the software allows you to select the appropriate attributes and types and combine them with just a few mouse clicks. Categories and sub-categories can be converted into case variables by establishing a data matrix and recording if and how frequently a given category has been assigned to a given respondent.

Table 8.4 Using QDA software for type-building QCA

Phase and respective computer support

1 *Determine purpose, aim, and focus of building types*

2 *Select relevant dimensions and determine attribute space*

Search and text retrieval functions make it easy to get a quick overview of the material and to check its suitability for type-building QCA.

3 *Code selected material*

Overview of categories, sub-categories and coding: is the information available for a sufficient number of cases? Do thematic or evaluative categories need to be combined?

Use the appropriate functionality of the QDA software for coding or grouping different categories.

4 *Determine type-building procedures and construct typology*

Under certain circumstances, experimental testing of different grouping possibilities.

(a) Formation of feature homogeneous types by combination, or	Combination of categories and formation of the groups (e.g., in an automatically generated, tabular case overview or a placement of the cases in a two-dimensional representation in which similar cases can be identified).
(b) Type-building through reduction, or	Combination of different categories and formation of suitable types through sensible reduction of the attribute space and grouping of certain attribute combinations (e.g., in an automatically generated, tabular case overview).
(c) Formation of polythetic types	Different variants are available for selection: (1) Assembling of the corresponding case summaries into homogeneous groups. (2) Use of suitable statistical methods such as cluster analysis or factor analysis and generation of case-related data on cluster memberships.

5 *Assign all cases to the types formed*

The typology is created in the QDA software as a new variable or category (e.g., with the label 'environmental mentality').

The various types formed are defined as values (e.g., as types of 'environmental mentality' the four types 'environmental rhetoricians', 'environmental ignoramuses', 'consistent environmentalists', and 'attitude-free environmentalists').

For each person, it is recorded to which of the educated types they belong.

6 *Describe typology and individual types; conduct in-depth case analyses*

For each type, the text passages of the categories representing the attribute space of the type building are compiled in a text retrieval. The condensed text written on this basis is stored as a memo for each type.

The type affiliation now serves as a selection criterion for the verbal data of selected individual cases. Individual cases are presented, contrasted, and interpreted. If necessary, an ideal type can also be synthesized within a type by assembling statements of different people of the same type.

(Continued)

Table 8.4 (Continued)

Phase and respective computer support
7   *Analyse relationships between types and secondary characteristics*
8   *Analyse relationships between types and other categories*
In these phases, both statistical and qualitative evaluations can be carried out. By means of correlations, cross-tabulations, and variance analyses, the connections between type affiliation and (socio-demographic) variables or other categories can be examined.
In the presentation of a topic matrix, statements on selected topics can be compiled according to types and compared with each other.
9   *Presentation of results*
With the help of tables, concept maps, locating cases on a surface, and other tools, the results can be visualized.

If you have conducted an evaluative text analysis, the appropriate assignments are already saved as case variables. Now you can examine the individual groups formed by combinatorics separately or compare them with each other. The characteristics saved as case variables can be statistically analysed directly in the QDA software (if the software provides corresponding functions) or the characteristics can be exported to statistical software in order to create crosstabs, which can then serve as the basis for building types via the method of reduction.

Type-building analysis benefits even more from the use of QDA software when you rely on statistical approaches (e.g., cluster analysis, factor analysis, and correspondence analysis) to help construct the types. This is particularly useful when you are working with a large number of cases and/or with an attribute space that contains a large number of attributes. After exporting the matrix of the attributes to be used to construct the types into a statistical software program, you can construct natural typologies using cluster analysis methods. The method assigns the respondents to types, which can then be imported back into the QDA software for the next phase of the analysis.

QDA software can also be useful for constructing types based on case summaries. In this case, you can start with the case summaries and manually assemble them in groups that are as homogeneous as possible according to their similarities. This can be done without computer assistance; however, you can still rely on the computer software to present your results, such as by creating diagrams to visualize the types and the respondents who have been assigned to them.

8.11 Advanced Analysis Using QDA Software

Qualitative content analysis, as described above, is not limited to developing categories, coding, and conducting category-based analyses; it also involves examining and working

through the texts extensively. QDA software can support such processes, which are characterized by exploration and serendipity – the accidental finding of what was not
originally sought (Merton & Barber, 2004). The programs offer a toolbox full of useful
features and procedures that can each be used creatively as well as usefully combined
with others (Kuckartz & Rädiker, 2019). Describing all of the available tools and their
features goes beyond the scope of this book; thus, we will present a brief outline of those
functions that go beyond building categories and coding data that are especially useful
for qualitative content analysis.

Integration of Multimedia Functionality

Modern QDA software enables you to use multimedia features in qualitative analysis,
which means that audio and video digital files can be synchronized with their transcriptions and used in the analysis. This also opens up new fields of application for QCA
beyond the analysis of texts. Space does not allow us to go into the analyses of these types
of data here. However, one innovation that is related to the extended multimedia functions also concerns the QCA of texts, namely that this synchronization introduces the
possibility of accessing the original sounds and/or images during the analysis process.

For a long time now, recording technology has made it possible not only to record a
qualitative interview in writing in key words or perhaps to take notes, but to record it
permanently. When such recordings were done on cassette tapes, transcribing and analysing the recordings was difficult because researchers could only move backwards and
forwards through the analogue recordings to locate specific moments with great difficulty. Everything changed, however, with the advent of digital recording devices, which
enable researchers to play nearly any part of the recording almost instantly, which
makes it possible to synchronize the recording and the transcription.

In general, researchers prefer to work with transcripts in the analysis despite the
existence of audio recordings, because transcripts are much easier to handle than audio
files. For example, you can search for a specific word of an interview text at lightning
speed, while it would take much longer to find the same spot in the audio file and listen
to it. However, integrating the multimedia functions offers many advantages. You can
always access the original recording, which is particularly advantageous if you would
like to take paraverbal characteristics into account and pay attention to pitch, delays,
volume, and the like. The same applies to video recordings, which provide even more
insight into the research situation and how the data were produced.

Theoretically, it is also possible to proceed in such a way that parts of an interview
that seem unimportant are not transcribed at all, but can be listened to in the original
sound if necessary. The transcript must contain time stamps so that you can directly
access the original recording. Clicking on these marks then plays the required sound
clip. Some programs also work in the opposite direction: when you play the audio file,
the transcription appears like subtitles. This can be particularly useful when verifying
the accuracy of a transcription.

Integrating multimedia features can also involve linking pictures, graphs, and more to the texts. This allows you to examine people or groups as well as places, which can increase the clarity of field research.

However, these new possibilities are accompanied by some quite serious problems. One of these is the problem of anonymity. This has always been a problem in qualitative research that should not be underestimated. Due to the new technology, this problem has increased dramatically. In fact, it is almost impossible to make qualitative data that include audio and video anonymous: voice and video recordings are difficult to edit in such a way that a participant's privacy is protected. Secondary analysis of this data is also problematic, as even if respondents provide written consent, researchers have to ask themselves if it is really necessary for the data to be circulating for decades.

Text Links, Hyperlinks, and External Links

In QDA software, you can also use hyperlinks, which are, generally speaking, electronic cross-references between two points. If you click on the starting point, you can jump to the other end of the link.

Hyperlinks can also be used as an additional tool in QCA. Text passages, whether in the same text, in different texts or in memos, can be linked to each other. This enables you to better understand the data independently of the categories and the coding of text passages. Creating links in QDA software is quite simple: select the text passages that will serve as your starting point and your destination, creating a permanent link between the two. Links in QDA software appear like those in conventional Internet browsers: if you click on the link, you will jump to the destination. If you click again, you will jump back to the starting point.

Using hyperlinks, you can create a network within your research project that makes it possible to navigate the data independently of the categories. Moreover, you can also use external links to connect given text passages with external files, such as photos, audio files, videos, and more. You can use geographical reference tools such as ArcGIS or Google Maps in combination with QDA software to gain a new understanding of social objects by examining their coordinates, which can be included in the QCA. This makes it possible to link any text passages with any related geographical reference, so that you can view the location on the globe that you are examining at any point during the analysis.

Geographical references provide valuable background information for systematic QCA. For instance, within the framework of her research on risks, Fielding analysed whether the respondents' assessed risk of flooding and other dangers associated with the climate are connected to where the respondents live (Fielding, 2008). Thus, objective dangers, such as proximity to rivers and elevation of the apartment or house, are related to how the respondents subjectively perceive the threat. Spatial aspects can be included as background information, but can also be the focus of research, for example in the special research area 'Re-Figuration of Spaces', set up at the Technical University

Berlin (www.sfb1265.de), in which the subjective experience of space, among other things, is studied through numerous projects.

Visualizations

In many scientific disciplines, visualizations are a standard part of an analysis and are used to assist in diagnosis and discovery as well as the presentation of results. Medical or climate research would not be the same without images, and in a variety of disciplines statistical approaches would not be the same without suitable graphs and diagrams of causal models. The idea of using diagrams, tables, and other visualizations within the framework of qualitative data analysis is not new; nearly two decades ago the proponents of grounded theory used diagrams to present their concepts (Strauss, 1991, pp. 238–273; Strauss & Corbin, 1996, pp. 169–192), and Miles and Huberman wrote their comprehensive book *Qualitative Data Analysis: An Expanded Sourcebook* as early as 1994, which presents visualization techniques in detail and is still very much worth reading because the authors draw attention to different forms of data presentation (cf. Kuckartz, 2010a; as well as the new edition of Miles et al., 2020).

Three of the various visualization techniques available in QDA software for presenting the results of QCA are described below: Visualizations that present the thematic progression of an interview; visualizations of the categories within each interview; and case-based concept maps.

Visualizations that Present the Thematic Progression of an Interview

Visualizing the structure and thematic progression of an interview is particularly interesting in structuring QCA. The more openly the interview is conducted, the more interesting the visualization will be. Likewise, if you rely on an interview guide and follow a strict sequence of topics in the interview, the visualization might not be as interesting.

Diagrams, such as the one presented in Figure 8.7 showing how a group discussion progressed, are particularly useful in analysing focus groups, when each speaker is coded or automatically identified by a corresponding function of the QDA software. It shows when each of the speakers (here abbreviated as A, B, C, D) participated in the discussion and what topics they discussed.[2] After an introduction by the moderator, speaker C, then B, and then again C continue the discussion. The moderator introduces the topic 'biggest problems in the world' rather generally at first. Speaker C touches on aspects related to 'nature and environment', speaker B focuses on the 'economy' which speaker C continues in paragraph 4 in connection with 'nature and environment'. Then, the moderator makes a reference to 'nature and environment' in paragraph 5 before speaker A shifts the discussion to address 'politics' in paragraph 6.

---

[2] The illustration was created with the help of MAXQDA's 'Codeline' function.

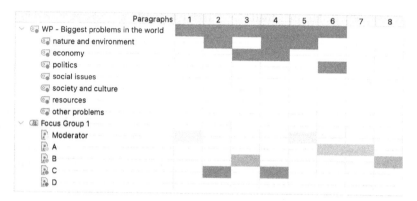

Figure 8.7 Visualization of the progress of a group discussion

Visualization of the Categories per Case

The concept of the profile matrix (cases by categories), particularly the thematic matrix, which is presented in Chapter 4, is central to QCA. A thematic matrix allows you to view cases and categories two-dimensionally. Creating visualizations of the codings increases their potential for analysis because in one glance you can see which categories have been assigned to which interviews. If applicable, you can also visualize how frequently each category has been assigned. Figure 8.8 presents this kind of visualization.[3] You can easily compare texts by arranging them side by side in the table; double-clicking on one of the nodes within the thematic matrix displays all of the text passages within the selected text that have been coded with this category.

The columns in Figure 8.8 display the cases (here interviews R01–R07) while the rows correspond to the categories and sub-categories. If you select the corresponding function of the software, the size of the symbols shows how often each category was assigned to each interview.

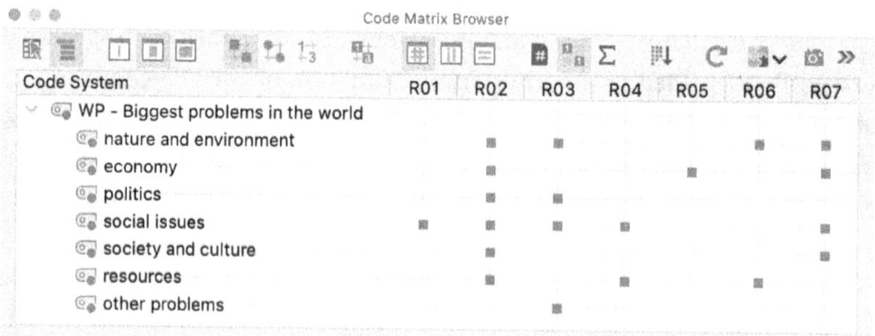

Figure 8.8 Visual representation of interviews and assigned categories

---

[3]This figure was created using the 'Code Matrix Browser' in MAXQDA.

Case-Based Concept Maps

Concept maps allow you to examine the relationships between the categories, sub-categories, and cases within a data sample. For example, you can arrange all of the categories that have been assigned to a given interview in such a map, and the categories, in turn, are linked to the appropriate passages in the text. These kinds of visualizations make it possible to determine which categories have been assigned to a given interview in just one glance. Moreover, by clicking on the symbol of a text passage, you can jump right to the underlying data. Concept maps are useful in QCA for two main reasons. First, they are especially suitable for presenting the results, such as for illustrating the background information as part of an in-depth interpretation of individual cases. Second, they can be used as a diagnostic tool for the actual analysis and work with the text.

Geographical links can also be inserted into concept maps so that if you click on the symbol for a geo-link, a geographical information program like Google Maps will begin the 'approach' to this very place and display exactly where the incident occurred.

Word-Based Techniques for Analysis

Taking a close look at words, sentences, and language in general is very important for qualitative data analysis. Thus, it also makes sense to use the word-based analysis capabilities of QDA software programs for QCA. As presented in Chapter 1, the classical content analysis of the 1940s has evolved to include a variety of computer-assisted possibilities for QCA that are based on words and process automatic codings on the basis of a dictionary. Two computer-assisted analysis techniques in particular can be used to supplement qualitative content analysis, namely, word frequency counts that display keywords in context, as well as dictionary-based word searches with subsequent automatic coding.

Word Frequency and Keyword-in-Context Lists

Going through a text sequentially to list all of the words alphabetically and count their frequencies can be quite useful in qualitative text analysis, particularly if you wish to compare selected texts or groups of texts. QDA software with corresponding functions for word-based analyses allows you to exclude insignificant words, such as articles and conjunctions, from the analysis by adding them to so-called 'stop lists' or 'exclusion lists'.

Word frequency lists can provide insight into the words that appear most frequently in the text as well as finding words that are seldom mentioned or words that you would not have expected to find within the given context. Because qualitative research aims to let people express themselves in their own words, it can be interesting to examine linguistic aspects of the interviews. A list of word frequencies can contain valuable information. This is illustrated by the list of most frequent words from the project 'Living Well in Germany' (Table 8.5), which is based on 84 statements. The list excludes the non-meaningful words collected in a stop list. Such a list of word frequencies does not replace careful QCA, but it gives a first overview quickly and may inspire the analysis. If the word frequency review is only carried out after the qualitative analysis, it also offers an interesting opportunity for comparison.

Table 8.5 Word frequencies: the 12 most frequent words in 84 statements

Word	Frequency	% of Words	Statements	% of Statements
Family	56	0.97	36	42.9
Security	51	0.88	30	35.7
Freedom	44	0.76	28	33.3
Health	41	0.71	28	33.3
Work	38	0.66	24	28.6
Children	32	0.55	18	21.4
Respect	21	0.36	12	14.3
Education	20	0.35	15	17.9
Citizens	18	0.31	14	16.7
Cooperation	18	0.31	13	15.5
Social	18	0.31	16	19.0
Peace	17	0.29	14	16.7

Particularly interesting in this context is the option to create keyword-in-context lists and explore the use of certain words in all or selected texts. In such lists, all instances of a selected word are displayed together with the surrounding text (Figure 8.9). The source of the quotation is displayed in an additional column, for example, in Figure 8.9 the first listed occurrence of 'family' stems from the statement of person S3, paragraph 4. It can be seen that the keyword 'family' occurs twice in the statement of person S10.

Pos.	Context	Keyword	Context
S3: 4	personal relationship with God. Marriage,	family	and friends. Health and happiness
S4: 4	like to have impact. My	family	and my friends should also
S5: 3	every life stands for this the	family	, which supports me where necessary
S10: 3	best in the interweaving of	family	, work and health. This is
S10: 6	to advance oneself and one's	family	. Perhaps not necessarily from the
S11: 2	We need all 3: health,	family	, work. For me personally, this

Figure 8.9 Keyword-in-context for the word 'family' (excerpt)

QDA software generates not only the output of frequencies for individual words but also listings of repeatedly occurring phrases, or multi-word combinations such as 'freedom and security' or 'with my family'. In so-called 'word trees' (Wattenberg & Viégas, 2008) such word combinations can be displayed in their broader context. In a sense, this is a combination of the keyword-in-context, word combinations, and word frequencies tools in one visualization. In the example in Figure 8.10, a word tree can be seen: In the texts analysed, the most frequent word before the word 'family' is the word 'my'. The most frequent word before 'my family' is 'with', which is therefore placed at the top, and the second most frequent word before 'my family' is 'for', placed in second position from the top.

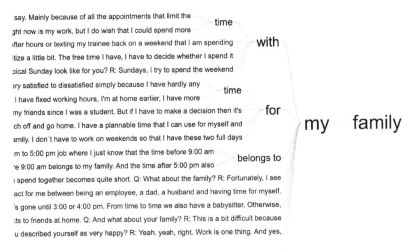

Figure 8.10   Word tree with focus on the word 'family' (detail)

Dictionary-Based Word Searches and Automatic Coding

The technique of creating dictionaries based on categories with search terms and using them to code automatically stems from computer-assisted quantitative content analysis (Krippendorff, 2004a, pp. 281–289).

Such a dictionary contains all of the categories combined with search terms that may appear in the text and that serve as indicators for their respective categories. For example, if you define the category 'craftsmanship' and compile a dictionary for it, you may include professions such as 'shoemaker', 'carpenter', and 'wood carver'. Then the passages in which any of these search words appear would be automatically coded and assigned to the category 'craftsmanship'. Ambiguous terms may not be coded correctly using this type of dictionary-based analysis; therefore it may be necessary to re-examine the context of the affected search terms. In our example, both 'Thatcher' and 'Carpenter' could denote the last names of respondents rather than their professions; thus, coding them to the 'craftsmanship' category may not be appropriate. A simple examination of the context in which the search words appear should clarify such ambiguities.

Dictionary-based coding is a method for reliably analysing a very large amount of data. You can conduct very efficient searches and access the corresponding text passages directly, if necessary. This type of analysis and coding forms a good basis for subsequent statistical analyses, but it can also simply be used to explore heuristically and make qualitative researchers aware of specific words or word combinations and the passages in which they appear. Dictionary-based content analysis is different from the other text analysis approaches presented in this book because it is an automated approach, which means that the coding is done by a computer rather than people. Thus, some research questions can be answered very quickly. For example, we conducted a dictionary-based analysis of statements that students made regarding the proposed increases to tuition fees. We were very quickly able to identify the different aspects and topics that the students named if they addressed social concerns or social inequality, if they thought that the quality of their studies would be improved by increased tuition and fees, or if they named legal aspects, such as the argument that the German constitution guarantees every individual's right to an education and that imposing additional fees would be illegal. Using the word frequency lists, the terms were assigned to categories within the dictionary and the statements were coded automatically. Then it was easy to test our hypotheses, such as 'Students connect the issues surrounding increased tuition fees more frequently with social inequality than with any improvements in the quality of their studies' or 'If a student names social aspects, he or she also names legal aspects'.

Since word-based analyses are limited to single words or short phrases and cannot decipher the ambiguity of words, they are of limited use when it comes to complex research questions. However, such techniques may sometimes supplement qualitative text analysis. They provide a different perspective on the data, draw attention to individual words, and thus allow additional forms of analysis that can help researchers to discover relationships within the data that may not have been visible in other ways. Furthermore, word-based analyses are not very time- or labour-intensive because they can be conducted on the data without further preparation.

8.12 Summary and Concluding Remarks

The emphasis of this chapter has been on the opportunities for using computer programs to effectively support and facilitate the process of QCA. This starts with the transcription of interviews or focus groups, either automatically or manually with software support. Particularly helpful for qualitative content analysis is QDA software, with which researchers can develop category systems, code data, retrieve coded text segments, and analyse them in a multi-stage process. Categories can be further refined in the analysis process. For example, they can be more finely differentiated or combined into more general, abstract categories. An advantage of computer-assisted work is that coding and categories remain linked to the original data through all phases of analysis. QDA software enables the definitions associated with each category, and supplementary examples from the original data, to be accessed instantly. In this way, a complete code book is automatically created that provides the framework for coding the data.

Researchers in a team can collaborate very well using QDA software, because every step of the work is recorded, so that it can be determined at any time, for example, who coded which parts of the text with which categories and who wrote which paraphrase or memo.

For all three strategies of qualitative content analysis described in this book – structuring, evaluative, and type-building QCA – we have described in detail in this chapter how to carry out the individual steps with QDA software. We have paid special attention to how QDA software can support the analysis phases after the coding of the data, and we have presented a variety of options for qualitative and quantitative analytical procedures. The options we have described are intended to serve as suggestions; there is no requirement for all of the possibilities described here to be realized, and we do not claim that our analysis suggestions are exhaustive. There are no limits to your creativity for further, new forms of analysis after coding.

9

QUALITY STANDARDS, RESEARCH REPORT, AND DOCUMENTATION

───────── Chapter objectives ─────────

In this chapter you will learn about:

- Quality standards within qualitative research
- Internal standards of quality, such as reliability, credibility, and authenticity
- External standards of quality, such as transferability
- Calculating coefficients of intercoder agreement
- Determining intercoder agreement in qualitative content analysis
- Consensual coding
- Preparing and composing your research report
- Including quotations in your report
- Documenting your qualitative content analysis process.

9.1 Quality Standards within QCA

How can you distinguish between a good and a poor qualitative content analysis? What standards exist? How should you plan and structure your research report? What should you document in your research report and what information should be placed in the appendix of the report? How should you cite quotations directly from the data? This chapter addresses practical questions like these, especially within the framework of a master's thesis or dissertation.

We cannot discuss quality standards within qualitative content analysis without considering the importance of standards in qualitative research. So, what standards generally apply to qualitative research? Do these standards differ from the classical standards of objectivity, reliability, and validity that have long been recognized in quantitative research? Discussions related to the standards within qualitative research date back to the 1980s and have been very controversial at times (Flick, 2007, pp. 487–510, 2009; Grunenberg, 2001; Guba & Lincoln, 1985; Kirk & Miller, 1986; Lamnek & Krell, 2016; Mayring, 2002; Spencer et al., 2003; Steinke, 1999, 2007). The points of reference for this debate were the classical criteria of standardization, measurability, accuracy, and reproducibility. These classical standards were all developed within the framework of psychological test theory, in settings that have little in common with qualitative research. In the discussions about quality criteria for qualitative research, three principal positions have emerged: universality of standards (i.e., there should be the same criteria for qualitative and quantitative research), specificity of standards for qualitative research, and rejection of standards for qualitative research (cf. Section 1.6). In the second variant ('specificity'), a distinction is also made between formulating new standards and reformulating classical standards.

Miles and Huberman (1994, pp. 277–280) formulated new criteria for qualitative research in the mid-1990s, based on the classical quality criteria of quantitative research (Table 9.1).

Table 9.1 Quality standards within quantitative and qualitative research

Quality standards within quantitative research	New quality standards within qualitative research (according to Miles and Huberman)
Objectivity	Confirmability
Reliability	Reliability, dependability, auditability
Internal validity	Credibility and authenticity
External validity	Transferability and adjustability

Ultimately, formulating quality standards will always be affected by epistemological assumptions or one's world view, as Creswell and Plano Clark (2018) note. The discussion regarding standards in qualitative research is complex and multi faceted; Döring and Bortz (2016) report on more than 100 catalogues of criteria. However, we will not address it any further here.

This book is oriented towards the pragmatic views of Creswell (2014), Seale (1999a), Flick (2018a), and others arguing for 'specificity'. These approaches are plausible because they attempt to find a new way to determine standards rather than simply blindly reject-ing or accepting the classical standards of quality. Their perspective encourages researchers to reformulate quality standards that are relevant to research institutions and can be used to analyse research proposals. Seale and Hammersley's *subtle realism* (Seale, 1999b, p. 469) serves as the basis for the following observations on the subject of quality standards within qualitative text analysis. Their observations are based on three premises. First, the validity of knowledge cannot be determined with certainty because assumptions can only be judged according to plausibility and credibility. Second, phenomena exist independently of our assumptions about them, although our assumptions can vary in closeness of fit. Third, reality is accessible from several perspectives we may hold on the phenomena. Research aims to present reality, not to reproduce it. In empirical qualitative research, the main question is how well the researchers' representations are founded in the data.

In the following, we will discuss quality standards for QCA. It seems useful to distin-guish between *internal standards of quality* (i.e., authenticity and credibility) and *external standards of quality* (i.e., how well you can transfer and generalize a study). The terms internal and external standards of quality intentionally refer to the terms internal and external validity, which stem from the classical hypothetical-deductive research para-digm. Our terms demonstrate that the classical standards cannot simply be copied over to qualitative research; rather, they have to be modified and extended in order to take into account the procedural nature of qualitative research (Flick, 2020). For QCA as a method of analysis, internal standards of quality are primarily relevant, while transfer-ring and generalizing the results depends more on the structure of the entire study – its design as well as the methods used for sampling. As with the classical quality standards of internal and external validity, internal quality is considered critical for a study's external quality.

9.2 Checklist for Internal Quality

Quality standards, such as credibility, authenticity, trustworthiness, transferability, and auditability, do not just apply to the approach used for QCA, but are regarded as quality standards for the entire research project. In fact, the quality of the collected data often only becomes clear during the analysis. Did the interviews achieve authenticity and depth? Did you conduct the interviews according to the rules laid out for the given type of interview? Are the interviewee's answers consistent and credible? Is the structure of the interview appropriate?

The following checklist contains key questions used to evaluate the internal quality of a study:

(a) In relation to data collection and transcription, these points are important:

- How were the data recorded? Using audio or video recordings, for example?
- Was an interview assessment document (postscript) prepared in which the interview situation and specifics were recorded? When was the postscript prepared?

- Was a full transcription of the interview made?
- Did you follow rules for transcription? Will you disclose these rules?
- What did the transcription process entail?
- Who completed the transcription? The researchers? Or others?
- Did you use specialized transcription software?
- Has the data been anonymized? In what way?
- Was it possible to synchronize the audio recording with the transcript?

(b) The following questions are important for the implementation of the QCA:

- Is the selected method of content analysis appropriate for the research question?
- How do you justify your choice of method?
- Did you implement the selected method correctly?
- Did you complete the content analysis with computer assistance?
- Were the data coded by multiple independent coders?
- How did you achieve consistency in the codings? How did you address any inconsistencies?
- Is the category system coherent?
- Are the categories and sub-categories well structured?
- How precise are the category definitions?
- Did you include typical examples for the categories?
- Does the qualitative analysis take all of the data into account?
- How often did you process the data in order to determine the final codings – that is, how many iterations or phases of coding work were completed?
- Is it possible to audit – that is, is the coding traceable?
- Have you considered any unusual or abnormal cases? How have you drawn attention to them and analysed them?
- Did you compose memos during the analysis? When? Did you apply any form or structure to them?
- Have you included quotations from the data in your research report? How did you select them? Did you select them according to their plausibility or have you also included counter-examples and contradictions?
- Can you justify your conclusions based on the data?
- What was documented and archived, how and in what form?

On the last point, additional information is provided in Section 9.6. Also, a decisive criterion for potential reviews and expert opinions is whether the methodological procedure for QCA is transparent and reflected. For reviewers, it is a considerable advantage if you have worked with QDA software, because then it is very easy to see how elaborate the categories are, how reliable the assignments of text passages to categories are, and what degree of reflection is shown in the written memos.

The criteria mentioned mostly focus on the procedural aspects of the research process, and place less emphasis on static evaluations as they are calculated in quantitative research, for example, in the form of coefficients of intercoder reliability. Since the process of coding is of central importance in QCA, the question of the quality of the codings and the agreement of the coders will be considered in more detail in the following section.

9.3 Intercoder Agreement

When the phrase 'quality criteria of qualitative content analysis' is mentioned, most people probably first associate it with 'intercoder reliability'. This is also what we will be dealing with in the following, but using the label 'intercoder agreement', which avoids the term 'reliability' which is inextricably linked with measurement theory and the demand for replicability. Whenever quantitative content analysis is mentioned, however, the term 'intercoder reliability' will be used.

In Chapter 3 it was argued that a distinction should be made between the *formation* of a category system and its *application*. No claim to intercoder agreement can be made on the formation of a category system. If several people develop categories on the basis of the same data, perfect agreement cannot be postulated as this cannot be achieved through detailed instructions and rules. Category development – whether inductively based on the material or deductive – is an act of construction based on the prior knowledge, experience, and not least the 'world-views' of the analysts. The more they agree in their knowledge and experience and the more similar they are in terms of general principles of category development, the more likely it is that independently formed category systems will be similar. But a coefficient of agreement here would say little about the quality of the category system; instead, it would probably measure something that was not intended to be measured at all. It could be, for example, that the analysts apply Charmaz's practice of category development, namely to develop only action-oriented categories in the form of the gerund, thereby showing a high level of agreement among themselves. However, this would not be evidence of the appropriateness and quality of the categories formed, but merely a measurement of the orientation towards Charmaz's approach.

The requirement for agreement between coders thus primarily refers to the application of the categories (i.e., the coding of data). With regard to the process of coding, however, there are now some serious difficulties for coding standards in the context of quantitative content analysis, which require more detailed treatment. The following considerations clearly show that a simple transfer of the classical quality criteria, in this case those of intercoder reliability, from quantitative content analysis is not possible. Instead, it is necessary to develop new criteria based on the classical criteria described above. In the first step, therefore, the mode of determining reliability in quantitative content analysis is presented; this is followed by reflections on determining intercoder agreement in qualitative content analysis.

Intercoder Reliability in Quantitative Content Analysis

In quantitative content analysis, the calculation of agreements between coders follows the model of measuring observer agreement or rater agreement. Following the terms used in psychological test theory, one usually speaks here of 'intercoder reliability'. The related term 'intracoder reliability' refers to a measurement in which the same person codes the same data again after a sufficient time interval.

In quantitative content analysis, the procedure is that coding units are defined in advance, before coding, and the coders assign categories or sub-categories of the category system to these units. For the sake of simplicity, we will consider the situation for only one category, two coders, and ten coding units. In Table 9.2, the value '1' indicates that the category has been coded and '0' that it has not been coded.

Table 9.2 Coding table for ten coding units, two coders, and one category

Coding unit	Coder 1	Coder 2
1	0	0
2	1	1
3	0	1
4	0	0
5	1	1
6	1	0
7	1	1
8	0	0
9	0	1
10	1	1

At first glance, it can be seen that many codings match (unit 1, 2, 4, 5, 7, 8, 10), but there are also some non-matches (unit 3, 6, 9). The table of all coding units can be condensed into a table with four cells as shown in Table 9.3. In the main diagonal, the matches are shown, namely in cell a (1/1 = both coders have coded the category) and d (0/0 = both coders have not coded the category). The non-matches are found in cells b (1/0 = only coder 1 coded the category) and c (0/1 = only coder 2 coded the category).

Table 9.3 Table of matches for one category and two coders (general form)

Coder 1	Coder 2		
	Coded	Not coded	Total
Coded	a	b	$a + b$
Not coded	c	d	$c + d$
Total	$a + c$	$b + d$	$N = a + b + c + d$

For the example of Table 9.2 with ten coding units, the agreement table is given in Table 9.4. In three coding units (1, 4 and 8) there is agreement in not coding the categories (cell d), in four units the category was coded in agreement (cell a), and in a total of three units we find non-agreement (once 0/1 in cell b; twice 1/0 in cell c).

Table 9.4 Table of matches for one category and two coders

Coder 1	Coder 2		
	Coded	Not coded	Total
Coded	4	1	5
Not coded	2	3	5
Total	6	4	10

A simple measure of agreement is to calculate the relative proportion of matching codings out of the total number of codings (N):

$$p_0 = (a+d)/N.$$

For the data in the example above, the result is 0.7 (i.e., 70% of all codings match).

More commonly used than this simple percentage measure of agreement is Cohen's kappa reliability coefficient. Kappa is based on the assumption that a certain level of agreement would be expected even if the coders were to assign categories to the coding units purely by chance. In our example, we proceed as follows. The corresponding probabilities are calculated via the marginal frequencies. The probability that coder 1 does not code a coding unit is

$$p_{1,\text{not coded}} = (c+d)/N = 5/10 = 0.5,$$

and that coder 1 does code a coding unit is

$$p_{1,\text{coded}} = (a+b)/N = 5/10 = 0.5.$$

The same calculations for coder 2 yield

$$p_{2,\text{not coded}} = (b+d)/N = 4/10 = 0.4,$$

$$p_{2,\text{coded}} = (a+c)/N = 6/10 = 0.6.$$

The estimated probabilities for random matches are now, for a random match in non-coding,

$$p_{e,\text{not coded}} = p_{1,\text{not coded}} \times p_{2,\text{not coded}} = 0.5 \times 0.4 = 0.2;$$

and for a match in coding,

$$p_{e,coded} = p_{1,coded} \times p_{2,coded} = 0.5 \times 0.6 = 0.3.$$

The estimated total proportion p_e of random match is the sum of the two probabilities:

$$p_e = p_{e,not\ coded} + p_{e,coded} = 0.2 + 0.3 = 0.5.$$

The kappa coefficient according to Cohen (1960) incorporates this expected frequency of random matches into the calculation of intercoder reliability. Kappa is defined as

$$\kappa = \frac{p_0 - p_e}{1 - p_e}.$$

Kappa here is therefore (0.7 − 0.5) / (1 − 0.5) = 0.4 and thus the coefficient is considerably lower than the relative or percentage agreement (p_0).

This calculation of kappa can easily be extended to more than one category, for example to four categories, resulting in Table 9.5. Cell *a* contains the number of coding units for which both coders have applied category 1 (so these are agreements). Cell *b* contains the number of coding units for which coder 1 has applied category 1 while coder 2 applied category 2 (so this is a disagreement). Therefore, only the cells *a, f, k,* and *p* on the diagonal contain the agreements; all other cells indicate disagreements.

Table 9.5 Table for two coders and four categories

Coder 1	Coder 2				
	Cat. 1	Cat. 2	Cat. 3	Cat. 4	Total
Cat. 1	a	b	c	d	a + b + c + d
Cat. 2	e	f	g	h	e + f + g + h
Cat. 3	i	j	k	l	i + j + k + l
Cat. 4	m	n	o	p	m + n + o + p
Total	a + e + i + m	b + f + j + n	c + g + k + o	d + h + l + p	N

The probabilities for each of the four categories are now calculated for both coders via the marginal frequencies and then the estimated probabilities of random agreement are determined for all four categories, summed and entered into the kappa formula.

So how is the level of the kappa coefficient evaluated? What is interpreted a good or very good value for intercoder reliability? As a rule of thumb, kappa values above 0.6 are assessed as good, above 0.8 as very good. It should be noted that the level of kappa is strongly dependent on the distribution of the marginal frequencies, and kappa values can be unreasonably small in the case of asymmetrical distributions (Feinstein & Cicchetti, 1990). There are alternative measures of intercoder reliability such as Krippendorff's alpha and Scott's pi (Krippendorff, 2004b; Zhao et al., 2012) which, however, are beyond the scope of this chapter.

Intercoder Agreement in Qualitative Content Analysis

How can the problem of intercoder agreement be addressed in QCA? There is no doubt that the agreement of two (or more) coders in the application of a category system is desirable and represents a quality criterion for the analysis. After all, what would the category-based analyses and the analyses of the interrelationships between categories be worth if one cannot rely on the codings?

However, many qualitative researchers will immediately ask themselves whether it is really useful to calculate a coefficient of agreement or whether such a calculation only makes sense within quantitative research. The calculation of percentage agreement, Cohen's kappa, and similar coefficients cannot be easily transferred to the logic of coding and segmenting in QCA:

> A very important difference is that in qualitative content analysis the data is usually not segmented in advance. The processes of segmenting and coding belong together – they form a unity. In most situations in qualitative content analysis, units of meaning are coded, that is, the coders are free to determine the beginning and end of such a meaning unit.

This means that a table like Table 9.2 cannot be created easily, because the coders may have segmented differently. And yet this table is the starting point for all subsequent calculations. Before discussing ways and means of calculating coefficients of agreement despite these difficulties, however, it should first be noted that there are two ways of ensuring the agreement of coders in QCA: a qualitative way via the collaborative checking of codings ('consensual coding') and a quantitative way via the calculation of percentage agreement and, if necessary, also of a suitable coefficient that takes the probability of chance agreement into account.

Consensual Coding in Qualitative Content Analysis

A procedure frequently employed in qualitative research to check the quality of coding is the method described as 'subjective assessment' by Guest et al. (2012, p. 91): two coders code the same text independently of each other and then compare their codings. Hopf and Schmidt have called such a procedure 'consensual coding' (Hopf & Schmidt, 1993, pp. 61–63).

In general, there is an important difference in research practice between qualitative and quantitative content analysis with regard to the coders themselves. While in quantitative content analyses it is usually a matter of using assistants (or student assistants) specially trained for this task, in qualitative content analyses it is usually the researchers (or members of the research team) who take on this extremely important task. So, what does consensual coding look like in practice? What problems arise? First of all, in a research team, care must be taken to ensure that pairs of researchers coding an interview are frequently reselected – that is, fixed pairs of coders should be avoided. Coding of the same interview is done independently with the same code book. Questions and uncertainties with applying the categories are noted, with memos or comments on the coding in question if QDA software is used. Next follows the joint part, which is much more effective if QDA software is used to visualize the codings of both persons simultaneously on the text. Differences in code applications are discussed and the coders look up the corresponding category definitions as their guideline. Where the differences are resolved with mutual agreement, this coding is recorded; possibly a suggestion for improving the category definitions is also noted, which can then be brought to the next team meeting.

What happens if the two coders still cannot agree? In this situation, a third person can be called in. It is best to appoint a person in the team beforehand who will take on the role of supervisor for the coding phase and then decide in each instance, after listening to the arguments, which coding should take place. With very important disagreements, the decision can be postponed to a team meeting. However, this should only be done in the case of differences of fundamental importance for the development of the category system.

What pitfalls should one expect? Consensual coding is laborious and requires a willingness to put forward good arguments for the codes applied. It is therefore not expedient or desirable to act according to the principle of 'the wiser head gives in'. Routine, as would be established by fixed coding pairs, should therefore be avoided.

Calculating the Intercoder Agreement in Qualitative Content Analysis

As stated above, due to the lack of fixed coding units, the procedure of calculating agreement, which is common in quantitative content analysis, cannot simply be transferred to qualitative content analysis. Solutions might be found in two ways: firstly, one can consider the issues around defining the boundaries of the coded segments; and secondly, one can try to carry out a modified calculation of agreement coefficients based on segment-oriented coding.

If one considers each interview or, in more general terms, each document, as a coding unit, a percentage agreement can be calculated for each of these units and from this an average agreement of two coders derived. This can be done by creating a coder-by-category table for each document, as illustrated in Table 9.6. A '1' means that the category was coded somewhere in the document, a '0' that it was not coded anywhere. For four of the categories in the example there is agreement, for one (category 3) there is not. This results in a percentage agreement of 4 / 5 = 0.8 = 80%.

Table 9.6 Comparison of coding for two coders and multiple categories

Category	Coder 1	Coder 2
Category 1	0	0
Category 2	1	1
Category 3	0	1
Category 4	0	0
Category 5	1	1

Of course, this extension of the coding unit to the entire case is associated with considerable loss of information. In contrast to the very fine-grained coding of segments, only the entire interview is considered here – highly aggregated. The loss of information by defining documents as coding units is reduced not only if the coders' comparison table takes into account whether the category was coded, but also when the frequency of coding of the category in the document is taken as a basis. The comparison table in Table 9.7 serves as an example. For this table, too, there is agreement in 4 out of 5 categories (i.e., 80%).

Table 9.7 Comparison of frequency of coding for two coders and several categories

Category	Coder 1	Coder 2
Category 1	4	4
Category 2	1	1
Category 3	3	4
Category 4	0	0
Category 5	5	5

The most difficult way to measure the level of coder agreement in QCA is to make a *segment-specific calculation*. Among others, the following situations can be distinguished:

1 Coder 1 and coder 2 both coded exactly the same text passage with the same category.
2 Coder 1 and coder 2 both coded the same text passage with the same category, but not with exactly the same segment boundaries (i.e., the codings overlap but are not identical).
3 Coder 1 has coded the text passage with category A, while coder 2 has coded exactly the same text passage with category B.
4 Coder 1 coded the text passage with category A, while coder 2 coded an overlapping passage with category B.
5 Coder 1 has coded the text passage with category A, while coder 2 has not.[1]

Before one can create a category-specific matching table similar to the one in Table 9.3 it is first necessary to clarify how a coding unit is to be defined and what is counted as a match. Let us consider the above five situations:

- Situation 1 and situation 3 are not problematic: the coding units are clearly defined ('the same text passage'). In situation 1 we have a match, in situation 3

---

[1] Not yet considered here are the complex cases where, for example, coder 1 has coded a segment with category A and coder 2 has coded the same segment with categories B, C, and D.

we do not. Situation 5 is also easy to manage. For coder 2, there is no coding unit in the text, but for the calculation of the coefficient it is assumed that there is a coding unit and that it has not been coded.

- Situation 2 needs to be clarified, because the same category was assigned, but the segment boundaries are different. It hardly makes sense to always demand a 100% match between the segment boundaries in qualitative coding; otherwise it would be considered a non-match if one coder had coded a punctuation mark or a space at the end and the other had not. It is therefore more appropriate to allow some tolerance, for example, if 90% of the characters in the two coded segments overlap, then this is counted as a match.

- Situation 4, in which two differently coded segments overlap, is still more unclear. Is this one coding unit that was coded differently (like situation 3) or two instances of situation 5? At first glance, it might be a good idea to follow the 90% rule, that is, if 90% of characters of the coded segments overlap, it is one coding unit, otherwise two separate coding units. In qualitative coding, however, it is common for several codings to overlap or be nested within each other, that is, ex-post definition of coding units does not work.

Instead of such an unsatisfactory ex-post definition of coding units, the following procedure is recommended. First, all codings of coder 1 are examined. Each coding is treated as one coding unit. It is considered a match if coder 2 has assigned the same category to the segment after allowing for an agreed range of tolerance over its boundaries. When all codings of coder 1 have been evaluated, the same procedure is followed for coder 2: examine all codings made by coder 2 and compare them with those of coder 1. Thus, the total number of coding units is equal to the sum of the numbers of codings made by each coder; implicit in this method is that even an exactly matched segment is counted as two segments. A contingency table for a new example can now be created, as in Table 9.8. The percentage agreement can be easily calculated from the table:

$$\frac{\text{Number of matching codings}}{\text{Total number of codings}} = \frac{a+d}{N} = \frac{6}{13} = 46\%.$$

Table 9.8 Match table for two coders

Coder 1	Coder 2		
	Coded	Not coded	Total
Coded	a = 6	b = 4	a + b = 10
Not coded	c = 3	d = 0	c + d = 3
Total	a + c = 9	b + d = 4	N = 13

But what about the calculation of a chance-corrected coefficient, namely kappa? Due to the method of qualitative coding, which normally takes place without a priori definition of coding units, the cell d always remains zero, because segmenting and coding are one and the same process and so logically there cannot exist any segments that were not coded by both coders, because, for a segment to exist, it must have been coded by someone. The calculation of the random agreement via the marginal totals is therefore not possible. Instead one can follow a suggestion by Brennan and Prediger (1981): the random agreement is calculated based on the number of different categories from which the two coders could choose. Supposing the category system consists of 10 categories. Then the expected value of random agreement is

$$p_e = \frac{1}{\text{Number of categories}} = 0.10,$$

while kappa is

$$\kappa = \frac{p_0 - p_e}{1 - p_e} = \frac{0.46 - 0.10}{1 - 0.10} = \frac{0.36}{0.90} = 0.40.$$

Usually, the number of categories and sub-categories in QCA is greater than 10, so that kappa is usually only slightly lower than the percentage agreement. However, it must be asked what 'chance-corrected' means in qualitative coding. With fixed coding units and mutually exclusive categories, it seems reasonable to assume that, for example, with 10 categories, the probability of randomly coding the 'right' one is equal to 1/10. With free segmenting and coding, one could accordingly calculate the random correction based on words. For example, given a text with 3000 words, how likely is it that one particular word or phrase will be randomly coded with the same category by two independent coders? That probability should asymptotically tend to zero as the size of text increases. It can be concluded that the calculation of kappa (or any other chance-corrected coefficient) only makes sense if coding units are defined a priori.

Consensual Coding and/or Coefficient of Agreement?

Should coefficients of intercoder agreement be calculated at all in QCA? Would it not be better to practise consensual coding and thus actually make all calculations of coefficients superfluous? If consensus is reached on all codings, the intercoder agreement becomes 100% and the calculation of kappa is then also superfluous, isn't it? In principle, the answer is 'yes, that's true', but there is usually not enough time in a research project to code all the data in a consensual way. In most situations, the laborious procedure of two people coding and then discussing differences will only be practicable at the beginning of the coding phase using a sample of the data set. However, when checking for agreement in the early stages of coding, the calculation of coefficients, especially the detailed calculation per category, can save a lot of time that can be well used elsewhere in the project. The percentage agreement figures can easily be used to identify the categories that are problematical and need to be worked on together; the category definitions can be inspected again and revised if necessary.

In this way, the calculation of intercoder agreements, if done with QDA software, can be an effective support in reaching a high level of agreement quickly and effectively in the team. It also becomes clear which coders deviate particularly frequently. Another advantage is that an overall coefficient is calculated, which might be a helpful indicator of the quality of coding.

In addition, the calculation of the coefficients may have a legitimizing function. Reviewers who come from the field of quantitative research and are committed to the hypothetico-deductive paradigm often request that information on the intercoder reliability be provided. A lack of such information is seen as a deficit. Similarly, preference is often given to the kappa coefficient over the calculation of percentage agreement. If kappa is not calculated, this is often considered a weakness, although the random effect in an analysis with a typical qualitative category system is usually very small. In qualitative coding with free segmenting and coding, the calculation of kappa makes little sense because here the model on which kappa is based is simply not appropriate for the reality of the coding process in QCA. If reviewers nevertheless require the calculation of kappa, then coding units should be defined a priori.

9.4 Validity Checks

Even if all items of the checklist presented in Section 9.2 are answered satisfactorily, this internal assessment of the study's quality does not guarantee validity – that is, the validity of the results. This is true even if consensual coding was practised and possibly even if checks were made on the coders' agreements, including the calculation of intercoder coefficients. The issue of validity of results plays an important role in all scientific research, but it is quite controversial in qualitative research (Whittemore et al., 2001). The positions of *methodological creativity* and *methodological rigour* form the extreme ends of the discussion. In Section 1.6, following Seale, we argued for the concept of subtle realism, that is, we took a position that is more oriented towards methodological rigour. This is logical for the method of QCA with its principles of systematics and structured procedures. There are several strategies for validity testing that have their usefulness in the practice of qualitative research, among them the following:

- *Discussion with experts (peer debriefing)*. This means regular meetings with competent persons outside the research team. These experts comment on the approach and the first results of the project and, if necessary, draw attention to phenomena and facts that are easily overlooked.

- *Discussion with research participants (member checking).* This means the discussion of the analysis results with the research participants themselves in order to receive informed feedback on the research results in the sense of 'communicative validation'.
- *Extended stay in the field.* A longer stay in the field or a return to the field can also help to avoid hasty diagnoses and false conclusions in the analysis of the material.
- *Triangulation or use of mixed methods.* Techniques of triangulation and the combination of different research methods (Creswell & Plano Clark, 2018; Denzin, 1978; Flick, 2018b; Kelle, 2008; Kuckartz, 2014b) result in more diverse perspectives on the research results and thus also the possibility of increasing generalizability.

9.5 Transferability and Generalization

How can it be ensured that the results of the analyses have relevance beyond one's own study, that they not only have situational validity but also can be generalized? This question not only concerns the process of using the method of QCA, but also is very important for the general *usefulness of* a study. Generalization or transferability of the results is clearly considered by numerous authors to be one of the goals of qualitative research (Flick, 2009, p. 26). The question of transferability should therefore be asked when writing up the results of a QCA. However, it should be noted that in qualitative research it is not *always* necessary to generalize. Think, for example, of ethnographic studies that deliberately do not strive for generalized theories. Such studies focus, for example, on life in a rural village, as a teacher in Bronx Park Middle School, or as a Bulgarian meat packer in a Polish factory. The dense description that is the goal in these studies has its own truth. The question of transferability is then left to the considerations and assessments of the academic audience, which is quite justified. However, it is equally justified to *want to generalize in* qualitative research as well.

In a hypothetical study where qualitative interviews were conducted, six male and six female teachers were asked about their perception of inclusive schooling of children in everyday school life. The data were analysed by means of structuring QCA in compliance with all rules. Can the results of this study be generalized? The first questions that should be asked in this regard concern the sample: Who was interviewed in the study? Are they teachers from a particular school? Perhaps even a particular type of school such as a private school, a religious school, or a school in a particular district? How were the interviewees selected? By chance, quota sampling, convenience sampling, snowball sampling? How transparent is the selection process? Were 'normal teachers' interviewed, or members of a particular group such as young teachers, politically active, or trade union members?

Let us look at another problem. If the result on a certain research question is the same for 100% of the teachers surveyed, then it seems plausible to transfer that result to other teachers outside the sample; but what happens if results were only observed in a subset of two-thirds or only one-third of the sample? In such situations, it is important to ask what your real motives are for extending the results. Why do you want to generalize at all? Often the answer is that it will not be enough for most researchers to only make statements about a small group of perhaps only 12 respondents after a relatively elaborate study. Such a minimalist claim would probably also disappoint the scientific community to whom the results are presented. But it is not only the problem of the small number of research participants that plays a role here. Even with 100 or 200 respondents, which is a large number of cases for a qualitative study, questions about the composition of the sample and the selection process are still relevant. For example, if I want to find out about the consequences of unemployment, then the selection of 100 respondents in a single small town in Saxony may not be adequate to answer far-reaching questions about the chances of success for political measures for the unemployed. The implicit claim by such a researcher is that the selected small town should be the laboratory for many towns, or at least for many small towns. Let us look at what generalization strategies are available in social science research:

1 *Probabilistic strategy.* This strategy assumes a defined population and a random sample. Probabilities and confidence intervals can be calculated, and generalization is done on this basis.
2 *Experimental strategy.* Experiments are conducted with randomized experimental and control groups. The context of the experiments is controlled as far as possible; before and after observations or measurements are carried out. Due to controlled random allocation, significant differences between experimental and control groups can be generalized.
3 *Saturation in repeated investigations.* For example, in a natural environment with different groups of children, I observe the children's behaviour when they play with marbles. Their negotiation processes and the dispute situations are recorded. The experiment is repeated several times and the results are always the same, that is, they can be replicated. Until proven otherwise, the results can be generalized.
4 *Theoretical strategy.* A theory forms the background, such as the assumption that all people are almost identical in terms of basic physiological functions: When a person cuts their wrists, a lot of blood comes out and the person bleeds to death if no one comes to help. For the purpose of generalization, a large sample is not necessary; $n = 2$ is sufficient to generalize the result to all people in the same situation.
5 *Abductive strategy.* A surprising result leads to a new theoretical assumption, a new rule that can explain the results obtained in a convincing way. In a study on 'fathers' months',[2] for example, the young fathers surveyed might show that an altered perception of fatherhood (and not, as initially assumed by the researchers, the parental allowance) was the decisive driving force. Of all five strategies, this generalization strategy has the highest risk of leading to wrong conclusions.

---

[2]"In Germany, both parents can receive a parental allowance for a maximum of 12 months. This can be extended by 2 months with the help of the so-called 'fathers' months' or 'fathers' time'.

It should be obvious that in qualitative studies, generalization strategies 1 and 2 are usually not available. Due to time and budget constraints, the third strategy is also rarely conceivable. So, if the classical critical-rationalist strategies with random sampling and inferential statistics are not applicable, then the argumentative justification of generalizations is required, that is, a new theory must be developed and it must be convincingly demonstrated that it can explain the research results as a 'case of'. In doing so, one should be aware of the risky nature of abductive inferences – as Peirce (1931/1974, p. 106) puts it: 'Abduction merely suggests that something *may be*'.

Because of this general problem, it seems to make sense to give preference to the term 'transferability' over 'generalization', because transferability has a certain inherent limitation of expansion, while generalization suggests boundlessness. The goal of generalization in the sense of critical-rationalist strategies is – as is well known in qualitative research – not achievable anyway. Furthermore, according to the self-understanding of qualitative research, this goal does not make sense at all, because of what is known about difference and diversity, about the context- and situation-bound nature of phenomena in the social fields. For example, there are working-class young people who study at universities, although all research shows that they are at a great disadvantage. This social fact is true even if it only applies to 5% of a group. Generalized statements are not the primary goal of qualitative research and probabilistic ones (e.g., 'The chances of a working-class child getting a degree are four times less than those of a middle-class child') are a matter for quantitatively oriented social research. When the researchers of the famous Marienthal study wanted to know how large was the proportion of the different types of attitudes they had identified, they did not rely on the numbers of their qualitative study but conducted a survey to determine the exact distribution of the identified types of attitudes. In the context of qualitative research, percentages and distributions can only be indications or rough estimates. So, beware of such generalizing statements as 'This is how doctors think', 'This is how nurses or teachers think', or even 'This is how Americans think'. If, however, random sampling was carried out within the framework of a qualitative study and the number of cases is sufficient, confidence intervals and parameters can of course also be calculated, but such studies are very rare.

Note that the generalization strategies common in quantitative research cannot be used, or can only be used very rarely, in qualitative research due to its sampling strategies and limited sample sizes. The question of transferability to external contexts should, however, be considered in the results report and, according to Flick (2009, p. 276), concrete steps should be taken to check and assess transferability.

9.6 Research Report and Documentation

A common misconception is that you cannot record the results until you have reached a certain point towards the end of the research process. This is simply not true. You should write continuously throughout the entire research process and particularly throughout the data analysis process. Doing so enables you to accumulate a good deal of material that you can use to write your final research report, which simply constitutes the last stage of this continuous writing process.

At the end of the research work there must be results – as was quoted at the beginning of this book in the forum contribution of a diploma student: 'One wants to report results, after all'. When integrating the various fragments of content that have emerged during the analysis, one should always ask oneself: What is my research question? Whatever you include in the report should answer this question, as it indicates how relevant and how useful the information is in practice or for further research.

Everything that you have written in the course of the analysis forms the basis for the research report, including:

- Memos that you have written, especially theory memos
- Category descriptions including typical examples
- Case summaries
- Excerpts from the literature or reviews
- Presentations and articles that you may have written over the course of the research project
- Graphical models and diagrams, such as concept maps
- Visualizations, such as relationships of categories
- Project diary or journal, in which not only the research process but also ideas, reflections and comments were recorded.

Thus, when you start writing the research report, you have a sort of inventory of everything that you have already produced over the course of the research process. If you are working in a team, gaining an overview of this inventory may prove to be a time-consuming task; however, it will also reveal any gaps or areas that require additional preparation. A good amount of literature has been published that provides instructions for writing research papers; thus, we will not list them here. As various authors correctly point out, not all researchers rely on the same writing process or structure. However, you should start with an outline, which could be based on the following general structure:

1 Introduction, including presentation of the state of research
2 Explanation of the research question and presentation of any hypotheses and theories on which it is based (if you have formulated hypotheses or your research is based on specific theories)
3 Description of your research methods
4 Results of your research
5 Conclusions.

Other important differentiations arise on their own. For example, the methods used to collect data, the type and rules for transcription, and the steps in the qualitative text analysis process will be described in your methods chapter. You can emphasize different elements of your project depending on whether you are writing an academic thesis, a research project funded by a third party, or an evaluation. Naturally, you may have to adhere to certain forms more rigidly and fulfil more specific and detailed requirements in the methods sections of academic theses than in other types of papers. In evaluations, the results, the assessments carried out by the evaluators and their consequences are usually of primary importance.

When writing the research report in qualitative research, researchers often encounter a phenomenon that Huberman and Miles refer to as 'data overload'. When you have collected so much interesting data, it can be difficult to see the wood for the trees, so to speak. Thus, it can be difficult to select the results and their underlying data. What should you report and what should you omit? Why should you include this case summary and not that one? Why are you focusing on a given category?

Unfortunately, researchers often use up most of their time and energy on transcribing and coding the data. These first few steps of the analysis process can understandably consume large amounts of time, which means that researchers lack the time and energy necessary to conduct complex analyses and compose their research reports. We recommend keeping the entire research process in mind, allotting sufficient time for writing and recording your results after you have completed the analysis, and – as mentioned above – thinking about what you would like to write throughout the entire analysis.

While writing, you might worry that your results could have repercussions on the field that you have researched. It is essential that you anticipate these potential effects and include them in your report. This is especially true for evaluations. The Standards for Evaluations, originally developed by the Joint Committee on Standards for Educational Evaluation (JCSEE; see Yarbrough et al., 2011), emphasize the need for fairness:

> P4 *Clarity and Fairness* Evaluations should be understandable and fair in addressing stakeholder needs and purposes.[3]

You should take such standards into account when writing a report and consult the client and stakeholders before finalizing your text, if necessary.

Quotations from the Original Data

When writing their report, quantitative researchers have a quasi-natural tendency to communicate *numbers* to the scientific community in the form of percentages, coefficients, correlations, etc., and in this way to make visible what the research has determined.

---

[3]See the program evaluation standards on the website of the American Evaluation Association at https://www.eval.org/About/Competencies-Standards/Program-Evaluation-Standards (accessed 20 March 2022).

Qualitative researchers feel the same way about *verbal data*, which should show the scientific community what the result of the analytical work looks like. Wanting to quote passages from the open interviews, for example, is perfectly natural and there is no reason not to include quotes in your research report. Every quote must be labelled as such and omissions must be noted. Like quotations from other sources, all quotes should contain information regarding their source, including the interview name and paragraph or line number. For example, '(R07: para. 14)' and '(Ms. Stone: lines 311–315)' represent valid citations with source information. The first example includes an abbreviated interview name and a paragraph number, and the second example contains an interviewee pseudonym and line numbers.

Quotations should be used sparingly; they should not comprise more than a quarter of the results section, even in a thesis. Reproducing authentic 'sound bites' may seem attractive, but it gives the scholarly paper or thesis a non-analytic character, which should be avoided.

Be aware of the danger of selective plausibility – using original quotations to justify each analytical finding. It can be tempting to do so, but it will likely make your readers suspicious. Thus, you should present contrasting statements in the research report and include a broad spectrum of answers using quotations.

Documentation

Transparency and auditability were mentioned above in Section 9.1 as special quality criteria of qualitative research. This means that good documentation should be prepared. What should you document and in what form, for example, in an academic thesis? What information must be kept confidential? What should your evaluators be able to understand and verify, if desired?

In the methods section of your research report, you should describe your chosen method of QCA clearly and comprehensibly:

- How were the data selected for the analysis? How voluminous was the material? What was the nature of the material?
- Which type of QCA did you use and with what aim?
- How did you explore the data?
- How was the category system developed? Did it consist primarily of deductive or inductive categories, and how did it change over the course of the analysis, and why? What types of categories were used? If inductive categories were formed, how much data was used for this?
- How was coding organized? What criteria were used to define the segment boundaries? How many people worked on the coding and how was the joint coding cycle organized, if applicable?
- What procedures were used to ensure and verify coding quality? Was coder agreement assessed? With what results? How were non-agreements dealt with?

- How were the coded data analysed? What role did case-oriented and category-oriented approaches play?
- Which QDA software was used and which functions facilitated the analysis?

At a minimum, the categories that were central to the analysis should be presented in the text itself. However, the following elements also should be included in the appendix of a thesis or research report:

- Written documents that are important to the study, such as covering letters
- Transcription rules and references to relevant standards (which can also be included directly in the text)
- The interview guide (if applicable)
- The accompanying questionnaire (if you have used one)
- Information regarding the length of the individual interviews or at least the average duration and the range of the lengths of the interviews
- The code book, that is, the documentation of the category system, including examples
- One or more transcripts that serve as examples of the data collected and the type of transcription, if requested by the evaluators.

Moreover, you should submit the following data in electronic form (if the evaluators ask for it):

- The final version of the project file, if QDA software was used in the analysis
- Transcripts of the anonymized original data in a conventional standard format (DOCX, RTF or PDF); this is not necessary when QDA software was used, as the project file contains the transcripts.

Secondary Use of Data

Particularly for publicly funded research studies, it is imperative to make the collected data available to the scientific community for subsequent use after completing the study (OECD, 2007). Several data repositories such as the UK Data Service[4] offer options to deposit qualitative data. The requirement to make collected data available for further use also applies to studies in which QCA was used. However, it is critical to note that the archiving and secondary analysis of qualitative data is not unproblematic and in practice there are often many hurdles to overcome. On the legal and research ethics side, the archiving of interviews, in particular, is confronted with data protection and personal rights; on the practical side, qualitative data are more difficult to archive due

---

[4]https://www.ukdataservice.ac.uk/deposit-data.aspx (accessed 20 March 2022).

to reduced possibilities for standardization. Laudel and Bielick (2019) report numerous practical research problems in archiving guided interviews, and Corti et al. (2005) discuss the potential benefits and problems of secondary analyses of qualitative data in their introduction to a special issue of the online journal *FQS – Forum Qualitative Social Research* (www.qualitative-research.net).

The following particular aspects should be taken into account when considering the secondary use of data collected and analysed with QCA: first, the informed consent of all respondents to storage and secondary use of their data; and second, the sufficient anonymization of the data. On the Qualiservice website of the Research Data Centre for Qualitative Social Science Data at the University of Bremen, Germany, you can find numerous helpful tips and handouts, including template forms for consent declarations.[5]

The preparation of research data for subsequent use is supported by QDA software with various functions:

- The original data can be exported (without the coding done by the analysts), whereby some software packages also allow the automatic masking of marked areas.
- Individual QDA packages offer special functions for archiving and exporting the documents analysed, optionally with the associated audio and video files, the standardized background information (e.g., socio-demographic data), and the category system used.
- Entire projects or even just the code book can be stored in a general exchange format for QDA programs, the so-called REFI-QDA standard (www.qdasoftware. org), which is considered the preferred data format by some data archives.

9.7 Summary and Concluding Remarks

Usually, to be regarded as scientific, studies must meet certain standards and quality criteria. This also applies to studies that work with the method of qualitative content analysis. For several decades now there has been a discussion in the scientific community about the standards for qualitative research. Should qualitative research adopt the standards established in quantitative research? Should qualitative research develop its own standards, or should it even forgo the development of standards? In this chapter we argue in the spirit of Seales's pragmatism for appropriate criteria tailored to qualitative research. In doing so, we distinguish between external and internal study quality, whereby standards of internal study quality are primarily relevant for QCA as a method of analysis, while questions of validity, transferability of results, and possible generalizability must be answered against the background of the entire research design, especially sampling. QCA standards primarily include a carefully developed

---

[5]https://www.qualiservice.org/en/the-helpdesk.html (accessed 20 March 2022)

and well-documented category system and trustworthy coding of the data. If the data are coded by several analysts, we recommend the procedure of consensual coding. If researchers are more oriented towards the classical quality criteria of reliability and validity, coefficients for intercoder agreement can also be calculated. We describe in detail how this can be done.

At the end of a project there is always a written product, perhaps a research report, a master's thesis, or a dissertation. It is often essential to defend one's work in front of a sceptical audience. Research always takes place under specific circumstances and restrictions. For example, researchers do not have enough time, or do not have enough financial resources, field access was not as expected, and many other unexpected circumstances may arise. There is much written in textbooks on methods and methodology that cannot always be realized satisfactorily in research practice. Our advice is: work carefully and trust your work. Remember that the most important thing is to achieve useful results – ultimately to change the world with your research and, if possible, to improve it. So do not be upset when you hear criticism from a sceptical audience. Sometimes the criticism is levelled at researchers who work with the method of qualitative content analysis that QCA has no background theory. Politely counter such criticism by saying that you see QCA not as a world-view or methodology but as a method, and that what matters to you is producing substantive results. Be proud of the grounding that your results have in the empirical data, in their empirical justification. In the end, it is the findings that matter. Methods can provide valuable support, but they are not an end in themselves.

FINAL REMARKS

As a method of analysis for qualitative data, qualitative content analysis is meeting with steadily growing interest and is being chosen by more and more qualitative researchers. The method is used for research in many academic disciplines and fields of practice, including education, sociology, political science, psychology, ethnology, social work and social pedagogy, nursing, and health science. The popularity in so many fields is understandable, because the different variants of QCA have numerous strengths. When compared with other methods for qualitative data analysis, QCA, as presented in this book, has many advantages:

- It allows you to conduct a systematic, understandable, and reproducible analysis.
- It is a collection of scientific techniques that can be clearly described and mastered.
- It offers a broad spectrum of different approaches, each of which is suitable for particular situations according to their different requirements.
- It can be conceptualized as a very open and explorative approach, such as in the form of a thematic analysis in which categories are constructed inductively. However, it can also be conceptualized as an approach that is based on hypotheses and predetermined categories, which means that it can also be a theory-driven approach.
- It allows you to analyse all of the data you have collected or do secondary analysis on data collected by others.
- It can process large amounts of text, if necessary.
- It facilitates a division of labour in teams of competent researchers.
- It requires researchers to develop a category system that includes detailed definitions and typical examples.
- It becomes increasingly reliable when conducted by multiple coders.
- It connects a hermeneutical understanding of the text with rule-governed coding.
- It can be carried out with excellent computer-assisted analysis software.
- It is a systematic approach that avoids anecdotalism and the suggestibility of individual cases.
- It avoids premature quantification (unlike quantitative content analysis).

If we take Kracauer's (1952) demand for codification from the beginnings of QCA as a yardstick, there has undoubtedly been great progress along this path in recent years. In some points there is still a need for further development, for example regarding the development of standards. Time does not stand still, and so empirical research and its methods are also subject to constant pressure to innovate. In recent years, it is above all the social media, which have grown considerably in importance, for which new forms of analysis and systematic methods are needed. This is certainly a field for the further development of QCA. Social media data differ considerably from the usual qualitative data such as that collected in the past, mainly by means of open interviews, focus groups, or field research. When analysing data from Twitter, it can easily happen that several thousand tweets are to be analysed, each of which is relatively short. Here, too, the case-oriented perspective we have emphasized in many places in this book can play a role: What kind of people are these, for example, who arouse widespread anger and attract attention by insults and abuse of the worst kind? However, some maxims of QCA can no longer be implemented when analysing data of this kind, such as the rule of gaining as much knowledge of the data as possible in the initiating phase of the analysis. No one can be expected to read 15,000 tweets. These new types of data demand methodological innovations, whereby a combination of human analytical understanding and algorithmic power is increasingly becoming a desideratum.

It may be surprising to read at the end of this book about a future turn towards analysis techniques that are based on machine learning and artificial intelligence. Further developments and methodological innovations will drive qualitative content analysis forward, and we believe AI will be a driving force in this. So we end, then, with the prophecy of a best-selling 1960s futurology book *The Year 2000: A Framework for Speculation on the Next Thirty-Three Years* (Kahn & Wiener, 1967): 'You will experience it.'

REFERENCES

Bailey, K. D. (1973). Constructing monothetic and polythetic typologies by the heuristic method. *Sociological Quarterly, 14*(3), 291–308.

Bailey, K. D. (1994). *Typologies and taxonomies: An introduction to classification techniques.* SAGE.

Barton, A. H. (1955). The concept of property-space in social research. In P. F. Lazarsfeld & M. Rosenberg, *The language of social research* (pp. 40–53). Free Press.

Bazeley, P. (2018). *Integrating analyses for mixed methods research.* SAGE.

Bazeley, P. (2021). *Qualitative data analysis: Practical strategies.* SAGE.

Berelson, B. (1952). *Content analysis in communication research.* Free Press.

Berelson, B., & Lazarsfeld, P. F. (1948). *The analysis of communication content.*

Bernard, H. R., & Ryan, G. W. (2010). *Analyzing qualitative data: Systematic approaches.* SAGE.

Blasius, J. (2001). *Korrespondenzanalyse.* Oldenbourg.

Boyatzis, R. E. (1998). *Transforming qualitative information: Thematic analysis and code development.* SAGE.

Brennan, R. L., & Prediger, D. J. (1981). Coefficient kappa: Some uses, misuses, and alternatives. *Educational and Psychological Measurement, 41*(3), 687–699. https://doi.org/10.1177/001316448104100307

Breuer, F., Muckel, P., & Dieris, B. (2019). *Reflexive grounded theory. Eine Einführung für die Forschungspraxis* (4th ed.). Springer VS.

Bryant, A., & Charmaz, K. (Eds.) (2007). *The SAGE handbook of grounded theory.* SAGE.

Bryman, A. (1988). *Quantity and quality in social research.* Routledge. https://doi.org/10.4324/9780203410028

Charmaz, K. (2014). *Constructing grounded theory* (2nd ed.). SAGE.

Cisneros-Puebla, C. A. (2004). 'To learn to think conceptually.' Juliet Corbin in conversation with Cesar A. Cisneros-Puebla. *Forum Qualitative Sozialforschung / Forum: Qualitative Social Research, 5*(3), Art. 32.

Cohen, J. (1960). A coefficient of agreement for nominal scales. *Educational and Psychological Measurement, 20*(1), 37–46. https://doi.org/10.1177/001316446002000104

Corbin, J. M., & Strauss, A. L. (2015). *Basics of qualitative research: Techniques and procedures for developing grounded theory* (4th ed.). SAGE.

Corti, L., Witzel, A., & Bishop, L. (2005). Potenziale und Probleme der Sekundäranalyse. Eine Einführung in die FQS-Schwerpunktausgabe über die Sekundäranalyse qualitativer Daten. *Forum Qualitative Sozialforschung / Forum: Qualitative Social Research, 6*(1), Art. 49. https://doi.org/10.17169/FQS-6.1.498

Creswell, J. W. (2014). *Research design: Qualitative, quantitative, and mixed methods approaches* (4th ed.). SAGE.

Creswell, J. W., & Creswell Báez, J. (2021). *30 essential skills for the qualitative researcher* (2nd ed.). SAGE.

Creswell, J. W., & Plano Clark, V. L. (2011). *Designing and conducting mixed methods research* (2nd ed.). SAGE.

Creswell, J. W., & Plano Clark, V. L. (2018). *Designing and conducting mixed methods research* (3rd ed.). SAGE.

Creswell, J. W., & Poth, C. N. (2018). *Qualitative inquiry & research design: Choosing among five approaches* (4th ed.). SAGE.

Denzin, N. K. (1978). *The research act: A theoretical introduction to sociological methods* (2nd ed.). McGraw-Hill.

Denzin, N. K., & Lincoln, Y. S. (Eds.). (2018). *The SAGE handbook of qualitative research* (5th ed.). SAGE.

Devi Prasad, B. (2019). Qualitative content analysis: Why is it still a path less taken? *Forum Qualitative Sozialforschung / Forum: Qualitative Social Research, 20*(3), Art. 36. https://doi.org/10.17169/FQS-20.3.3392

Dey, I. (1993). *Qualitative data analysis: A user-friendly guide for social scientists*. Routledge.

Diekmann, A. (2007). *Empirische Sozialforschung: Grundlagen, Methoden, Anwendungen* (4th ed.). Rowohlt Taschenbuch Verlag.

Dietrich, M., & Mey, G. (2019). Visuelle Jugendkulturforschung: Trends und Entwicklungen. *Diskurs Kindheits- und Jugendforschung / Discourse Journal of Childhood and Adolescence Research, 14*(3), 293–307. https://doi.org/10.3224/diskurs.v14i3.04

Dilthey, W. (1977). Ideas concerning a descriptive and analytic psychology (1894). In W. Dilthey, *Descriptive psychology and historical understanding* (pp. 21–120). Martinus Nijhoff. https://doi.org/10.1007/978-94-009-9658-8_2 (Original work published 1894.)

Dittmar, N. (2009). *Transkription. Ein Leitfaden mit Aufgaben für Studenten* (3rd ed.). VS Verlag für Sozialwissenschaften.

Dresing, T., Pehl, T., & Schmieder, C. (2015). *Manual (on) transcription: Transcription conventions, software guides and practical hints for qualitative researchers* (3rd ed.). Self-published. https://www.audiotranskription.de/wp-content/uploads/2020/11/manual-on-transcription.pdf

Döring, N. & Bortz, J. (2016). *Forschungsmethoden und Evaluation in den Sozial- und Humanwissenschaften* (5th ed.). Springer.

Elo, S., Kääriäinen, M., Kanste, O., Pölkki, T., Utriainen, K., & Kyngäs, H. (2014). Qualitative content analysis: A focus on trustworthiness. *SAGE Open, 4*(1), 1–10. https://doi.org/10.1177/2158244014522633

Esser, H. (2001). *Soziologie – Spezielle Grundlagen, Band 6: Sinn und Kultur*. Campus.

Feinstein, A. R., & Cicchetti, D. V. (1990). High agreement but low Kappa: I. The problems of two paradoxes. *Journal of Clinical Epidemiology, 43*(6), 543–549. https://doi.org/10.1016/0895-4356(90)90158-L

Fenzl, T., & Mayring, P. (2017). QCAmap: Eine interaktive Webapplikation für Qualitative Inhaltsanalyse. *Zeitschrift für Soziologie der Erziehung und Sozialisation, 37*(3), 333–340.

Festinger, L. (1957). *A theory of cognitive dissonance*. Stanford University Press.

Fielding, J. (2008). Double whammy? Are the most at risk the least aware? A study of environmental justice and awareness of flood risk in England and Wales.

In W. Allsop, P. Samuels, J. Harrop, & S. Huntington (Eds.), *Flood risk management: Research and practice*. Taylor & Francis. https://doi.org/10.1201/9780203883020

Flick, U. (2007). *Qualitative Sozialforschung: Eine Einführung* (8th ed.). Rowohlt Taschenbuch Verlag.

Flick, U. (2009). *Sozialforschung: Methoden und Anwendungen. Ein Überblick für die BA-Studiengänge*. Rowohlt Taschenbuch Verlag.

Flick, U. (2018a). *An introduction to qualitative research* (6th ed.). SAGE.

Flick, U. (2018b). *Doing triangulation and mixed methods*. SAGE.

Flick, U. (2020). Gütekriterien qualitativer Forschung. In G. Mey & K. Mruck (Eds.), *Handbuch Qualitative Forschung in der Psychologie: Band 2: Designs und Verfahren* (pp. 247–263). Springer. https://doi.org/10.1007/978-3-658-26887-9_30

Flick, U., von Kardoff, E., & Steinke, I. (2017). Was ist qualitative Forschung? Einleitung und Überblick. In U. Flick, E. von Kardorff, & I. Steinke (Eds.), *Qualitative Forschung: Ein Handbuch* (12th ed., pp. 13–29). Rowohlt Taschenbuch Verlag.

Friese, S. (2019). *Qualitative data analysis with ATLAS.ti* (3rd ed.). SAGE.

Früh, W. (2017). *Inhaltsanalyse: Theorie und Praxis* (9th ed.). UVK Verlagsgesellschaft mbH.

Gadamer, H.-G. (1960). *Wahrheit und Methode*. J. C. B. Mohr.

Gadamer, H.-G. (2013). *Truth and method*. Bloomsbury.

Glaser, B. G. (2005). *The grounded theory perspective III: Theoretical coding*. Sociology Press.

Glaser, B. G., & Strauss, A. L. (1967). *The discovery of grounded theory*. Aldine.

Glaser, B. G., & Strauss, A. L. (1998). *Grounded theory: Strategien qualitativer Forschung*. Huber.

Gläser, J., & Laudel, G. (2004). *Experteninterviews und qualitative Inhaltsanalyse*. VS Verlag für Sozialwissenschaften.

Gläser, J., & Laudel, G. (2010). *Experteninterviews und qualitative Inhaltsanalyse* (4th ed.). VS Verlag für Sozialwissenschaften. https://doi.org/10.1007/978-3-531-91538-8

Grunenberg, H. (2001). Die Qualität qualitativer Forschung. Eine Metaanalyse erziehungs- und sozialwissenschaftlicher Forschungsarbeiten [Diplomarbeit]. Philipps-Universität Marburg.

Guba, E., & Lincoln, Y. S. (1985). *Naturalistic inquiry*. SAGE.

Guest, G., MacQueen, K. M., & Namey, E. E. (2012). *Applied thematic analysis*. SAGE.

Guetterman, T. C., Creswell, J. W., & Kuckartz, U. (2015). Using joint displays and MAXQDA software to represent the results of mixed methods research. In M. T. McCrudden, G. J. Schraw, & C. W. Buckendahl (Eds.), *Use of visual displays in research and testing: Coding, interpreting, and reporting data* (pp. 145–176). Information Age Publishing.

Guetterman, T. C., & Fetters, M. D. (2022). Data visualization in the context of integrated analyses. In J. H. Hitchcock & A. J. Onwuegbuzie, *The Routledge handbook for advancing integration in mixed methods research* (pp. 301–323). Routledge.https://doi.org/10.4324/9780429432828-24

Guetterman, T. C., Fetters, M. D., & Creswell, J. W. (2015). Integrating quantitative and qualitative results in health science mixed methods research through joint displays. *Annals of Family Medicine*, *13*(6), 554–561. https://doi.org/10.1370/afm.1865

Gugushvili, T., & Salukvadze, G. (2021). Using MAXQDA for analyzing documents: An example of prioritization research design in urban development. In M. C. Gizzi & S. Rädiker (Eds.), *The practice of qualitative data analysis: Research examples using MAXQDA* (pp. 107–120). MAXQDA Press.

Hammersley, M. (1992). *What's wrong with ethnography?* Routledge.

Helfferich, C. (2011). *Die Qualität qualitativer Daten: Manual für die Durchführung qualitativer Interviews.* VS Verlag für Sozialwissenschaften. https://doi.org/10.1007/978-3-531-92076-4

Hempel, C. G., & Oppenheim, P. (1936). *Der Typusbegriff im Lichte der neuen Logik: Wissenschaftstheoretische Untersuchungen zur Konstitutionsforschung und Psychologie.* Sijthoff.

Höld, R. (2009). Zur Transkription von Audiodaten. In R. Buber & H. H. Holzmüller (Eds.), *Qualitative Marktforschung* (pp. 655–668). Gabler. https://doi.org/10.1007/978-3-8349-9441-7_41

Hopf, C. (2016). *Schriften zu Methodologie und Methoden qualitativer Sozialforschung* (W. Hopf & U. Kuckartz, Eds.). Springer VS.

Hopf, C., Rieker, P., Sanden-Marcus, M., & Schmidt, C. (1995). *Familie und Rechtsextremismus. Familiale Sozialisation und rechtsextreme Orientierungen junger Männer.* Juventa.

Hopf, C., & Schmidt, C. (1993). Zum Verhältnis von innerfamilialen sozialen Erfahrungen, Persönlichkeitsentwicklung und politischen Orientierungen: Dokumentation und Erörterung des methodischen Vorgehens in einer Studie zu diesem Thema. *Institut für Sozialwissenschaften der Universität Hildesheim.* https://nbn-resolving.org/urn:nbn:de:0168-ssoar-456148

Hsieh, H.-F., & Shannon, S. E. (2005). Three approaches to qualitative content analysis. *Qualitative Health Research, 15*(9), 1277–1288. https://doi.org/10.1177/1049732305276687

Jackson, K., & Bazeley, P. (2019). *Qualitative data analysis with NVivo* (3rd ed.). SAGE.

Jahoda, M., Lazarsfeld, P. F., & Zeisel, H. (2002). *Marienthal: The sociography of an unemployed community.* Transaction Publishers. (Original work published 1933.)

Janssen, M., Stamann, C., Schreier, M., Whittal, A., & Dahl, T. (Eds.). (2019). FQS special issue 'Qualitative Content Analysis I'. *Forum Qualitative Sozialforschung / Forum: Qualitative Social Research, 20*(3). http://www.qualitative-research.net/index.php/fqs/issue/view/65

Johnson, B., & Christensen, L. B. (2020). *Educational research: Quantitative, qualitative, and mixed approaches* (7th ed.). SAGE.

Kahn, H., & Wiener, A. J. (1967). *The year 2000: A framework for speculation on the next thirty-three years.* Macmillan.

Kan, M. P. H., & Fabrigar, L. R. (2017). Theory of planned behavior. In V. Zeigler-Hill & T. K. Shackelford (Eds.), *Encyclopedia of personality and individual differences* (pp. 1–8). Springer. https://doi.org/10.1007/978-3-319-28099-8_1191-1

Kelle, U. (2007). Theoretisches Vorwissen und Kategorienbildung in der 'Grounded Theory'. In U. Kuckartz, H. Grunenberg, & T. Dresing (Eds.), *Qualitative Datenanalyse: Computergestützt* (pp. 32–49). VS Verlag für Sozialwissenschaften.

Kelle, U. (2008). *Die Integration qualitativer und quantitativer Methoden in der empirischen Sozialforschung* (2nd ed.). VS Verlag für Sozialwissenschaften. https://doi.org/10.1007/978-3-531-91174-8

Kelle, U., & Kluge, S. (2010). *Vom Einzelfall zum Typus: Fallvergleich und Fallkontrastierung in der Qualitativen Sozialforschung* (2nd ed.). VS Verlag für Sozialwissenschaften.

Keller, R. (2011). *Wissenssoziologische Diskursanalyse: Grundlegung eines Forschungsprogramms* (3rd ed.). VS Verlag für Sozialwissenschaften.

Kirk, J., & Miller, M. L. (1986). *Reliability and validity in qualitative research.* Sage Publications.

Klafki, W. (2001). Hermeneutische Verfahren in der Erziehungswissenschaft. In C. Rittelmeyer & M. Parmentier (Eds.), *Einführung in die pädagogische Hermeneutik. Mit einem Beitrag von Wolfgang Klafki* (pp. 125–148). Wissenschaftliche Buchgesellschaft. (Original work published 1971.)

Kluge, S. (1999). Empirisch begründete Typenbildung: Zur Konstruktion von Typen und Typologien in der qualitativen Sozialforschung. *VS Verlag für Sozialwissenschaften.* https://doi.org/10.1007/978-3-322-97436-5

Kowal, S., & O'Connell, D. C. (2014). Transcription as a crucial step of data analysis. In U. Flick, *The SAGE handbook of qualitative data analysis* (pp. 64–78). SAGE. https://doi.org/10.4135/9781446282243.n5

Kracauer, S. (1952). The challenge of qualitative content analysis. *Public Opinion Quarterly, 16*(4, Special Issue on International Communications Research), 631–642. https://doi.org/10.1086/266427

Krippendorff, K. (1980). *Content analysis: An introduction to its methodology.* SAGE.

Krippendorff, K. (2004a). *Content analysis: An introduction to its methodology* (2nd ed.). SAGE.

Krippendorff, K. (2004b). Reliability in content analysis: Some common misconceptions and recommendations. *Human Communication Research, 30*(3), 411–433. https://doi.org/10.1111/J.1468-2958.2004.TB00738.X

Krippendorff, K. (2018). *Content analysis: An introduction to its methodology* (4th ed.). SAGE.

Kriz, J., & Lisch, R. (1988). *Methoden-Lexikon.* PVU.

Kuckartz, U. (1991). Ideal types or empirical types: The case of Max Weber's empirical research. *Bulletin of Sociological Methodology/Bulletin de Méthodologie Sociologique, 32*(1), 44–53. https://doi.org/10.1177/075910639103200103

Kuckartz, U. (2006). Zwischen Singularität und Allgemeingültigkeit: Typenbildung als qualitative Strategie der Verallgemeinerung. In K.-S. Rehberg (Ed.), *Soziale Ungleichheit, kulturelle Unterschiede: Verhandlungen des 32. Kongresses der Deutschen Gesellschaft für Soziologie in München* (pp. 4047–4056). Campus. https://nbn-resolving.org/urn:nbn:de:0168-ssoar-142318

Kuckartz, U. (2009). Methodenkombination. In B. Westle (Ed.), *Methoden der Politikwissenschaft* (pp. 352–263). Nomos.

Kuckartz, U. (2010a). *Einführung in die computergestützte Analyse qualitativer Daten* (3rd ed.). VS Verlag für Sozialwissenschaften.

Kuckartz, U. (2010b). Nicht hier, nicht jetzt, nicht ich – Über die symbolische Bearbeitung eines ernsten Problems. In H. Welzer, H.-G. Soeffner, & D. Giesecke (Eds.), *Klimakulturen: Soziale Wirklichkeiten im Klimawandel* (pp. 144–160). Campus.

Kuckartz, U. (2014a). *Qualitative text analysis: A guide to methods, practice & using software.* SAGE.

Kuckartz, U. (2014b). *Mixed methods: Methodologie, Forschungsdesigns und Analyseverfahren.* Springer VS.

Kuckartz, U., Dresing, T., Rädiker, S., & Stefer, C. (2008). *Qualitative Evaluation: Der Einstieg in die Praxis* (2nd ed.). VS Verlag für Sozialwissenschaften.

Kuckartz, U., & Rädiker, S. (2019). *Analyzing qualitative data with MAXQDA: Text, audio, and video.* Springer Nature Switzerland. https://doi.org/10.1007/978-3-030-15671-8

Kuckartz, U., & Rädiker, S. (2021). Using MAXQDA for mixed methods research. In R. B. Johnson & A. J. Onwuegbuzie (Eds.), *The Routledge reviewer's guide to mixed methods analysis* (pp. 305–318). Routledge. https://doi.org/10.4324/9780203729434-26

Kuckartz, U., & Rädiker, S. (2022). *Qualitative Inhaltsanalyse. Methoden, Praxis, Computerunterstützung* (5th ed.). Beltz Juventa.

Kuckartz, U., Rädiker, S., Ebert, T., & Schehl, J. (2013). *Statistik: Eine verständliche Einführung* (2nd ed.). VS Verlag für Sozialwissenschaften.

Lamnek, S., & Krell, C. (2016). *Qualitative Sozialforschung* (6th ed.). Beltz.

Laudel, G., & Bielick, J. (2019). Forschungspraktische Probleme bei der Archivierung von leitfadengestützten Interviews. *Forum Qualitative Sozialforschung / Forum: Qualitative Social Research, 20*(2), Art. 10. https://doi.org/10.17169/fqs-20.2.3077

Lazarsfeld, P. F. (1972). *Qualitative analysis. Historical and critical essays.* Allyn and Bacon.

Legewie, H., & Schervier-Legewie, B. (2004). Anselm Strauss: Research is hard work, it's always a bit suffering. Therefore, on the other side research should be fun. *Forum Qualitative Sozialforschung / Forum: Qualitative Social Research, 5*(3), Art. 22. https://doi.org/10.17169/FQS-5.3.562

Maksutova, A. (2021). Using MAXQDA's summary features: Developing social types in migrant integration studies. In M. C. Gizzi & S. Rädiker (Eds.), *The practice of qualitative data analysis: Research examples using MAXQDA* (pp. 135–147). MAXQDA Press. https://doi.org/10.36192/978-3-948768058

Marshall, C., & Rossman, G. B. (2011). *Designing qualitative research* (5th ed.). SAGE.

Mayring, P. (1983). *Qualitative Inhaltsanalyse: Grundlagen und Techniken.* Beltz.

Mayring, P. (2002). *Einführung in die qualitative Sozialforschung (5th ed.).* Beltz.

Mayring, P. (2014). Qualitative content analysis: Theoretical foundation, basic procedures and software solution. http://nbn-resolving.de/urn:nbn:de:0168-ssoar-395173

Mayring, P. (2015). *Qualitative Inhaltsanalyse: Grundlagen und Techniken* (12th ed.). Beltz.

Mayring, P. (2019). Qualitative Inhaltsanalyse – Abgrenzungen, Spielarten, Weiterentwicklungen. *Forum Qualitative Sozialforschung / Forum: Qualitative Social Research, 20*(3), Art. 16. https://doi.org/10.17169/fqs-20.3.3343

Mayring, P. (2020). Qualitative Inhaltsanalyse. In G. Mey & K. Mruck (Eds.), *Handbuch Qualitative Forschung in der Psychologie* (pp. 495–511). Springer Fachmedien. https://doi.org/10.1007/978-3-658-26887-9_52

Mayring, P. (2021). *Qualitative content analysis: A step-by-step guide.* SAGE.

Mayring, P., & Gläser-Zikuda, M. (Eds.). (2005). *Die Praxis der qualitativen Inhaltsanalyse.* Beltz.

Medjedović, I. (2014). *Qualitative Sekundäranalyse: Zum Potenzial einer neuen Forschungsstrategie in der empirischen Sozialforschung.* Springer VS.

Medjedović, I., & Witzel, A. (2010). *Wiederverwendung qualitativer Daten: Archivierung und Sekundärnutzung qualitativer Interviewtranskripte.* VS Verlag für Sozialwissenschaften. https://doi.org/10.1007/978-3-531-92403-8

Merten, K. (1995). *Inhaltsanalyse: Einführung in Theorie, Methode und Praxis* (2nd ed.). Springer Fachmedien.

Mertens, D. M. (2018). *Mixed methods design in evaluation*. SAGE.

Merton, R. K., & Barber, E. (2004). *The travels and adventures of serendipity: A study in sociological semantics and the sociology of science*. Princeton University Press.

Mey, G., & Mruck, K. (2011). *Grounded Theory Reader* (2nd ed.). VS Verlag für Sozialwissenschaften.

Miles, M. B., & Huberman, A. M. (1984). *Qualitative data analysis: A sourcebook of new methods*. SAGE.

Miles, M. B., & Huberman, A. M. (1994). *Qualitative data analysis: An expanded sourcebook* (2nd ed.). SAGE.

Miles, M. B., Huberman, A. M., & Saldaña, J. (2020). *Qualitative data analysis: A methods sourcebook* (4th ed.). SAGE.

Miller, D. C., & Salkind, N. J. (2002). *Handbook of research design & social measurement* (6th ed.). SAGE.

Mollenhauer, K., & Uhlendorff, U. (1992). *Sozialpädagogische Diagnosen: Über Jugendliche in schwierigen Lebenslagen*. Juventa.

Morgan, D. L. (2014). *Integrating qualitative and quantitative methods: A pragmatic approach*. SAGE.

OECD (2007). OECD principles and guidelines for access to research data from public funding. http://www.oecd.org/science/inno/38500813.pdf

O'Leary, Z. (2018). *Research question*. SAGE.

Oswald, H. (2010). Was heißt qualitativ forschen? Warnungen, Fehlerquellen, Möglichkeiten. In B. Friebertshäuser, A. Langer, & A. Prengel (Eds.), *Handbuch qualitative Forschungsmethoden in der Erziehungswissenschaft* (3rd ed., pp. 183–201). Juventa.

Peirce, C. S. (1974). *Collected papers of Charles Sanders Peirce* (C. Hartshorne & P. Weiss, Eds.; 4th ed.). Belknap Press of Harvard University Press. https://books.google.de/books?id=G7IzSoUFx1YC. (Original work published 1931.)

Popper, K. R. (2010). *Die beiden Grundprobleme der Erkenntnistheorie: Aufgrund von Manuskripten aus den Jahren 1930–1933* (T. E. Hansen, Ed.; 3rd ed.). Mohr Siebeck. (Original work published 1979.)

Preisendörfer, P. (1999). *Umwelteinstellungen und Umweltverhalten in Deutschland*. VS Verlag für Sozialwissenschaften. https://doi.org/10.1007/978-3-663-11676-9

Prosch, B., & Abraham, M. (2006). Gesellschaft, Sinn und Handeln: Webers Konzept des sozialen Handelns und das Frame-Modell. In R. Greshoff & U. Schimank (Eds.), *Integrative Sozialtheorie? Esser – Luhmann – Weber* (pp. 87–109). VS Verlag für Sozialwissenschaften. https://doi.org/10.1007/978-3-531-90259-3_5

Przyborski, A., & Wohlrab-Sahr, M. (2014). *Qualitative Sozialforschung: Ein Arbeitsbuch* (4th ed.). Oldenbourg Verlag.

Pürer, H. (2003). *Publizistik- und Kommunikationswissenschaft: Ein Handbuch*. UVK.

Rädiker, S., & Kuckartz, U. (2020). *Focused analysis of qualitative interviews with MAXQDA: Step by step*. MAXQDA Press. https://doi.org/10.36192/978-3-948768072

Rehbein, J., Schmidt, T., Meyer, B., Watzke, F., & Herkenrath, A. (2004). *Handbuch für das computergestützte Transkribieren nach HIAT*. https://www.exmaralda.org/hiat/files/azm_56.pdf

Ritchie, J., & Spencer, L. (1994). Qualitative data analysis for applied policy research. In A. Bryman & R. G. Burgess (Eds.), *Analyzing qualitative data* (pp. 173–194). Taylor & Francis. https://doi.org/10.4324/9780203413081_chapter_9

Ritchie, J., Spencer, L., & O'Connor, W. (2003). Carrying out qualitative analysis. In *Qualitative research practice: A guide for social science students and researchers* (pp. 219–261). SAGE.

Ritsert, J. (1972). *Inhaltsanalyse und Ideologiekritik: Ein Versuch über kritische Sozialforschung.* Athenäum.

Rorty, R. (1979). *Philosophy and the mirror of nature.* Princeton University Press.

Rössler, P. (2017). *Inhaltsanalyse* (3rd ed.). UVK Verlagsgesellschaft mbH mit UVK/Lucius.

Rust, I. (2019). Theoriegenerierung als explizite Phase in der qualitativen Inhaltsanalyse: Auf dem Weg zur Einlösung eines zentralen Versprechens der qualitativen Sozialforschung. https://t1p.de/Theoriegenerierende-Inhaltsanalyse

Saldaña, J. (2013). *The coding manual for qualitative researchers* (2nd ed.). SAGE.

Schmidt, C. (2000). Analyse von Leitfadeninterviews. In U. Flick, E. von Kardorff, & I. Steinke (Eds.), *Qualitative Forschung: Ein Handbuch* (pp. 447–455). Rowohlt Taschenbuch Verlag.

Schmidt, C. (2010). Auswertungstechniken für Leitfadeninterviews. In B. Friebertshäuser & A. Prengel (Eds.), *Handbuch qualitativer Forschungsmethoden in der Erziehungswissenschaft* (3rd ed., pp. 473–486). Juventa.

Schreier, M. (2012). *Qualitative content analysis in practice.* SAGE.

Schreier, M. (2014). Varianten qualitativer Inhaltsanalyse. Ein Wegweiser im Dickicht der Begrifflichkeiten. *Forum Qualitative Sozialforschung / Forum: Qualitative Social Research, 15*(1), Art. 18. https://doi.org/10.17169/fqs-15.1.2043

Schutz, A. (1962). *Collected papers I. The problem of social reality.* Martinus Nijhoff.

Seale, C. (1999a). *The quality of qualitative research.* SAGE.

Seale, C. (1999b). Quality in qualitative research. *Qualitative Inquiry, 5*(4), 465–478. https://doi.org/10.1177/107780049900500402

Seale, C., & Silverman, D. (1997). Ensuring rigour in qualitative research. *European Journal of Public Health, 7*(4), 379–384. https://doi.org/10.1093/eurpub/7.4.379

Silver, C., & Lewins, A. (2014). *Using software in qualitative research: A step-by-step guide* (2nd ed.). SAGE.

Spencer, L., Ritchie, J., Lewis, J., & Dillon, L. (2003). *Quality in qualitative evaluation: A framework for assessing research evidence.* https://www.gov.uk/government/publications/government-social-research-framework-for-assessing-research-evidence

Sprenger, A. (1989). Teilnehmende Beobachtung in prekären Handlungssituationen: Das Beispiel Intensivstation. In R. Aster, H. Merkens, & M. Repp (Eds.), *Teilnehmende Beobachtung: Werkstattberichte und methodologische Reflexionen* (pp. 35–56). Campus.

Stamann, C., Janssen, M., & Schreier, M. (2016). Qualitative Inhaltsanalyse – Versuch einer Begriffsbestimmung und Systematisierung. *Forum Qualitative Sozialforschung / Forum: Qualitative Social Research, 17*(3), Art. 16. https://doi.org/10.17169/fqs-17.3.2581

Stamann, C., Janssen, M., Schreier, M., Whittal, A., & Dahl, T. (Eds.). (2020). FQS special issue 'Qualitative Content Analysis II'. *Forum Qualitative Sozialforschung / Forum: Qualitative Social Research, 21*(1). http://www.qualitative-research.net/index.php/fqs/issue/view/66

Steigleder, S. (2008). *Die strukturierende qualitative Inhaltsanalyse im Praxistest: Eine konstruktiv kritische Studie zur Auswertungsmethodik von Philipp Mayring*. Tectum.

Steinke, I. (1999). *Kriterien qualitativer Forschung: Ansätze zur Bewertung qualitativ-empirischer Sozialforschung*. Juventa.

Steinke, I. (2007). Qualitätssicherung in der qualitativen Forschung. In U. Kuckartz, H. Grunenberg, & T. Dresing (Eds.), *Qualitative Datenanalyse: Computergestützt* (pp. 176–187). VS Verlag für Sozialwissenschaften. https://doi.org/10.1007/978-3-531-90665-2_11

Strauss, A. L. (1991). *Grundlagen qualitativer Sozialforschung: Datenanalyse und Theoriebildung in der empirischen soziologischen Forschung*. Fink.

Strauss, A. L., & Corbin, J. M. (1990). *Basics of qualitative research: Grounded theory procedures and techniques*. SAGE.

Strauss, A. L., & Corbin, J. M. (1996). *Grounded theory: Grundlagen Qualitativer Sozialforschung*. Beltz PVU.

Strauss, A. L., & Corbin, J. M. (1998). *Basics of qualitative research: Techniques and procedures for developing grounded theory* (2nd ed.). SAGE.

Tashakkori, A. M., Johnson, R. B., & Teddlie, C. B. (2021). *Foundations of mixed methods research: Integrating quantitative and qualitative approaches in the social and behavioral sciences* (2nd ed.). SAGE.

Tesch, R. (1990). *Qualitative research: Analysis types and software tools*. Falmer Press.

Uhlendorff, H., & Prengel, A. (2013). Forschungsperspektiven quantitativer Methoden im Verhältnis zu qualitativen Methoden. In B. Friebertshäuser, A. Langer, & A. Prengel (Eds.), *Handbuch Qualitative Forschungsmethoden in der Erziehungswissenschaft* (4th ed., pp. 137–148). Beltz Juventa.

Vogt, J. (2016). *Einladung zur Literaturwissenschaft* (7th ed.). Wilhelm Fink.

Wattenberg, M., & Viégas, F. B. (2008). The Word Tree, an interactive visual concordance. *IEEE Transactions on Visualization and Computer Graphics, 14*(6), 1221–1228. https://doi.org/10.1109/TVCG.2008.172

Weber, M. (1988). *Gesammelte Aufsätze zur Soziologie und Sozialpolitk* (M. Weber, Ed.; 2nd ed.). http://www.zeno.org/nid/20011442131 (Original work published 1911.)

Weber, M. (1964). *Wirtschaft und Gesellschaft: Grundriss der verstehenden Soziologie* (J. Winckelmann, Ed.). Kiepenheuer und Witsch.

Wenzler-Cremer, H. (2005). Bikulturelle Sozialisation als Herausforderung und Chance: Eine qualitative Studie über Identitätskonstruktionen und Lebensentwürfe am Beispiel junger deutsch-indonesischer Frauen [Dissertation, Universität Freiburg]. https://freidok.uni-freiburg.de/data/2267

Whittemore, R., Chase, S. K., & Mandle, C. L. (2001). Validity in qualitative research. *Qualitative Health Research, 11*(4), 522–537. https://doi.org/10.1177/104973201129119299

Witzel, A., & Reiter, H. (2012). The problem-centred interview: Principles and practice. SAGE.

Yarbrough, D. B., Shulha, L. M., Hopson, R. K., & Caruthers, F. A. (2011). *The program evaluation standards: A guide for evaluators and evaluation users* (3rd ed.). SAGE.

Zhao, X., Liu, J. S., & Deng, K. (2012). Assumptions behind intercoder reliability indices. In C. T. Salmon (Ed.), *Communication Yearbook* (pp. 419–480). Routledge.

INDEX

Page references to figures or tables will be in *italics*.

Printed in the USA
CPSIA information can be obtained
at www.ICGtesting.com
JSHW050507181123
52020JS00008B/52